MW01174774

COMBINING TWO CULTURES

McMaster University's Arts and Science Programme: A Case Study

Edited by Herb Jenkins, Barbara Ferrier, and Michael Ross

University Press of America,® Inc.
Dallas · Lanham · Boulder · New York · Oxford

Copyright © 2004 by
University Press of America,® Inc.
4501 Forbes Boulevard
Suite 200
Lanham, Maryland 20706
UPA Acquisitions Department (301) 459-3366

PO Box 317
Oxford
OX2 9RU, UK

Library of Congress Control Number: 2004106841
ISBN 0-7618-2928-8 (hardcover : alk. ppr.)
ISBN 0-7618-2929-6 (paperback : alk. ppr.)

∞™ The paper used in this publication meets the minimum
requirements of American National Standard for Information
Sciences—Permanence of Paper for Printed Library Materials,
ANSI Z39.48—1984

To our students

CONTENTS

Preface

For many years writers concerned with higher education have called attention to widespread disillusionment with the research-intensive university as a place for undergraduate education. Prominent among them are Christopher Lucas in his scholarly and balanced book, *Crisis in the Academy*[1] and Charles Anderson in his provocative and philosophical book, *Prescribing the Life of the Mind.*[2] Recently Tom Pocklington and Allan Tupper have raised the theme of disillusionment and failure for Canadian research universities in *No Place to Learn.* Although the roots of disillusionment are seen somewhat differently by these authors, they share the common view that the underlying cause is an evasion of the universities' responsibility to put the instruction of undergraduates first. The consequences of this failure are cited as an over-specialized, incoherent curriculum dominated by the research interests of departments. There is, too, a consensus that, to quote Lucas, "...today's professoriate has a professional obligation to struggle anew with the age-old problem of restoring greater coherence and intelligibility within a common undergraduate curriculum." This book is a critical account of one such struggle, and what has come of it over the more than 20 years since it began. The struggle was not to reform all of undergraduate education in our university, but to produce an alternative to the discipline- and department-centred programmes for students who aspire to both a liberal education encompassing the arts and sciences, and to engagement as citizens or professionals in the concerns of a democratic society.

Despite a measure of agreement in the recent literature urging reform in higher education there have been few notable or enduring successes in providing alternatives to the department-centred curriculum. In Anderson's book, cited above, he writes

> To be sure, even the most modest effort to specify a working relationship among the disciplines will seem to some hopelessly naive and optimistic. Years ago, C. P. Snow spoke of the "two cultures" of the university—the sciences and the humanities—that coexisted in mutual incomprehension. Since that time matters have probably gotten somewhat worse. Anyone familiar with the contemporary university knows that it is not simply indifference and ignorance that divide the disciplines, but far too often suspicion, derision, and contempt as well. (123)

Our Programme is based on the belief that Snow's description of the two cultures in his 1959 book, *Two Cultures and the Scientific Revolution*[4] does not imply that by nature, minds are either "of the arts type" or "of the science type." Rather than reflecting a great divide in the propensities or capacities of minds, the isolation of the sciences from the arts reflects the historical evolution of a now prevalent university structure that is better suited to the needs of faculties and departments as purveyors of specialized knowledge and skills than to the needs of many undergraduates.

But even for those ready and willing to respect the values of both the arts and sciences, there is another formidable obstacle to successful innovation. The consensus on the broad direction of needed change tends to fracture into competing views when it comes to the task of deciding what to teach—a task which includes identifying the most important intellectual skills, and agreeing on how they might best be fostered.

Our decisions about what to teach were guided by three commitments: to provide a substantial introduction to the arts, the sciences, and mathematics; to pay attention throughout to the development of broadly applicable intellectual skills; and to give high priority to teaching the art of inquiry into problems of our society that do not lie within the province of a single discipline. Our emphasis on developing the skills of inquiry, which include formulating critical questions and pursuing them effectively through research, was subsequently reinforced by the publication of the influential Boyer Commission report, *Re-inventing Undergraduate Education*,[5] whose recommendations in almost all respects parallelled our practices.

There is an extensive and valuable literature which through

philosophical debate and argument develops prescriptions for higher education, but this book was written to serve a different purpose. It aims to provide a critical case study of one long-standing programme of liberal education for our times. Although we do not offer this account as the one best way to provide a vital undergraduate experience for students who aspire to a liberal education, we hope it will contribute to such efforts in several ways.

First, there are many competing and worthy claims for attention which a plan for any such programme must recognize and resolve. To cite but one example, What is the right balance in the curriculum between breadth in the arts and sciences and the opportunity to develop strength through concentration? We examine a host of such competing claims and offer evidence, as well as argument, on the consequences of the choices we have made. Second, our experience with the teaching of inquiry is a basis for discussing its strengths and limitations as an approach to learning and acquiring knowledge. Third, from our experience with the programme in practice we have learned some things that would surprise those who wrote the blueprint. One happy example is the emergence of a strong sense of community in teachers and students alike. That raises the question of what makes for a community of learning.

Finally, while we do not claim to give a universal answer to the question of what and how to teach, we do claim to demonstrate the possibility of developing an agreed upon framework for a curriculum which both allows teachers to exercise their initiatives and maintains a satisfactory degree of coherence in the whole.

The ultimate measure of worth for an effort of this kind lies in what it means to its participants. The best way we know to explore that is to let them speak for themselves. Accordingly, you will find, unedited except for modest reductions in length, commentaries from teachers, current students, and especially from graduates. In the case of graduates, we invited contributions from a sample of those who span the history of the Programme from its first class and who would reflect the diversity of paths our graduates' lives trace out. In our view, the invitees were not otherwise special, and we wish all our graduates could have been included. We asked our invitees not for testimonials, but rather for information about how their lives have unfolded. That in their responses they reflect on their university years is not of course surprising, but perhaps you will find, as we have, something heartening in the way they speak of how that experience has contributed to the way they now live.

Notes

1. Christopher Lucas, *Crisis in The Academy: Rethinking Higher Education in America* (New York: St. Martin's Press, 1966).
2. Charles Anderson, *Prescribing the Life of the Mind: An Essay on the Purpose of the University, the Aim of Liberal Education, the Competence of Citizens, and the Cultivation of Practical Reason* (Madison: The University of Wisconsin Press, 1993).
3. Tom Pocklington and Alan Tupper, *No Place to Learn: Why Universities Aren't Working* (Vancouver: UBC Press, 2002).
4. C.P. Snow, *Two Cultures and the Scientific Revolution* (New York: Cambridge University Press, 1959).
5. Boyer Commission on Educating Undergraduates in the Research University, *Re-inventing Undergraduate Education: a Blueprint for America's Research University* (Princeton, N.J.: Carnegie Foundation for the Advancement of Teaching, 1997).

Acknowledgments

We set out to create a record of what has been the most rewarding teaching experience of our lives. To do that we have relied on the good grace, eloquence, and creativity of others who have shared it. We will frequently describe the Arts and Science Programme as a community, and in keeping with that character, this book is a community effort. Students, graduates and instructors have participated, both through their formal contributions and informally in many discussions. Louis Greenspan, in addition to writing a chapter, gave valuable editorial advice at many stages of this long project. We are very grateful to them all; their eagerness to participate bolstered our belief that the project was worth undertaking.

We would like to thank Dr. Harvey Weingarten, the former Provost and Vice-President (Academic) of McMaster University for his encouragement and financial support, and Dale Roy, Director of McMaster University's Centre for Leadership in Learning, for his wise counsel and financial support through the J.W. McConnell Family Foundation.

We are grateful to Warner Bros. Publications for permission to quote from *Once in a Lifetime*, by David Byrne and Chris Frantz.

We also wish to express our appreciation to Sue Fletcher for her devotion to the task of converting the original manuscripts to consistent camera-ready copy. The errors that remain belong to the editors.

Hamilton, Ontario, Canada, November, 2003.

I

The Programme Takes Shape

1   Quest for Meaning in Undergraduate Education

Leslie J. King

This book is about an innovative venture in undergraduate education begun at McMaster University in 1981. Called the Arts and Science Programme, it is still flourishing, admitting about sixty students each year from an applicant pool many times that number. Its instructors are drawn from many disciplines and its graduates are in all walks of life; some of them will be heard from in this account.

In its presentation of a radically new approach to undergraduate education, the Arts and Science Programme had been preceded into the McMaster calendar by the revolutionary medical programme introduced a decade earlier, and the Engineering and Management Programme begun in the early 1970s. The hard-won success of the medical programme in particular, with its emphasis upon self-directed, problem-based learning,[1] did much to ease the way within the University for the acceptance of later innovations such as the Arts and Science Programme.

For a university that had begun as a small, religious institution in late nineteenth-century Toronto,[2] these developments marked its final transformation into a secular institution of the twentieth century. At the same time they were products of a quest for meaning and purpose in undergraduate education that had been going on for decades, and that at McMaster, as at other places, had been impeded by many disappointments and frustrations.

The university that opened its doors to students in the fall of 1930 in Hamilton was committed to liberal education. Its head, Chancellor Howard Whidden, who had worked hard to arrange the relocation from Toronto, had expressed his vision of the institution's role in his 1923 inaugural address:

> The chief business of the smaller university is to furnish a liberal education... Liberal education should seek to relate the individual to his universe. I refer more specifically to the universe of things... As a result of the application of scientific knowledge the stellar spaces have been measured and brought near, the subtle forces hidden in air and earth and sea have been harnessed and made to serve man's need. The whole development and structure of material things in past ages is brought within our ken; the life of plant and animal is so much better understood that human life is conserved in previously unthought of ways. In connection with all this there has gone on steadily an emancipation of the mind of man with regard to the dominance of the material... It is not through science, nor through literature that human nature is made whole, but through a fusion of both.[3]

This was a view of liberal education unconstrained by any religious tenets and clearly supportive of learning in all fields of the arts and sciences. And indeed, in its new setting of Hamilton and under the leadership of Whidden and then George Gilmour, McMaster grew steadily both in its student numbers and in the range of arts and science courses offered. It remained, however, until 1957 an institution under the administrative control of the Baptist Convention of Ontario and Quebec, and the commitment to a liberal education by way of a core curriculum had to acknowledge that fact. Writing in 1948, just prior to his departure to the Presidency of Acadia University, Watson Kirkconnell, the Head of English, noted that:

> At McMaster University... it has long been a principle that every student should enter with Senior Matriculation in Mathematics, English and one foreign language, and that he should take, in his first two university years, at least one course in science, one course in philosophy (or psychology), one course in English, one course in history, and two courses in a foreign language; while the University's statute of incorporation requires each undergraduate in each year to take a course in Scripture or its equivalent—the present curriculum calling for the New Testament in Year I, the

Old Testament in Year II, and in Year III a choice as amongst Comparative Religion, Science and Religion, Ethics, and Advanced New Testament.[4]

This insistence upon a set of core courses was, in Kirkconnell's view, "conducive to the stimulus and growth of all sides of the human personality," and he observed,

> minds so trained...are of the greatest worth in every walk of life. Men who can think clearly, who can grasp the essential points in an argument, and who can express themselves with effectiveness and economy, are extremely useful in industry, in the professions and in public administration.[5]

Similar arguments in support of a liberal education had been heard and debated in one form or another in English-speaking universities ever since Newman presented his famous Discourses in Dublin in 1852,[6] but they were arguments that were losing out at McMaster even as Kirkconnell wrote. The university's new Chancellor, George Gilmour, lamented the change in words written only a few months later:

> The defensible broadening of secondary school training seems to mean that those students who proceed beyond senior matriculation will be less intensively trained in university prerequisites than formerly. On the other hand, these students are usually required to reach a higher level for a bachelor's degree in a given honours area than was the case a generation ago. The ceiling demanded may be unreasonably high. In order to get undergraduates up to it, specialization has crept gradually down from the senior years to the junior and even to the freshman level. Little wonder that the cry for more general education meets resistance from academic departments which feel that their specialized products must compare favourably with the analogous products of other places, which in turn are watching still other places. University presidents cry for more liberal education and are heard only with difficulty.[7]

Gilmour's cries would not be heeded. The trend towards greater specialization and an erosion of the support for a university-wide core curriculum as the foundation of a liberal education would continue down through the decades to come, not just at McMaster but at universities around the world.[8]

A major force behind these developments was the accelerated growth of the sciences in the universities during and following World War II. Science courses had been part of the McMaster curriculum from the early 1890s, and a BSc degree had been introduced in 1908. Scientific research and training at the University had been boosted by the demands of the First World War,[9] but they received even greater support and promotion during the global conflict of the 1940s. At McMaster the building of the nuclear reactor and the incorporation of the new Hamilton College as the home for the science and applied science departments were the physical manifestations of this heightened emphasis. Johnston describes the tensions that resulted on the campus and how one outcome was the founding of a short-lived Metaphysical Club as a forum in which faculty members from the arts, theology and science might seek common ground.[10] The quest was unsuccessful and the changing curriculum reflected that fact. The span and depth of scientific knowledge were increasing so rapidly that only concentrated and specialized study could achieve mastery of a subject; for the undergraduate student that required a four-year honours programme.

It was not just in science that the specialization in undergraduate education was occurring. The McMaster calendar for 1955-56 listed as many as 20 honours programmes in arts and eight in science, and together these programmes accounted for just under a quarter of the total enrolment of 956 students. A decade later, the corresponding numbers of programmes were 36 and 11 and the proportion of honours students had risen to 25.4% of the total arts and science enrolment which then stood at 2,647. This pattern was similar to that which had developed in the province as a whole.[11]

Specialization in undergraduate education was reinforced by the development of post-graduate programmes. Masters degree courses had been offered at McMaster even prior to the move to Hamilton, where the scientists led the drive that resulted in Senate's approval of the first PhD programme in 1949 (in chemistry); others soon appeared, including some in the arts disciplines. By 1957 a Faculty of Graduate Studies had been created and over the next few decades McMaster participated fully in the expansion of graduate studies within the province and built a reputation as one of the country's leading centres for graduate work and research.[12] This development, critics later would charge, further distorted the priorities in undergraduate education. Honours programmes were seen as being tailored to attract the more able students and to satisfy the requirements for admission into graduate work, while the general baccalaureate courses and the students in them were treated with an indifference bordering on neglect.

The changed circumstances within the universities of the Western world in the aftermath of World War II, in particular the heightened relative importance of science and technology programmes, the favouring of specialized over general courses of study, the increased concern for vocational training at the expense of liberal education, the funding of research and graduate studies and the increased numbers of students, provided the subjects for many committee reports and reflective treatises in the 1940s and 50s.

In Canada, the Royal Commission on National Development in the Arts, Letters and Sciences (the Massey Commission) observed in its 1951 report that the "purpose of the university is, through a liberalizing education, to enable persons to live more complete lives; this should be true of any training which has a proper place in the university."[13]

But though the Commission bemoaned the "plight of the humanities" and insisted that "humanistic studies... should pervade the professional schools... and permeate the entire university," it seems, in hindsight, that its report had little direct impact upon the curriculums of universities across the country. Certainly none was discernible at McMaster.

Even before the Second World War ended, some universities in the United States had already done a great deal of soul searching about undergraduate education. The two such efforts chosen for mention here anticipated some of the arguments and proposals that later went into the fashioning of McMaster's Arts and Science Programme. The first was the publication in 1944 of a book by Algo Henderson, then President of Antioch College, long noted for its educational innovations. The case for a vitalization of liberal education, Henderson insisted, was rooted in the premise that the real function of such education "is to provide leadership for the progressive solution of the essential problems of society."[14] The basis of the curriculum, he suggested, should be "significant social problems – many of them highly controversial"and the primary aim "must always be that of developing the power to think – which in itself assumes the proper function of knowledge, the use of the scientific method, and learning to apply thinking to the practical problems of life."[15]

The second and much more celebrated study came out of Harvard University a year later.[16] The committee that prepared the report conducted comprehensive reviews of education at all levels in the United States and of the theories that shaped those activities. These reviews provided the basis for a number of prescriptions having to do with general education at Harvard. Notable among these was the proposal that of the sixteen courses required for the bachelor's degree, six should be in general education with at least one taken in each of the humanities, social sciences and sciences. In each of these three areas there would be one specially designed course that would be required of all students – for humanities it was suggested that it be on the "Great Texts of Literature," for social sciences "Western Thought and Institutions,"and for science there should be a choice between a course on the "Principles of Physical Science" and one on the "Principles of Biological Science."Rosovsky provides an interesting description of the evolved form of this core requirement at Harvard some forty or so years later.[17]

The Harvard report was cited by Eric Ashby, Vice-Chancellor of The Queen's University, Belfast, in his treatise on *Technology and the Academics*, as one of many adaptations by universities in response to the debate over what Ashby regarded as the "mischievous" antithesis of "specialisation versus a liberal education." The debate, he felt, was confused and ignored both the fact "that liberality is a spirit of pursuit, not a choice of subject," and the dilemma that "if the university repudiates the call to train technologists, it will not survive; if it repudiates the cultivation of non-practical values, it will cease to merit the title of university." Ashby's answer in a nutshell was that "the university must use specialist studies as the vehicle for a liberal education."[18]

McMaster in the late 1950s was concerned mainly not with matters of curriculum but with what Johnston called "the long game,"[19] the issue of severing its ties with the Baptist Convention and becoming a public institution supported by government funding. The game was completed in 1957 and only then did the Senate turn its attention to the task of reviewing "the whole matter of curriculum," including the core curriculum and honours courses. The work under the chairmanship of Jack Graham, an economist, took more than three years to complete, and the committee report, transmitted in February 1961, sounded the death knell for a university-wide core curriculum.[20]

The committee's view on liberal education was akin to that of Ashby mentioned above. The "true hallmark"of a liberal education, the report noted, "is to be found as much in such intangibles as attitudes and temperament as in specific knowledge or in particular habits of thought." The committee expressed no regret that "the curriculum of a modern university has long since ceased to present a unified body of knowledge which is the central concern of all students," but insisted that "if the purpose of the core curriculum is to be achieved, the content of the core might well depend on the nature of the liberal deficiencies evident in the various fields of specialization." Hence, it should be left to each of the divisions of Humanities, Social Science, and Science to decide on which courses in the other two divisions would "serve the purpose of the core curriculum for their areas of study." The only exception to this devolution of curricular authority would be the requirement that all students complete a course in English and in a foreign language.

The Graham Report provided the framework for undergraduate education at McMaster through the 1960s and, although its recommendation that all students complete English and foreign language courses failed to win acceptance, a great deal of time and effort was spent in fashioning the "basic requirements" that students in a particular subject would have to complete in the other divisions.[21]

The 1960s were a troubled decade for universities around the world, as student discontent and disillusionment with the institutions found expression in protest movements.[22] McMaster was spared from any serious disruptions, but the discontent was not far below the surface.

The charge, often levelled at that time, that universities had lost their way and had departed from their proper mission of educating young persons had a strong local advocate in the person of George Grant, principal intellectual architect of McMaster's Department of Religious Studies. In Grant's eyes, the promotion of the "dynamism of technology" had become the over-riding purpose in Western civilization and the multiversity, with its emphasis on research in all fields, including the humanities, now existed to serve that purpose. Its curriculum, "the essence of any university," favoured those subjects and approaches that "facilitate the production of personnel necessary to that type of society." Missing, in his judgement, was any serious debate and consideration about "what it concerns a human being to know," about "what we think human life to be," and about "what activities serve human fulfilment."[23]

Grant's arguments won little open support from the local university community that prided itself on being one of Canada's leading research institutions, but there were many who quietly shared similar feelings of unease over the university's priorities. The Senate responded to some of these concerns in late 1969 by charging a committee with the task of considering afresh "the objectives of undergraduate education ...and the means whereby such objectives may be achieved."

The resulting Vichert Report presented a comprehensive and insightful analysis of the forces that had shaped McMaster and its curriculum. The authors insisted it was "a tentative and uncertain document, reflecting a university which no longer has a clear vision of itself, or perhaps has too many clear, and conflicting, visions of what it ought to be."[24] The two minority reports from the committee provided some immediate support for that judgment.

The committee observed that "those noble gestures toward a liberal education, the basic requirements, have slipped out of the calendar," and that "liberal education in the sense of a common body of knowledge has perished at McMaster." Its resurrection was considered impossible in a setting where "there is no longer a clear sense of what the relationship between faculty and students ought to be, or of what kind of education the university should be providing." The challenge lay with the faculties and departments, the committee felt, "to liberalize their own curricula and stop expecting the university to provide the liberal component in education." To this end, the committee directed some 39 recommendations that dealt not only with curricular matters but also with the physical settings within which learning took place.

Three broad issues concerning the curriculum were given prominence. The student's first year, it was felt, should involve at least two-fifths of supervised study, conducted either independently or in small groups of no more than 15 students, with the supervision being given by faculty drawn from across a Division[25] rather than from one department. A second matter was the bold idea that an Individual Studies Programme be established as a separate Faculty of the University. This would be designed for "able and highly motivated students" who would enter after the first year of university work and then spend three years ideally on a "project-oriented rather than course-oriented programme" of their own choosing. The instructors/advisers would come from across the university and would typically work in the new Faculty on one-year renewable appointments. The third issue was the general or "pass" degree, intended for the student "who wants simply to be better educated." This stream, "now so generally considered second-rate", was seen as "potentially one of the most exciting programmes in the university" if, within it, "courses, possibly of an interdisciplinary nature, be devised for the purpose of general education rather than specialization."

Though few quarrelled with its diagnoses, the Committee's prescriptions for a cure proved unpalatable. Academic administrators were lukewarm to its more radical proposals and so too were most departments, concerned as they were about protecting their domains in a period of shrinking resources. Faculty members, for the most part, lacked the will and confidence to move beyond their disciplinary boundaries; to them, as to their colleagues in most universities, interdisciplinary work appeared as "an attenuated and popularized mode of education, chiefly useful for beginning students, and peripheral to the really serious business of specialized learning."[26]

There were attempts at change made in the early 1970s that followed the spirit, though not the exact letter of Vichert, but they were short-lived. One was an effort directed by a member of the Vichert Committee to fashion a Special Topics Programme for a selected class of up to 50 first-year students in Social Sciences. Its inspiration, drawn mainly from similar undertakings at Berkeley and The University of British Columbia, was that for students, "a disciplined approach to issues and ideas which transcend the boundaries of individual disciplines, with close personal supervision, could be more valuable than the introduction to the subject matter of the several disciplines which usually constitutes a first year course of study."[27] The programme focussed, by way of an integrated combination of lectures, seminars, tutorials and individual sessions with a group of faculty members drawn from the social sciences, on the theme of man's attempt to come to terms with his social environment through the accumulation of knowledge, the evolution of social institutions and the development of instruments of social change and control. As an experimental programme it enjoyed success for a half dozen or so years, but once its champion departed from the University its cause was lost.

A more ambitious proposal for an Independent Studies programme that "would not recognize any division between science and non-science spheres"[28] commanded the attention and support of a wide cross section of faculty members in the mid 1970s but it never moved beyond the level of committee discussion.

In 1977 another proposal surfaced. By then, strategic university planning had become the order of the day, and the first such plan for McMaster dealt with all aspects of its academic work. In respect to undergraduate education, the Report concluded that there was "a widespread faculty confidence" that the existing four-year honours programmes were both educationally sound and academically desirable for the able and highly motivated students who chose them but that there was less satisfaction with the aims and achievements of the three-year, mini-specialist Pass programmes. The University, it was suggested, had abandoned its obligation "to shape and provide appropriate three-year undergraduate programmes that give reality to a meaningful contemporary concept of what it means to be an educated individual citizen in our kind of society, as distinct from a professional man or woman."[29]

To correct this situation, it was recommended that the University explore in detail the possibility of creating a new baccalaureate degree programme that would assist students seriously to consider and come to know in some depth what the arts and sciences are and how they function, or can be made to function, in society. Students in the new programme, it was proposed, would deal with "certain key matters" such as "science, technology and the organization of the scientific and technological enterprise in modern society," "the nature of human societies, both Western and non-Western, and how they change through time," and "the arts, both as an area of study and as an activity in which the individual can engage."

The ad hoc committee that subsequently was charged with the task of dealing with this recommendation was chaired by a member of the Health Sciences Faculty (Dr. Dugal Campbell), and it reported in the spring of 1979.[30] Its response was strongly supportive of the Plan's recommendation, carefully measured in content, and shrewd in approach. Rather than enmesh itself in the details of programme requirements, course design and admission standards, the committee focussed on the principles that should underlie the new programme. It should provide students with a broad outline of contemporary knowledge, with a certain level of expertise in a specific subject, with an understanding of the connections between different fields of knowledge, and with the essential techniques for dealing with various kinds of information. The programme should have its own director reporting to the Vice President (Academic) and be staffed by faculty seconded from departments across the campus. The Director would be responsible at the outset for bringing together a planning council that would design the programme and the new courses that would be essential to its existence and success. Students successfully completing a three-year course of study would be awarded the BA; those completing a four-year programme would be awarded an Honours BA degree.

In the discussion of this report that followed, there was some concern expressed that the probable honours-level nature of the new programme would not address the need for an integrative approach to general education in the three-year Pass degree, but this criticism was not strong enough to thwart the enthusiastic endorsement of the proposal by the University's Senate in late June, 1979.

The task then was to find a director who could bring the programme into being. It was a search in which this author personally was involved. Any retrospective claim of success by a former academic administrator inevitably is a disputed one, but the very confident assertion made here is that the choice of Dr. Herb Jenkins was an outstanding one. Herb brought to the position a very genuine interest in the nature of undergraduate education, a warm and engaging manner with students, and a dogged persistence in dealing with academic administrators at all levels. As a dedicated teacher and distinguished researcher he understood the symbiosis between the two activities, and his fashioning of the inquiry seminars that became an essential part of the new programme reflected this understanding. But at this point, the narrative should be in his hands and it will be passed to him after one or two closing comments.

The Arts and Science Programme has given an excellent general education to the hundreds of students who have passed through it, and many of their commentaries contained in the following pages will attest to that fact. Why has it been so successful? Several reasons stand out. The first, already touched on, was the leadership of the founding Director, Herb Jenkins. Without his commitment and genius, the venture would never have developed its strong foundations and survived the subsequent university retrenchments. The high quality of the students was another important factor. From the outset, the admissions process sought to ensure that the students chosen were intellectually very able and committed to the goals and values of the new programme. With its enrolment of these bright, enthusiastic young students and its fashioning of new courses that had significant intellectual content, the Programme was able then to attract some of the University's outstanding faculty members into its teaching ranks. Their interaction with exceptional students was a wonderful catalyst for success. Another important factor was that from its earliest days the Programme was backed strongly by the senior academic administration, who committed significant resources to its development. Finally, the fact that from the beginning the Programme was assigned its own physical space and home quarters facilitated the fostering of a strong sense of identity and community among its students and instructors. This will be apparent in the discussion that follows.

Notes

1. See, William B. Spaulding, *Revitalizing Medical Education: McMaster Medical School, the Early Years 1965-1974* (Hamilton: B.C. Decker, 1991).
2. For its official history, see, C.M. Johnston, *McMaster University, vol.1, The Toronto Years* (Toronto: University of Toronto Press, 1976), *vol. 2, The Early Years in Hamilton, 1930-1957* (Toronto: University of Toronto Press, 1981).
3. The quotations appear in G.A. Rawlyk, "A.L. McCrimmon, H.P. Whidden, T.T. Shields, Christian Education and McMaster University," in G.A. Rawlyk, ed., *Canadian Baptists and Christian Higher Education* (Kingston &

Montreal: McGill-Queens University Press, 1988), 52-53. See also A.B. McKillop, *Matters of Mind: The University in Ontario, 1791-1951* (Toronto: University of Toronto Press, 1994), 314-315.

4. Watson Kirkconnell, "Liberal Education in the Canadian Democracy" (McMaster University, 1948), 14.
5. *Ibid*, 14-15.
6. See, F.S.L. Lyons, "The idea of a university: Newman to Robbins," in N. Phillipson, ed., *Universities, Society, and the Future* (Edinburgh: Edinburgh University Press, 1983), 113-144.
7. G.P. Gilmour, "Higher Education in the Canadian Democracy" (McMaster University, 1948), 14.
8. Ian Gregor, "Liberal education: an outworn ideal," in Phillipson, ed., *Universities, Society, and the Future*, 145-166.
9. Johnston, *McMaster University, vol. 1.*, 143-144.
10. *Ibid., vol. 2.*, 107-108.
11. The report, *From the Sixties to the Seventies* (Toronto: Committee of Presidents of Universities of Ontario, 1966), 77-79, notes that full-time undergraduate enrolment in the arts and science grew by over 300% from 1955-56 to 1965-66 and that by the end of the period about one-third of the students were in "Honour" courses. See also Committee of Presidents of Universities in Ontario; Subcommittee on Research and Planning, *Towards 2000: The Future of Post Secondary Education in Ontario* (Toronto: McClelland & Stewart, 1971), 73-80.
12. See Claude Bissell, *Halfway up Parnassus* (Toronto: University of Toronto Press, 1974), 78-80; Mel A. Preston and Helen E. Howard-Lock, "Emergence of physics graduate work in Canadian Universities 1945-1960," *Physics in Canada* (March/April 2000): 153-162.
13. *Report of the Canada Royal Commission on National Development in the Arts, Letters and Sciences* (Ottawa: Government of Canada, 1951), 138.
14. Algo D. Henderson, *Vitalizing Liberal Education* (New York: Harper & Bros., 1944), 26.
15. *Ibid.*, 104, 181-182.
16. Harvard University Committee on the Objectives of a General Education in a Free Society, *General Education in a Free Society* (Cambridge, Mass.: Harvard University Press, 1945).
17. Henry Rosovsky, *The University. An Owners Manual* (New York: W.W. Norton & Co., 1990), 113-130.
18. Eric Ashby, *Technology and the Academics* (London: Macmillan, 1958),77-81.
19. Johnston, *McMaster University, vol. 2.*, 240-267.
20. "Report of the McMaster Senate Committee on Curriculum Review" (McMaster University, 1961).
21. See "McMaster Faculty of Arts and Science, Final Report to the Senate Concerning Curriculum" (McMaster University, 1961).

22. See Eric Ashby, *Masters and Scholars* (London: Oxford University Press, 1970), 50-81; also, Bissell, *Halfway up Parnassus,* 122-159.
23. See George Grant, *Technology and Empire: Perspectives on North America* (Toronto: Anansi Press, 1969). The chapter in this book entitled "The University Curriculum" was reprinted as, "The University Curriculum and the Technological Threat," in W.R. Niblett, ed., *The Sciences, the Humanities and the Technological Threat* (London: University of London Press Ltd, 1975), 21-35. The quotations are taken from this reprinted version. See also William Christian, *George Grant. A Biography* (Toronto: University of Toronto Press, 1993), 271-275, 326-330.
24. "Report of the McMaster Senate Committee on Undergraduate Education" (McMaster University, 1971).
25. The 1968/69 McMaster Act organized the academic departments into three Divisions: *Arts,* which included the humanities, social sciences and business, *Science and Engineering,* and *Health Sciences.* The divisions were abolished in 1974, creating the present arrangement of six Faculties, each headed by a Dean who reports to the Provost.
26. Leo Marx, "Technology and the study of man," in Niblett, *The Sciences, the Humanities and the Technological Threat,* 13.
27. S. Lanfranco, "Social Sciences Experimental Year I Programme: A Midyear Progress Report" (McMaster University, 1971).
28. R.H. Hall, "Independent Studies Programme at McMaster University. A Brief History" (McMaster University, 1974).
29. "A Plan for McMaster, Report of the Joint Board/Senate Committee on Long Range Planning" (McMaster University, 1977).
30. "Report of the Ad Hoc Committee on a General Studies Programme Leading to a New Baccalaureate" (McMaster University, 1979).

2   Planning and Approval of the Arts and Science Programme

Herb Jenkins

My purpose here is to tell the story of the development by the Planning Council of what came to be known as McMaster's Arts and Science Programme. The story revolves around the tensions inherent in making choices among alternative pathways in the design of a programme of this kind. Those tensions first played out in the Planning Council as we struggled to outline the curriculum, and then in the larger university community as it reacted critically to the choices we had made. The record will show, I think, sufficient evidence of folly, of some wise choices, and of good luck, to be of interest to anyone who is given to contemplating questions about what a contemporary liberal education should aim to do, and how it might be fashioned to do it.

In the late summer of 1979, the Vice President Academic, L.J. King, asked whether I would accept a Senate appointment as Director of the new baccalaureate programme in general studies. My appointment stemmed from the Senate's endorsement in the spring of 1979 of the Campbell Committee Report, which recommended the development of a general studies programme at McMaster (p.12). At this stage the task was to form a planning council, and to bring a specific proposal for a programme to Senate for approval. Should the programme be approved, I would serve as its first Director.

I did not see the invitation coming. I was not involved in the work of the Campbell Committee. Although my academic life was centred on experimental psychology, and was as specialized as most, my experience as an undergraduate as part of a social-intellectual culture of engagement at Oberlin College, a relatively small liberal arts college, planted a seed of discontent with what I saw as the typical undergraduate educational experience in such research-intensive universities as McMaster. That experience suffered, I thought, from narrowness, and from the absence of a lively, social, intellectual community discussing and arguing about a wide spectrum of issues. Although I had only the vaguest conception of how to foster such a community, or to shape a curriculum for liberal education within a research-intensive university, I knew that I could not pass up this once-in-a-lifetime opportunity to try.

The Campbell Committee articulated in broad terms the aims of a general studies a programme. They were: to provide students with an outline of contemporary knowledge, to develop the relations and connections among different fields of knowledge, to provide a moderate degree of specialization in a discipline, to teach techniques of obtaining and processing information and communicating through speech and writing, and to teach mathematical reasoning and a second language.

The report recommended using a mix of existing and new courses for the new programme, which was to lead to a BA degree. New courses in general studies would be concerned with multi-disciplinary approaches to certain topics and would be jointly taught by several faculty members from different disciplines. The report left to the new planning council the task of designing a specific programme that would be appropriate to the aims of general studies as articulated by the Campbell Committee.

The report left unanswered an important question: was the new programme to be at the honours level (four years with a higher admission average), or at the level of pass programmes (three years with a lower admission average) (p.12). They did, however, recommend an admission average of 60% (equivalent to C– on the grading system used at McMaster in the era of the Campbell Report) which was at the level of our Pass programmes. The debate in Senate leading up to the decision to appoint a Director to plan a programme was also divided on the issue of whether the new programme should be at the pass or honours level. Dissatisfaction with three-year Pass programmes had been one of the spurs for devising a general studies programme. Yet, several Senators expressed their belief that the aims of the programme envisioned by the Campbell Committee pointed toward students with strong intellectual interests and the ability to handle a wide range of subjects – from mathematics to poetry. The Senate left a decision on the level of the programme to the new planning council.

With advice from the Academic Vice President, L.J. King, I began in late August of 1979 to put together a broad-based planning council. Partly as a counterweight to the prejudices of many faculty against anything connected with the words "general studies," I sought outstanding academics at McMaster whose achievements in research and scholarship were widely recognized. The six I approached said yes, confirming my belief that the opportunity to design a new, more liberal programme of undergraduate education is hard to resist.[1]

Overview

An overview of the major steps in the process of developing the Programme and obtaining approval from various bodies at the University may make the story easier to follow. The Planning Council reformulated the aims as stated by the Campbell Committee report while trying to remain faithful to the ideals of general education. It put forth an outline of its proposed programme in mid-March of 1980. Near the end of March, the proposal was discussed and vigorously criticized in an All-Faculties General Meeting. Subsequently, an invitation to all faculty members to express their views of the Programme was issued by the Vice President, and many responded. The first proposal was revised in the light of criticism and by early May was ready for consideration by the various committees of Senate.[2] It went first to the Curriculum Committee of Undergraduate Council, and then to Undergraduate Council. After approval by Undergraduate Council, The Board-Senate Committee on Long Range Planning assessed the Programme's potential value in relation to its anticipated costs. On May 21st the Proposal was voted on and approved by Senate as a whole.

Between the end of May of 1980 and September of 1981, when the first group of students entered the Programme, instructors for the Programme's new courses were appointed. They comprised an Instructional Council in which plans for individual courses were discussed. The final course outlines were approved by Senate's Undergraduate Council, and we made ready to welcome the first class.

Philosophy of the Programme

The Planning Council got down to work in September of 1979.[3] Our first task was to agree on the philosophy of the Programme. In a memorandum to the Council I put forth for discussion my views. I thought that the Programme should try to challenge able students who wanted to prepare themselves to lead an effective intellectual life in society although they might not wish to become practitioners of a departmentally-based discipline. Much of the memo was concerned with a question that proved central to our deliberations, "What is it that a student who does not intend to become a specialist should learn from the disciplines?"

My proposal was that they should learn how the core disciplines go about creating new knowledge. In other words, the programme should help them to understand the modes of inquiry that characterize the different disciplines. I thought that this would make the disciplines accessible to the students so that they would be able to read the literature of the discipline, or seek advice from experts, with some understanding of what the discipline was about. In those early days it was my view that the larger purpose of being introduced to the ideas and methods of the disciplines was to enable our students to take a multi-disciplinary approach to the investigation of questions that arise from living in society (rather than from the state of the art in a discipline). I used the term "practical inquiry" to distinguish questions of this kind from those that arise within academic disciplines, but I had no doubt that practical inquiry needed to be scholarly as well.

Developing the skills of inquiring into questions of human concern that do not lie in the province of a single discipline, was, I thought, a central and distinctive purpose of the Programme. Through this effort, students would have reason to try to integrate what they were learning from their work in the disciplines of arts and science. So, inquiry, both within the established disciplines as well as inquiry directed to the understanding of issues that arise more immediately from living in society, should, I thought, be the unifying philosophy of the Programme.

My conviction that teaching the art of inquiry should be an important part of our Programme developed from several sources: an experience at Oberlin College, a discussion with a colleague at McMaster University, and readings in the philosophy of higher education. At Oberlin College, where I was a student in the late 40s, a professor whom I greatly respected, L.E. Cole, gave an invited talk entitled "Integration" in a college-wide lecture series (Senior assembly, May 15, 1945, Oberlin College). He addressed a prevalent concern among students about what their courses really added up to. Is there a larger meaning to a university education than the sum of courses taken? He argued that no professor could presume to the kind of omniscience that would be required to develop the connections among the disciplines and make them speak to a larger purpose. Moreover, attempts to achieve the same end in a capstone course taught by many teachers would likely result in a loosely joined series of mini-courses in which the difficulty was reproduced in the very remedy. A more promising way to see the relations among the several arts and sciences was, he thought, to investigate a complex, multi-dimensional issue in depth. In the process of focussing the knowledge and the methods of several disciplines on such an issue, one might be able to appreciate both their distinctive roles and how, together, they can lead to a fuller understanding of an issue than could be had from a narrower perspective. I thought this was a good argument.

I was also encouraged to pursue the idea of inquiry by a discussion with a McMaster colleague, B.G. Galef (Psychology), who had led a small seminar group of students within the Experimental Year I Programme in the Social Sciences (p.11). He spoke of the work of the seminar as "inquiry", and I thought that was a good name for what I hoped we could develop in our new programme. After my appointment as Director, I began discussing the idea with many colleagues at McMaster, including those who later became members of the Planning Council. I found that it was generally well received—often enthusiastically.

I also found in readings on the philosophy of the curriculum support and further arguments about the place of inquiry in a programme of liberal education. Daniel Bell wrote convincingly, I thought, about the centrality of inquiry.

> I do not think that the distinction between general education and specialism really holds. One must embody and exemplify general education through the disciplines: and one must extend the concept of specialism so that the ground of knowledge is explicit. The common bond of the two is the emphasis on conceptual inquiry. To this extent, in the reconciliation of liberal education and specialism, training cannot deal with techniques in the narrow sense, but with the foundations of knowledge itself: i.e., how a particular discipline establishes its concepts; how these concepts, seen as fluid inquiry, need to be revised to meet new problems; how one establishes the criteria of choice for one, rather than another, alternative patterns of inquiry. In effect, general education is education in the conduct and strategy of inquiry itself.[4]

While the inquiry of which Bell writes is discipline centred,

J.J. Schwab's writing, which also influenced my thinking, gave an important place to inquiry focussed on contemporary issues of a kind that cannot be encompassed by one or another of the disciplines. Schwab wrote about the place of "practical and current" problems in the liberal curriculum, and gave as examples those of "energy shortage, environmental deterioration, urbanism, democratization of industry, multinational corporations, individual rights and freedoms, and making democracy safe from the US presidency." It would be a mistake, he said, to view these matters as though they could be understood as examples of perennial concerns, to view them as instances of general issues, and "to make them appear to be well within the compass of the typically academic, amenable to its great strength—which is its greatest weakness as far as practical problems are concerned—its passion for generality, neatness, and order."

What one needs to approach these messy issues, he said, is to recognize the particulars of the circumstances that give rise to them, to see how these particulars might enter into the formulation of the questions to be understood, to weigh alternative ways of formulating the question, to be eclectic in the use of discipline-based knowledge and methods, to anticipate and weigh alternative "answers" to these questions, and to decide if and when deliberation warrants taking a position, or even taking action to remedy a problem.

Schwab concludes his rather brief treatment of these matters thus:

> The arts of the eclectic and the practical are not presently arts typical
> of the university. Yet they depend, in part, on the fruits of academic
> arts. And if they are necessary arts and if they can be taught, they
> ought to be taught. And if they are not taught by universities, then
> by whom shall they be taught?[5]

I circulated these readings to the Council. We agreed that the "arts of inquiry" were "necessary arts", that they could be taught, and, of course, should be taught in the university, and, specifically, in our programme. Moreover, I even hoped that becoming especially accomplished in the ways of scholarly investigation into current issues of public concern could be a professional goal for our students—one that could be considered, although somewhat paradoxically, as a form of specialization in itself.

In addition to a new emphasis on the aim of fostering the art of inquiry, our discussions of philosophy for the Programme led to an agreement that we should aim to provide a balanced and substantial introduction to arts and sciences, and to develop skills in writing, speaking, and in critical and quantitative reasoning. We had reformulated the expression of aims in the Campbell Committee report while remaining, we thought, faithful to its spirit.

Early Agreement on Major Features

By mid-November we appeared to have made rapid progress toward a broad outline of the Programme. We had identified the sectors and given them approximate weights. For the core of required courses we settled on sectors and weights as follows: natural science and technology–20%; society and conceptions of man–20%; competence in language and mathematics–30%; creative Arts–10%; art of practical inquiry–20%.

We seemed to be making good progress, but we did not foresee how difficult it was going to be to move from this broad conception to a description of the individual courses that would constitute the curriculum, especially for that part of the Programme which was labelled "society and conceptions of man." To jump ahead of the story, we later recast this part as "humanistic learning and the social sciences," but rather than helping us toward outlining the courses that would convey this part of the Programme, our decision to put humanistic learning and the social sciences together probably exacerbated the problems.

In other areas, certain decisions were taken rather easily. First, although one Council member believed we should develop the Programme for Pass students, the view that we should place the Programme at the honours level prevailed. I think it did so for several reasons. The aims we set out were ambitious, even idealistic, and would, we thought, appeal only to students with a thirst for knowledge. We found ourselves designing a Programme for budding intellectuals who were able and willing to undertake studies in a wide spectrum of disciplines. Second, we thought it important to challenge the association of "general" or "liberal" education with lower standards and less demanding work than in specialist programmes. We believed that the equation of breadth with superficiality needed to be overturned. If we could attract very able and highly motivated students, and satisfy their intellectual needs in this Programme, we would be taking a step toward breaking the association of "liberal" with "superficial". Then, too, we thought that even a modest infusion of students who were especially able and eager to learn could have a good effect on the intellectual life of the University as a whole.

Second, we came to the view that we should aim for a small programme with a yearly intake of no more than 40 or so students. We thought that the aims of the Programme required a kind of teaching that simply could not be done with large classes. In particular, the inquiry courses, as well as other courses in which skill development was a major objective, would require a great deal of attention to individual work. To accomplish that in a larger programme would require a greater diversion of the University's resources from existing programmes to our Programme than we thought would be acceptable, or wise.

Third, we made up our minds to argue that the Programme should lead to its own distinctive degree. The Campbell Committee had recommended that a general studies programme should lead to the BA degree. We had settled on "Arts and Science" to describe the Programme and hoped that we could get approval for the degree, Bachelor of Arts and Science. Although we recognized the possible confusion with a Faculty of Arts and Science in our proposed name for the Programme, The Arts and Science Programme, we could not live with any of the alternatives that came to mind: "Integrated Studies"; "General Studies"; "Liberal Studies", "Multi-disciplinary Studies"; and so on. We had also decided that both a three-year and a four-year degree should be offered, that honours level performance should be required throughout, and that the first three years should be substantially the same whether or not the fourth year was undertaken. We thought a three-year Programme would appeal to students who want to go on to professional schools, or to use all of a fourth year to prepare for a particular graduate programme, without extending too greatly their years of formal schooling.[6]

The weights given to different sectors of the curriculum reflected our view that the Programme should pay a lot of attention to developing intellectual skills—skills in thinking, writing and speaking clearly, and skills in quantitative reasoning. If we needed a rationale for that emphasis, our commitment to inquiry was ready to hand. But even putting that aside, these skills were seen as essential parts of a liberal education that would, in the long run, open many doors to satisfying work.

The important role we assigned to the sciences reflected a consensus in the Council that in our times, the sciences were playing an ever increasing role in shaping conceptions of man, society and the universe. A liberally educated person must have some understanding of the methods and achievements of the sciences. We soon came to the view that the core curriculum should include biology as well as the physical sciences. Modern biology, with its relatively recent understanding of the genetic code, was too important to be merely an optional study. The inclusion of technology in the core acknowledged that much of the way we live on this planet is shaped by technology.

We had also decided against one version of a liberal programme – a year or two of broad-sweep courses followed by a conventional but reduced departmental specialization. We decided not to insist on specialization, to steer away from survey courses, and to design a programme with a substantial core curriculum required of all students. Each of the core courses was to extend for a full year. Electives, we thought, should increase in number in the later years of the programme, but in every year some core courses would be taken. In the fourth or final year of the programme a thesis or individual study course would be part of the required core. Whereas electives are used to broaden the curriculum in the typical specialized degree programme, in our proposed programme, breadth was carried by the required core courses while more specialized work could be pursued, for students who so chose, through a departmentally concentrated use of electives.

In the Campbell Committee report, a foreign language course was advocated, but we decided not to require it. The arguments that prevailed were that unless one devoted enough time to the study of a second language to become fluent, and had cause to use the language regularly, the skill would soon decay. Moreover, there was so much to be accomplished in developing English-language skills broadly conceived, that we felt it unwise to require a course in a foreign language.

We also considered the question of whether the degree was to be earned in the traditional way in North American universities or in a new way. Traditionally, degrees are earned by the satisfactory completion of a number of required and elective courses. We considered a departure in which satisfactory performance in non-course, or area, examinations would be a substitute for, or a supplement to, course-based examinations. In favour of non-course examinations was the idea that if properly designed and well described in advance, they might motivate students to take more interest in the bigger picture, might give them more responsibility for thinking creatively about the relations among areas of knowledge, and might even liberate them from having to jump all the hurdles involved in a piecemeal, course-by-course definition of academic success. On the other hand, the use of non-course examinations would put us radically out of step with the way credits are accumulated and degrees are earned in the rest of this University and in other institutions. Then, too, there was the question of how well students unaccustomed to such examinations would be able to deal with them. In the end we dropped the option of non-course examinations.

The particular issues raised by the possibility of substituting comprehensive examinations for the traditional course-based exams are part of a more general issue: In the design of a new programme with distinctive goals, how far can one afford to depart from the traditional organization of undergraduate education in the parent university? That question was implicit in other decisions about the curriculum as well, and I later return to it.

Getting to Courses

Getting from an overall conception of the Programme to a description of courses required decisions on a number of general issues. How far could we go in establishing new courses to meet the goals of the Programme? How much use should be made of existing courses and in what parts of the Programme? Should we create optional sets of courses within the core Programme among which students might choose, or should there be just one set of core courses for all? For those courses that were to be newly designed for the purposes of the Programme, what was the appropriate level of specificity in our proposal about content or method of teaching? Although it was expected that some members of the Council at one time or another would teach in the Programme, we were not designing courses for ourselves to teach. They would be taught by others who would not be recruited until after the Programme was accepted. If we outlined courses in too much detail, we might find ourselves with prescriptions no one was able or willing to fill. University teachers, we recognized, must have the freedom to bring their own insights to the design of a course. On the other hand, too vague a characterization of courses might lead to a programme whose parts were not much more closely related or coherent in design than a collection of courses from a university calendar. Although we did not seek to formulate explicit answers to these questions, we were aware of them, and we tried to steer a mid course and to avoid the hazards of going too far in one direction.

Our decision on whether to provide optional sets of courses within the prescribed core was conditioned by a prior decision about the prerequisites for admission to the Programme. We did not wish to narrow the pool of potential students by requiring specific high-school credits. We wanted above average students with a serious interest in learning, but we did not expect them to have made an early commitment to a subject area. We believed that one of the potential advantages of our Programme was to allow students, who might be undecided about where to concentrate, a chance to explore the academic landscape at university before making that decision. It would be inconsistent with that aim to require an applicant to have done, for example, a course in physics, chemistry, or many courses in advanced high school mathematics. Although somewhat modified later (p.45) our first statement of admission requirements stipulated only the senior high school course in English (Grade 13 English), and at least one senior course in mathematics, not necessarily calculus. Accordingly, we could expect students to enter our Programme with quite different levels of preparation for courses, especially in mathematics and science. That argued for offering some optional courses within the required core to accommodate students with different backgrounds.

Inquiry

The inquiry courses would be newly developed for the Programme. We thought of them as an opportunity to develop the wide spectrum of skills involved in research: formulating incisive questions, deciding what information is needed, finding and evaluating the information, and reporting the findings and conclusions. These courses, we hoped, would also serve to motivate the application of skills and knowledge developed in other parts of the Programme and show the need to integrate the arts and sciences when trying to understand complex issues. We thought that three, year-long inquiry courses should be required. In the first-year course, special attention would be given to developing skills of inquiry. They included library research skills, an introduction to certain basic ideas of data analysis, and the use of computers. We also thought the first inquiry course was a place to provide a more extended orientation to the work of the University than was available elsewhere. We envisioned a series of lectures and discussions led by faculty members from different academic disciplines explaining what their subject was about, why someone might want to study it, and where the frontiers of research in the subject might lie.

Mathematics, Science, and Technology

In mathematics, we decided to rely entirely on existing courses. Students with high school calculus would take a more advanced calculus course than would those without that prerequisite. All students would follow up with an existing course in statistics and probability theory. In the sciences, we incorporated the existing first-year biology course which had been recently redesigned by the Department to give a broad view of adaptation, evolution, structure and function.

For the physical sciences, however, we felt it desirable to develop a new course. We wanted a course which, although centred on physics, would include some fundamental concepts in chemistry. We also wanted to include an historical perspective on turning points in the development of modern physical and chemical theory. We did not expect this course to cover all of the topics usually encountered in a first-year physics or chemistry course.

To teach what we hoped our students would learn about the nature and impact of technology clearly required a new course. We thought that part of that course could focus on technologies flowing from physical sciences and engineering, while another part might focus on technologies more closely associated with the biological sciences, including, of course, medical technology. We thought that students should learn something about how technology works as well as about the place of technology in society.

The Arts

From early in our deliberations it became clear that we intended to emphasize the development of broadly transferable intellectual skills, which, on the arts side, included skill in the uses of language and in clear thinking. Although we considered the possibility that these skills might be developed as an integral part of more content-oriented courses in the arts, we came to the view that we were more likely to get a stable commitment to furthering these skills by making their development the aim of a separate course. We believed that if we were to leave the development of these skills entirely to courses with broader, more content-oriented aims, we would run the risk that not enough would be done. Then too, teaching these skills is an academic specialization and benefits from experience. An instructor well qualified to teach a content-oriented course in the arts might not have the background for teaching these skills.

Since, in our view, much of what ails student writing can be ascribed to weakness in logic, or critical thinking, we thought it made sense to combine writing and logic in one course. That eventually led to the course: "Writing and verbal reasoning," later called "Writing and informal logic." As this course subsequently developed in practice, instructors took steps to link it closely with other courses in which there were major writing assignments.

The Council also moved rather quickly to the view that a course in the creative arts would add a valuable dimension to the programme. The proposal was to pay special attention to the creative process in both music and the graphic arts as a way into a deeper appreciation of artistic achievements. We spent rather little time discussing alternative approaches, or specifics of any kind, for this course. Perhaps that was because only one of us could claim much insight into its subject matter. In any case, we did not anticipate just how difficult it would be to teach this course consistently well.

To our surprise, designing the remaining, more content-oriented courses, in the humanities and social sciences was the most difficult and time-consuming part of the Council's work. Moreover, our recommendations for this area attracted the most concerted criticism when our initial proposal was put before the University community. I begin this part of the story by indicating what we said about this area in the first proposal, and I then turn to an account of how we arrived at that position. That will involve a look at other options we considered and why we did not adopt them.

Recall that we developed the view that what our students should learn from the disciplines had to do with their modes of inquiry. How did the different disciplines go about generating new knowledge? But we recognized that questions about modes of inquiry were quite abstract– they needed to be coupled with knowledge of the major achievements of a discipline. We felt that we should be more specific about what our students should be learning in these courses.

Our view was that our students should, wherever possible, be reading and discussing great books in the humanities and social sciences throughout these courses. We believed that great books could be used to illuminate perennial concerns of human kind about how to live a life. Through their study one could develop a critical appreciation of different approaches to understanding the human condition and the search for a good life. Our statement of a theme owed something to Sidney Hook, who, in an essay on what students should encounter in a curriculum for a liberal education, had written:

> Every student needs to be informed, not only of significant facts and theories about nature, society, and the human psyche, but also of the conflict of values and ideals in our time, of the great maps of life, the paths to salvation or damnation, under which human beings are enrolled He must learn how to uncover the inescapable presence of values in every policy, how to relate them to their causes and consequences and costs in other values, and the difference between arbitrary and reasonable value judgments.[7]

The decision that our courses in both the humanities and the social sciences should speak to the same, or closely related, fundamental questions of living led us to refer to the entire course sequence as humanistic learning and the social sciences (HL&SS). These courses, we believed, would exemplify both differences and complementarity in modes of inquiry in the humanities and in the social sciences. We hoped that our students would develop an appreciation of the place of each mode of thought in the larger scheme of things so that they would continue to learn from both.

We came to the view that there should be three full-year courses in HL&SS. We recommended that the first should explore our overarching theme—the search for understanding and for the good life—in religious and philosophical thought, and in the scientific world view as it emerged from the Enlightenment. The second would examine conceptions of man and society as they developed in the social sciences. The third course would continue to explore the same broad theme through literature. These courses would be newly designed to meet our objectives for this part of the Programme.

I turn now to consider other options for the curriculum in the humanities and social sciences which we considered and ultimately rejected.

1) The work in the humanities and social sciences might be carried largely by selections from among existing departmental offerings, followed, perhaps, by a new capstone, or integrative seminar that would explore a major theme. Alternatively, we could create a new set of courses and require them of all the Programme's students.

We took the latter path and decided to develop new courses for the entire area. This rather risky decision was made for several reasons. We thought that we could create a more coherent, better connected set of courses by designing them for the aims of this Programme. If successful, our students would share an intellectual experience which could stimulate good discussions, and help to build a vital intellectual climate. Designing our own courses would also provide an opportunity to recruit excellent teachers to the Instructional Council.

2) We could structure the entire set of courses in humanistic learning and the social sciences on the literature, thought, and history of selected centuries or periods. The member of Council who put forth this proposal (E.P. Sanders, Religious Studies) recommended a study of the Mediterranean world in the first century; the Renaissance; the eighteenth century; and the twentieth century. Attention to the social sciences could be subsumed under "thought."

Although we found this proposal to be innovative and attractive, in the end we thought that the resulting set of courses would depart too radically from discipline-centred courses in the University. We thought that doing all of the work in humanistic learning and the social sciences in this structure was especially risky. We wondered whether we could find faculty willing and able to teach the courses. Some of us thought that the periods approach did not provide definite occasions on which the work of the social sciences would be treated. Some preferred to see literature studied in a separate course which would create a place in the Programme for instructors with a depth of knowledge and experience in introducing students to the values and forms of literature. Some thought that the periods approach might become too descriptive and that a thematic approach would be more attractive to students.

3) A year-long, global history course could be developed as the first course in a two-year sequence in the humanities and social sciences. The history course would provide a context for the examination in more depth of selected topics or themes in a second course, as well as providing useful historical context for the study of selected literature in the third course.

The option of a global history course stemmed from discussions I had with a member of the Department of History, T.E. Willey, about ways of structuring the work in humanities and the social sciences. He wrote a thoughtful proposal, which was read by members of the Council, in which he argued for the value of a broad survey of world history from the 1500s to the modern age. It would attempt to "convey the dynamic of change in the modern world, [and] the interaction between material development and culture."

Although this proposal also had its appeal, we felt that a broad survey was not compatible with our commitment to the examination of great books as a way into some of the central ideas in the humanities as well as the social sciences. If we used one of the courses in the sequence as a survey, that would virtually preclude the examination in reasonable depth of ideas in religious and philosophical thought and the emergence of a scientific world view, unless, of course, we were willing to give up on a separate course devoted to thought in the social sciences, or to literature. For some of the same reasons that led us to reject the period approach to thought, history, and literature, we decided against world history for the first course in the sequence.

4) We might develop a major course on the Western intellectual

tradition. In one version, the course would be based on great books in literature, science, and philosophy. We had before us a model for such a course that was being taught successfully at the University of Utah. It was entitled "The Intellectual Tradition: Philosophical, Literary, and Scientific Landmarks of the West." A course of this kind might be supplemented with selected courses from existing Departmental offerings in order to deal with the social sciences, or other areas, in a more comprehensive way.

Although this option was certainly consistent with our desire to make heavy use of great books, it posed other problems. At least as structured by the University of Utah, it did not provide definite occasions for treating the social sciences. It also contained more readings in science than we thought appropriate for this part of our Programme. Moreover, because of the very broad range of matters dealt with in such a course, it would undoubtedly have to be jointly taught by several faculty. We feared that courses taught by several faculty would become several mini courses, rather than a coherent view of intellectual history. We decided that the Utah course was not quite the right prescription for course work in the humanities and social sciences in our programme.

5) Cutting across issues of what should be studied was the matter of the method or format for teaching. We knew that the inquiry courses would be aimed at developing skills in self-directed learning and would not be dominated by the lecture format. But should we recommend a non-traditional format for other courses as well? More specifically, we considered the possibility of using for courses in the humanities and social sciences a seminar format in which instructors would act more as tour guides than as lecturers.

We decided against recommending a seminar format as the dominant approach to teaching in the humanities and social sciences. Our classes were going to be small, they could include time spent in even smaller sections, and they would certainly involve our students in writing, presenting papers, and discussing issues to a greater degree than would be expected in the usual course. We thought students could profit from considerable guidance in understanding and interpreting the great books, and that lecture courses would lend themselves better to this kind of instruction than would the seminar format. As in many of our other decisions, we chose the more conventional approach to undergraduate education—lecture courses rather than seminars.

Critics Have Their Day

A General Faculty Meeting was called for March 27th to discuss the proposal entitled "Outline of a New Baccalaureate Degree Programme in Arts and Science," which had been distributed to all faculty. The meeting was not well attended, perhaps one hundred from a faculty of one thousand or more, but what the meeting lacked in numbers it made up in the vigour of the criticisms.

Most of the criticism came from faculty members in the humanities. It was said that the curriculum lacked any serious study of the humanities, and that the absence of a course in history was a particularly serious mistake. More than one said that the Programme was one in applied social science. The proposed inquiry courses, one speaker said, lacked a framework to guide investigation and showed too much faith in method. Another critic asserted that the framers showed a naive optimism that the world's problems could be solved by students who had learned a little science while learning nothing in depth about any discipline and suffering from an ignorance of the past and the value of humanistic learning. One said that the Programme manifested the shallowness of scientism, positivism, and presentism. In a similar vein, another remarked that it would seem to have come from an institute of technology rather than a university.

Although the major tenor of the criticisms from those in the disciplines of the humanities was that the proposed programme contained too much of the social sciences and showed a misplaced belief in the ability of applied social science to solve society's problems, members of the social science faculty did not express approval of the treatment of their disciplines. No specific place had been given, for example, to the study of anthropology, sociology, psychology, or economics. Although the disapproval was not explicitly voiced, it seemed as though the attempt to consider together humanistic and social scientific approaches to fundamental issues about the way we live in society was applauded by neither the social scientists nor the humanists.

In addition to serious reservations about the content of the curriculum criticisms were voiced about the feasibility of a Programme of this kind. Some doubted that students could be found to take the Programme, or faculty willing to teach in it. Others claimed that our graduates would have great difficulty in finding work, and even those who used their electives to specialize might lack the credits necessary for acceptance to graduate schools.

It was said that the Programme's small size meant that scarce resources would be devoted to a few students, while broader concerns about undergraduate education at McMaster would not be addressed. One speaker criticized the proposal for a lack of detail about the content of courses, expressed the fear that the Programme would be hastily approved without due deliberation, and recommended that the proposal be reviewed by each of the Faculties before being considered by Undergraduate Council.

Although a few speakers expressed their support for the Programme as proposed, there was no mistaking the dominant expression of dissatisfaction with the proposal. We of course expected criticism and suggestions for changes, but the members of the Planning Council were surprised by the extent of the rejection of its plan by most of those who spoke at this meeting. Our informal discussions with colleagues over the months as the proposal was taking shape had been generally positive and did not prepare us for this outcome. We decided that although we were prepared to make revisions in an attempt to strengthen the proposal, before proceeding we needed to know the views of a larger number of faculty.

There was another reason to seek the views of a wider group. We believed that particularly threatening to our cause was the position of one of the speakers at the General Faculty Meeting that the proposal should go to each of the Faculties for their assessments before it went to Undergraduate Council. Had the proposal been referred to faculties it would no doubt have been reviewed by each department. It is in the nature of a broad core programme that no one discipline receives quite as much attention as disciplinary, departmental adherents think desirable or even necessary to a liberal education in the arts and sciences. If the referral to Faculties took place we believed the programme would be lost. We believed that the programme should be the legitimate concern of all faculty members as individuals, rather than as members of one or another faculty, and we later argued successfully against a referral to faculties.

To obtain the views of more faculty, I turned for help to the Vice President, Academic. He agreed to write a letter and send it to all members of faculty inviting them to write to Undergraduate Council, with a copy to the Planning Council, expressing their views of the proposed Programme. In his letter, he reminded faculty that in the next few months Undergraduate Council would judge the academic merits of the Programme as fashioned, while the detailed description of courses, which would have to await the identification of instructors, would at a later time also be subject to their approval. His letter expressed his own view of the proposal in these words: "In all of its essentials the new programme has my full and enthusiastic support."

In response to the Vice President's letter, or earlier on their own initiative in response to the General Faculty Meeting, forty-five members of faculty wrote to express their views. Thirty-two expressed strong support with no substantial reservations. Three writers, while not commenting on the merits of the Programme as a whole, advocated the inclusion of the study of Eastern religious thought, or more broadly, Eastern thought and culture. Two clearly supported the Programme, but wanted to see some significant changes. Four had more serious reservations and recommended substantial changes in the curriculum. Finally, four others were comprehensively and almost completely negative.

The responses showed far more support for the Programme at McMaster than one would have thought existed from the speakers at the General Faculty Meeting. Supporting letters came from a wide spectrum of disciplines including the humanities and social sciences as well as the sciences and the Faculty of Health Sciences. The letters often cited the emphasis on inquiry as innovative and aimed at an important educational objective. Many praised the attention paid to intellectual skills. Several found the proposal to be coherent, and well balanced in the arts and sciences. The provision for an examination of technology was mentioned as appropriate to a liberal education for our times.

The proposal also received support from members of the University community who were not faculty members. The Chairman of McMaster's Board of Governors wrote a strong letter of support for the structure of the Programme as well as for its aims. The senior staff of the student counselling service jointly authored a letter in which they strongly endorsed the principles of the Programme and said: "The types of learning and intellectual skills emphasized in the program are precisely those which employers from both the private and public sector identify as highly important and desirable in university graduates." They went on to say: "From our intensive contact with students, we are aware that problems in deriving academic satisfaction from the university experience, and in developing those qualities required for satisfying careers are most prevalent among Pass degree students." The staff regretted that the Programme was intended for especially able students and would do little to address the problems of other students. However, they gave their support to the Programme in the hope that it would serve as a model and its advantages extended to a larger number of students, especially to those who normally follow Pass degree programmes.

Negative letters repeated the lines of criticism voiced at the General Faculty meeting, which was not surprising since several of them were written by speakers at that meeting. One new, and comprehensively negative letter from a member of the history department attacked, among many other things, the choice of examples of readings students might encounter in the HL & SS, and remarked: "The real problem lies in the humanities component, which betrays less an intention to plan a general education than the need for the planners to acquire one." *Touché*. The Departments of Philosophy, History, and Religious Studies accounted for a large share of the negative letters.

A Revised Proposal

While letters from faculty were coming in, the Council began a revision of the proposal (see note 2). We tried to see what changes would strengthen the Programme in the light of those criticisms which we could accept, and to make, overall, a stronger case for the merits of the proposed Programme.

We began with another look at the option of a history course, and at other ways of encouraging an historical perspective in the Programme. Through its Chairman, we asked the Department of History to develop their recommendation. Some of the members met to consider the matter. They reached the conclusion that the proposal for a global history course as described in the letter from T.E. Willey, which I noted previously, reflected their views. The Planning Council continued, however, to think that a broad historical survey course would do little to encourage historical thinking about fundamental issues in the humanities and social sciences. We did, however, decide to increase opportunities for the study of history, or the use of an historical approach to understanding issues, in another way. In the revision we allowed the substitution of a course in which another age or culture was studied for the third inquiry course. In addition to increasing opportunities for developing a comparative historical approach to understanding our own age and culture, it was intended to open the door more widely to the study of Eastern religious thought and cultures.

Many critics focussed on the three-course sequence in humanistic learning and the social sciences. As we studied the criticisms we came to the view that our proposal was too prescriptive of what was to be studied in these courses. Although we intended only to give examples of writings that might be studied, some critics took them to be prescriptions and voiced objections to the particular choices. Moreover, we now thought that we had related these courses too strongly to a theme—"the search for understanding, maps of life, and pathways to salvation." Perhaps by so doing we had invited the fear that the integrity, methods, and achievements of the disciplines would be slighted. We may well have added to that fear by labelling the entire three-course sequence as "humanistic learning and social science." We needed to make it clearer that accomplished scholars at McMaster with deep knowledge of their disciplines would be sought to teach these courses. We decided to rework this part of the proposal.

In the revised proposal the three courses were entitled Western Thought I, Western Thought II, and Literature. We continued to advocate the study of great writings that changed human consciousness in Western civilization, but we no longer tried to identify an overarching theme. Rather, we simply said that these courses should help students to deepen their understanding of central issues of life. We continued to recommend that Western Thought I should focus on religious thought, philosophical thought, and the emergence of a scientific world view. Western Thought II would examine important writings in political science, economics and psychology. These courses, we noted, could be structured as intellectual history. That could highlight the interconnectedness of thought about central issues of living. Alternatively, the courses might trace the development of selected themes more vertically within intellectual traditions. That would be well suited to bring out both continuity and change in Western thought. These matters, as well as the selection of readings were, we said, best left to instructors. We left the study of Eastern Thought or other cultures as an option which could be substituted for the third inquiry course.

The third course, Literature, would examine works drawn from a variety of genres and cultural periods. Using wording suggested by Michael Ross, a member of the English Department who later served as the first instructor of the course, the proposal said: "The literature of the past, as well as of the present, has much to say about persistent, vital questions of existence in human societies. We believe it is possible to deepen one's sense of the human condition through literature while respecting the essential truth that literary works say what they have to say in specifically literary ways, and that, for a proper understanding of them, their imaginative integrity must be recognized, not violated."

Our revised proposal continued to give an important place to inquiry. We tried to respond to the criticism that inquiry courses lacked a framework by suggesting one. Borrowing from unpublished writings by Leo Marx on the Kenan Colloquium at Amherst College, we suggested that the search for a balanced relation between the interests of individuals and the natural, social, and cultural environments could serve as a recurrent theme. We identified four broad areas of inquiry with examples of more specific topics within each area. The broad areas, and an example of a topic within each area, shown in parentheses, were: technology and human purposes (the possible use of computers for surveillance and regulation of individuals by government, business, or other institutions); culture and the arts (the role of censorship in arts and entertainment); government, other institutions, and political systems (patterns of employment and the problem of unemployment); the commonweal and the clash of interests and ideologies (the rise of special interest groups and their increasing influence on government policies). We also included in an appendix outlines for inquiries submitted by individual faculty members. Reluctantly, we relinquished our plan to include an orientation to the University within the first inquiry course in response to the criticism that it should not be given course credit.

We hoped our revision would change the perception on the part of some that the planners thought of inquiry as solving problems through applied social science. In our view, the essential purpose of inquiry was to help students to a better understanding of how to approach important issues by giving them guidance in asking good questions and pursuing them through research.

Finally, we tried to allay fears that, without extensive additional course work beyond the Arts and Science Programme, our graduates would be inadmissible to medical schools or to academic graduate programmes. Even the most prescriptive requirements for admission to any of Ontario's medical schools could be met, we pointed out, by a student within our Programme through an appropriate use of electives. We also suggested that other judicious substitutions for required courses would be allowed to meet the needs of students who were concentrating their electives in a departmental discipline and might be preparing for graduate work in that discipline. As it turned out, a clearer answer to the very important question of the suitability of the Programme for students who at some point decide they wish to put down roots in a discipline and perhaps to do graduate work within it, was not developed until after the Programme had been in operation for few years and Combined Honours Programmes were developed (p.46).

The curriculum as it appeared in the revised proposal is shown in Table I.

TABLE I		
Core curriculum of the Arts and Science Programme as of May 1981		
	Science & Mathematics	Humanities & Social Science	Interdisciplinary
Year I	Biology Calculus	Western Thought I Writing & Informal Logic	Inquiry I
Year II	Physical Science Statistics & Probability	Western Thought II	Inquiry II
Year III		Literature Technology & Society	Inquiry III
Year IV		Creative arts	Thesis

Notes: Underlined courses were newly created for the Programme. All courses extend over the full year (6 units). A typical sequence of courses by years is shown, but there was flexibility in sequencing. In place of Inquiry III, 6 units of study of another age or culture could be taken. A typical full-load four-year programme at McMaster consists of the equivalent of 20 full-year courses, or five courses each year. Fourteen such courses constituted the core (required) programme. The equivalent of 6 full-year courses (36 units) was therefore available for electives.

Running the Gauntlet

By the third week of April, the revised proposal was sent to Undergraduate Council, and copies were made available to other members of the University community. Meetings with the Curriculum Committee of Undergraduate Council followed in the next weeks. My memory of the particulars has faded, but I recall my disappointment at the Committee's final vote. Although none voted to reject the proposal, as many abstained as voted in its favour. Next was a debate and vote in Undergraduate Council as a whole.

Leading up to that debate, I had a useful discussion with someone who had a long-term interest in undergraduate education, was a member of the Department of English, Associate Dean of Humanities Studies, and a member of Undergraduate Council, Maureen Halsall. She would speak against its approval at Undergraduate Council. Although she believed that the Programme had strong positive features which would, in a time of more adequate funding and expansion, warrant approval, she did not believe it should be instituted at this time when McMaster was experiencing persistent underfunding which threatened our ability to maintain the quality of existing honours programmes. In her view the most serious problem with undergraduate education at McMaster was the unsatisfactory state of Pass programmes whose students needed many of the things the new Programme proposed to offer to a small number of honours level students– courses to develop intellectual skills and such courses in the humanities and social sciences as the Western Thought courses, which take a broader perspective than traditional Departmental offerings. She had an alternative proposal. She would advocate requiring such courses of all Pass students and making their delivery the responsibility of faculties and departments. The money so spent would, she believed, have a greater impact than if spent on the proposed Arts and Science Programme.

I thought that these arguments on the best use of very tight resources might prove persuasive to many, and I asked for a meeting with the President, Arthur Bourns, and Vice President, L.J King, to discuss the question of funding. The University had recently obtained a generous bequest from Harry Lyman Hooker, and from the endowment income it had created a general fund for University advancement. I urged that the Arts and Science Programme, if approved, be funded for a start-up period from this fund, while other initiatives designed to enhance undergraduate education, could also be considered for support from this source. I also suggested that approval of the Programme by Undergraduate Council might include provision for a review of the Programme's performance by Undergraduate Council in three years' time. Both suggestions were supported by the President and Vice President, and were put forward in the subsequent debate at Undergraduate Council, and may have played a role in gaining the support of its members for our proposal.

Members of the Planning council were invited to be present at the meeting of Undergraduate Council and were given opportunities to respond to the weightier critiques. The debate was long and vigorous. Virtually all of the arguments we had encountered to this point were voiced again. We expressed our strong belief that by attracting excellent students, and by providing leadership in educational innovation, the programme would benefit the University as a whole. At the end, the motion to approve passed without a dissenting vote.

The next step in the approval process was in the hands of the Board-Senate Committee on Long Range Planning (CLRP). It was their responsibility to examine the resource requirements of the new Programme and to judge the potential gains against the costs. A report to CLRB estimating the resources required and discussing potential benefits to the University was submitted by the Vice President and myself. The CLRP reported its assessment, which was positive, to Senate.

The final step, at the Senate meeting of May 12, was surprisingly simple. The Chairman of Undergraduate Council, gave a clear and positive summary of the deliberations of Council, and, with a favourable assessment from CLRB, Senate quickly gave its approval without a dissenting vote. Quite a good party ensued.

Reflections on a Successful Launch

In closing this chapter, I would like to reflect on circumstances that appear to have contributed to our success in launching the Arts and Science Programme, and to identify one important issue about planning new undergraduate programmes to which we will turn more fully in the closing chapter of this book.

One of the circumstances of success was the strong and visible support of University administrators and leaders: the President, Arthur Bourns; the incoming president, Alvin Lee; the Vice President, Academic, Les King; the Dean of Science, Don Sprung; The Vice President of Health Sciences, Fraser Mustard; and the Chairman of the Board of Governors, John Panabaker. The proposal was also supported by the chair of Undergraduate Council during the approval process, Lorraine Allan (Psychology), and the previous chair during the deliberations following the Campbell report, Mel Kliman (Economics). Although critical of the treatment of humanities in the first proposal, the revised proposal was supported by the Dean of Humanities, Al Berland, who later taught in the Programme and was an influential member both of the Instructional Council, and of the smaller Advisory Council, which was established following the approval of the Programme by the Senate.

The climate at McMaster for entertaining new approaches to education was made more favourable by the success of its new medical programme, which departed radically from traditional programmes. This programme was designed to be problem-, not department-centred. It put much responsibility on students for their own learning. It sought to go beyond an exclusive reliance on the biological sciences to bring to bear the contributions of people with different backgrounds, including the social sciences, on the treatment of medical problems. Although the Planning Council did not take the medical programme as a model for a liberal education in the arts and sciences, it shared many of the same convictions—the need for more self-directed learning, and the integrative value of focussing on problems that require multi-disciplinary approaches. Moreover, our proposal found many allies in the members of McMaster's Faculty of Health Sciences.

The Planning Council worked hard and well together. Its members were widely known on campus and respected for their achievements in research and scholarship. They represented a broad spectrum of academic traditions. A similar proposal from a less committed or respected group might not have succeeded. The Council's willingness to revise following the concerted and weighty criticisms in the General Faculty Meeting probably contributed to the almost complete support the proposal eventually received from Undergraduate Council and the Senate.

The Programme filled a need at McMaster that our specialized honours programmes were not fulfilling. Intellectually able students with a high level of eagerness to learn needed the alternative of a broader, less specialized programme. The proposed programme attracted the support of many on McMaster's campus who found the emphasis on intellectual skills, including the important skills of scholarly inquiry, the use of a great books approach in the humanities and social sciences, and the attention to issues raised by technology in our culture innovative and exciting. Although, as we have seen, cogent arguments were levelled against the small size of the Programme and the setting of a high admission standard, there were also strong positive implications of those features of the Programme. Every ambitious university wants outstanding students, and recognizes their potential for contributing to the intellectual quality of the university as a whole. Small numbers meant that the Programme did not threaten to weaken existing departmental programmes in the way that a proposal for large scale shift in student numbers and of resources to a new programme would certainly have done. Most important, the small size of the Programme, coupled with the intellectual quality of the students, made it possible to create a climate for learning that worked very well for students and faculty. Later chapters will explore these matters.

There were three major phases in the planning and approval process: The Campbell Committee report advocating a new general studies programme, the Planning Council's report outlining a curriculum for the Arts and Science Programme, and the year of preparation following approval in which instructors were appointed and course outlines were produced. In retrospect, it is hard to defend the logic of more than two phases–a first phase in which the aims are articulated and an appropriate curriculum is outlined in broad strokes; a second in which instructors are appointed and courses are designed in detail. But, as it turned out, the Campbell report left open too many basic choices about the curriculum, and even about aims, to serve as a basis for appointing instructors to design courses. Although perhaps not efficient, this might be seen as a fortunate development. McMaster University may have needed the longer time involved by the second planning effort to adjust to the idea of an Arts and Science Programme that was the responsibility of neither a faculty nor of a department.

How far should planners go in prescribing what should be studied, or how it should be studied, in the courses that make up a programme? Did the planners of this Programme manage to strike a reasonable balance between saying too much and too little on these matters? The argument for saying very little and putting a great deal of discretion in the hands of the ultimate instructors is perhaps obvious. University teachers, if they are to be fully engaged, must be free to bring their insights to the design of a course. That argues for not going beyond the articulation of broad educational goals in the description of courses at the planning stage. The case for going beyond that rests in part on the conviction that certain contents, ideas, skills, or understandings are so fundamental to being a liberally educated person that their inclusion should be specified in the planning. Moreover, planners might hope to achieve greater intellectual coherence, encourage a mutual reinforcement among courses, and avoid undesirable repetition, by prescribing, recommending, or exemplifying course content. Finally, planners may attempt these things because they anticipate the criticism of being so vague as to provide no basis for others to judge the educational quality of a proposal.

Did we achieve a proper balance among these considerations in our proposal? To shed light on this question we need to consider the ways in which the Programme has changed from the one described in the Planning Council's proposal to Senate twenty-some years ago. We also need to reflect on what those changes might mean for the question of how far one should go in prescribing the content of courses when trying to establish a curriculum of liberal education in the arts and sciences.

While most of these are matters best left to a concluding chapter, one comment may be appropriate at the close of the present chapter on the planning of the Arts and Science Programme. When a programme comes off the page and comes to life, a new dynamic arises from the interaction of students, instructors, and directors. Good communication among them leads quite naturally to new approaches to teaching and learning within courses. Wise planning should anticipate this unpredictable, uncontrollable, but healthy dynamic.

Notes

1. Their names and Departments were: Dennis McCalla (Biochemistry), Jules Carbotte (Physics), Edward Sanders (Religious Studies), William Wallace (Music), G. Papageorgiou (Geography), Dugal Campbell (Psychiatry) and former chair of the Campbell Committee. They joined me (Psychology) to comprise the seven-person council. Four of McMaster's six Faculties were represented: Science, Social Sciences, Humanities, and Health Sciences.

2. "Revised Outline: A New Baccalaureate Degree Program in Arts and Science" (Report of the Planning Council chaired by H.M. Jenkins to the Senate, McMaster University, May 1980).

3. Our meetings were not minuted, but quite a good record of our deliberations exists in the memoranda we exchanged on the questions that had to be resolved in order to generate a proposal. My fading memory of what transpired has been refreshed by that record.

4. Daniel Bell, *The Reforming of General Education* (New York: Columbia University Press, 1966), 157.

5. J.J. Schwab, "On Reviving Liberal Education" in *The Philosophy of the Curriculum*, ed. Sidney Hook et al. (New York: Prometheus Books, 1979), 48.

6. Until very recently there were five years of high school, grades 9 through 13, in the Province of Ontario, but now grade 13 has been eliminated.

7. Sidney Hook, "General Education: The Minimum Indispensables" in *The Philosophy of the Curriculum*, ed. Sidney Hook et al. (New York: Prometheus Books, 1979), 32.

3   The Programme in Practice

Barbara Ferrier

The Curriculum

The original plan for the curriculum (Table 1, p.39) has proved to be robust, and relatively few changes have been made over the more than twenty years that the Programme has been in existence. The changes that have been made are discussed below, but mention should be made here at the outset of one significant change made not in the curriculum as such, but in the number of core courses which the Programme was responsible for delivering.

Shortly after the Programme's inception in 1981 the Calculus course and the course on Probability and Statistics were made its responsibility. This had the advantage of allowing the Programme Directors a much stronger voice in the choice of instructors and in formulating the aims of the courses in ways appropriate to the overall aims of the Programme. It also meant a change in the admissions requirements in mathematics. While originally any advanced high school mathematics was acceptable, now only high school Calculus would meet the requirement. These developments made it possible to raise the overall level of mathematical skill achieved within the Programme and to increase the intellectual coherence in the set of core courses. With these changes, of the fourteen courses in the core curriculum (Table 1, p.39), all but one—the Biology course—were now delivered through through the Arts and Science Programme and for its students exclusively.

45

An important new development, which was begun in 1982, was the introduction of a route by which a student who develops a deep interest in a discipline can pursue its study. The challenge of providing both breadth and depth in The Programme was an issue for the planners. They hoped that the availability of electives in the curriculum and freedom of choice of an honours thesis topic would go far to address this. It became clear, however, that some students, while not prepared to give up the breadth of education that the Arts and Science Programme provided, did seek more experience in the discipline of their interest than these choices allowed, often to facilitate their admission to graduate studies. There already existed at McMaster the opportunity to graduate with a Combined Honours Degree, which usually satisfied requirements for graduate work, but these programmes combined two disciplines. The concept was now extended to apply to the combination of the Arts and Science Programme core requirements with those of another subject. This decision was not reached without much careful debate in the Programme's Council of Instructors from which the recommendation came. Some members believed that it went counter to the Programme's purpose of providing a broad interdisciplinary education and surrendered to some of the career oriented pressures that were operating, while others believed that depriving students of the opportunity to delve into a subject of their choice and possibly prepare for graduates studies would be irresponsible. Others were torn. Eventually it was agreed that the new combined programmes went a long way toward meeting the needs for specialization while preserving the breadth of the Arts and Science Programme. Information on the students' involvement in them is given on pp.198-9.

The Director of the Arts and Science Programme and the Chair of the Department involved in each Combined Honours Programme negotiated agreements by which students could meet the requirements for an honours degree in both. Sometimes compromises were made; for example, a student wishing to do a combined honours degree with Sociology would complete the research methods course required by that Department in place of the Arts and Science statistics course; a student with a similar interest in Political Science would be excused from taking the introductory course normally required by that Department because the content of some required Arts and Science courses was judged to be adequate preparation. In three science disciplines, Biology, Chemistry and Physics, it was found to be necessary to extend the length of the combined honours programme to five years in order to accommodate the sequence of science courses and laboratories. Students graduating from a combined programme, for example with Biology, would graduate with the degree of B.ArtsSc. (Honours Arts and Science and Biology). In order to complete a combined degree, students usually assign all of their elective time to the discipline of their choice and choose an honours thesis within it. New combinations are considered at a student's request.

At the outset, students were required to take the first year Inquiry course and two additional ones from a list of four in upper years. They were permitted to substitute for one of the upper year Inquiry requirements a course addressing "another age or culture." It became increasingly difficult to establish criteria for what could be considered another culture, and this option was dropped. The upper year Inquiry course requirement has now been reduced to one, selected from three offered. This was done to survive a budget cut, of which there were several for all undergraduate programmes in the 1990s. While there is agreement that the development of inquiry skills remains a crucial objective of the Programme, it became clear to the members of the Council of Instructors that those skills were also being developed in other courses, notably Technology and Society (p.177), in which inquiry-type projects were part of the requirements.

Thesis and Individual Studies supervisors found that students in their final year were mostly able to get started on their research without needing to spend additional time on skill development.

Another course that had to be sacrificed to additional budget reductions was Creative Arts. This was done with great reluctance and after open meetings with students and full discussion in the Council of Instructors and the Programme Advisory Committee. The selection of this course for elimination was based on the arguments that courses in the creative arts are available to students as electives and that the course had proved to be difficult to teach with consistent effectiveness. The original intention had been to use it to explore the cultural role of the creative arts and the nature of artistic creativity, but it seemed that the students' eagerness to explore their own creativity drove the course in directions in which the great range of their backgrounds and skills created obstacles to presenting a coherent course. The pattern of having two different instructors treat two different arts appears to have contributed to the problem. It is hoped that a course with the original objectives that addresses a very important dimension of the human experience can be reintroduced if the budget permits.

The original names of the Western Thought I and Western Thought II courses were changed to Western Civilization and Modern Western Civilization respectively to reflect broader content than the original names implied, and the different historical periods emphasized in the two courses (p.55). For some time, students exerted pressure to do something to correct what they saw as an exclusively Western focus in these intellectual and cultural history courses, but no agreement could be reached about what could be displaced. The elimination of the Creative Arts course, however, allowed for the introduction of Eastern Studies. At first, students were required to take two one-term courses on aspects of Indian and Chinese religious tradition, from the Department of Religious Studies. These courses were later supplemented by others from University offerings. Students select from this list.

An early change was the replacement of the required course in the Physical Sciences by a course in Physics. The former course had dealt very largely with Physics but had included some basic material from Chemistry. This Chemistry did not, however, meet the requirements for admission to medical school, a career of interest to many students, and many students were taking Chemistry as an elective. Further, the planning group had agreed at the outset, after much discussion, that some knowledge of Physics and Biology in particular can be of great help to the educated citizen who is considering problems in the public domain. Matters of energy generation, particularly from nuclear reactors, reproductive technologies, and genetic manipulation are examples of areas in which thorny questions have to be addressed. Other candidate sciences for inclusion would be Chemistry, Earth Sciences, and Psychology, and while all are of obvious importance, the chosen sciences appear to be the most basic and therefore the most appropriate choices for the core curriculum.

Governance and Administration

The Programme was established as a free-standing teaching unit of the University, accountable to the Office of the Provost and Vice-President (Academic). As is the case for the undergraduate faculties, ultimate authority for matters of policy and curriculum lies with the University Senate, and for matters of budget with the Board of Governors. The Programme Director reports to the Associate Vice-President in the Provost's Office on all issues except those relating to curriculum, which are submitted directly to the Undergraduate Council, a sub-committee of the Senate.

Within the Programme, two committees exist to deal with undergraduate matters. These committees parallel those in the undergraduate faculties. The Council of Instructors, made up of all current instructors and student representatives, acts as a Departmental Curriculum

Committee and makes recommendations to the Programme Advisory Committee, on which there are elected instructors and students and faculty members representing the University. The latter committee acts as a Faculty Council. Other Programme committees are appointed to deal with the necessary review of student progress, nominations for student awards, and student admission and hearings. With the exception of those dealing with student progress and awards, all committees and working groups have student membership.

At times there have been suggestions that the Programme be relocated to a faculty or be managed by a group of Deans of the Faculties of Humanities, Science and Social Sciences. The reason given for these suggestions has been to simplify and reduce the cost of administration. It is, however, questionable that the Programme would continue to get the attention it needs and now enjoys as a distinct and different teaching unit reporting to the Office of the Provost, if it were administratively incorporated within a faculty.

For its first three years the costs of the Programme were covered from the Hooker bequest (p.40). Following an internal review at the end of its first three years, the budget allocation for the Programme was shifted to regular University operating funds and became part of the Provost's budget. As is true in the undergraduate faculties, by far the largest part is devoted to teaching costs and salaries. The teaching costs are largely in the form of payment to the University faculties from which Arts and Science instructors are released and for occasional part-time appointments, usually to cover the absence of an instructor on research leave. There may also be an additional cost to compensate for the release of the Director, and there are salaries for an administrator and secretary. It was understood from the start that the Programme's instructors would be recruited from McMaster's faculty members in an effort to make it an integral part of the undergraduate structure, and departments were expected to consider the work of their faculty members in the Programme (and subsequently in other interdisciplinary programmes) as part of their normal teaching duties. Later, as funding of all teaching was constrained and as the number of interdisciplinary programmes increased, it became increasingly difficult to get an agreement from departmental chairs and faculty deans to continue this practice. An arrangement was made to centralize some funds from faculty budgets to support those interdisciplinary programmes that reported directly to the Provost. These funds, along with others, were allocated to programme budgets to allow them to negotiate release of faculty members in return for a standard amount paid to each instructor's home faculty.

At various times the claim has been made within the University that the Programme is an extravagance that it cannot afford. But estimates of cost per student do not support that claim. In most Departments the first year courses have a large number of students but upper level courses and seminars may have very small enrolments. In contrast, the Programme's courses are of relatively uniform size throughout.

Student Recruitment and Selection

When the Programme was planned and approved it was not clear that students would be attracted to it because the conventional undergraduate curricula in Canada were commonly based on a model of specialization, particularly for the most able students. However, the University was persuaded of the need for graduates who knew enough of a wide range of disciplines to be able to contribute to the management of complex public problems and to be able to work with and to understand the contribution of professionals in different areas. As a result of recruiting efforts, twenty-four students with disparate high school academic records joined the first class. In later years, with only modest recruitment efforts, numbers of applicants rose rapidly as knowledge of the Programme increased, and the class reached its size limit. It appears, based on where the applications came from, reports from admitted students, and patterns of applications from many of their younger siblings, that in-course students and graduates were largely responsible for the increase by speaking favourably of their experiences to their families, friends and former high school teachers. As numbers of applicants grew, the grade-point averages needed to be considered for admission rose steadily, being admitted gathered esteem, and the Programme became more attractive to high achievers. It now has one of the highest academic standards of admission in the country.

It is also very likely that a myth about the Programme contributed to its appeal. It became widely believed, particularly it seems in the Toronto high schools, that admission to it gave an advantage in subsequent competition for admission to McMaster University's School of Medicine. This myth has proved hard to dispel, possibly because each year several of its students have been successful in that competition. The fact that others were admitted to other medical schools was largely ignored. The point that these students might well have been equally successful if they had been in other McMaster programmes or other universities proved to be unconvincing in the face of what many high school students and their parents and teachers believed to be evidence to the contrary. (The goal of being admitted to medical school fades for many students; see p.200 for a summary of career interests of graduates.)

In order to be considered for admission, applicants now must have successfully completed the high school diploma including final level courses in English and Calculus. The application average is calculated using the grades in these two courses and in the four strongest final level courses from those presented, with three of the four coming from a list of academic (rather than skill-based) courses. Very early it was recognized that students who flourished in the Programme and who met the planners' hopes for their active contributions to the life of the University as a whole had records of achievement in high school that went beyond their academic success. A supplementary application form was designed to collect appropriate information about their interests and achievements. The assessment of this form became very important in discriminating among applicants as their grade-point averages soared. Initially, each form was evaluated by two Programme instructors and one senior student, with each group of three being responsible for between a hundred and a hundred and fifty applications. Later, it became apparent that the students were at least as careful, rigorous and insightful as the instructors, and the composition of the teams was changed to one instructor and two students. The score assigned was from a range of -5 to +5 and the mean of the three rating scores was added to the admission average, which had not been revealed to the assessors, to form a composite admission score. Often applicants with high application averages also were awarded high supplementary scores, but for approximately 20% of the applicants the decision to accept or reject was changed by their score on the supplementary application.

Some general principles for selection have evolved. Students were sought who had not only performed well in subjects from the arts, the sciences and mathematics but had enjoyed their studies in all of these areas. If they had emphasized one group of subjects at the expense of the others, evidence to restore a balance was looked for in their extracurricular activities. Evidence of their having made a serious commitment to being involved in some aspects of the world around them was also a requirement. Those who viewed their undergraduate years as providing a rich opportunity for expansion of their minds and not merely as a necessary step on the road to a career were thought to be more suitable. Another principle that became entrenched was that senior students of the Programme would be involved in the selection process, both as members of the selection committee and as assessors of the supplementary applications. It has usually been the case that students were somewhat harsher in their assessment than were faculty members, perhaps because they are closer to the experience of being a high school student and were aware that some of the extracurricular activities described were not very demanding. As a result they may be better detectors of "padding." The more generous rating from instructors may stem in part from the belief of many of them that what they could have written at this stage would have shown them to be less impressive than were the applicants they were reviewing. Even very careful efforts to apply selection principles cannot claim to be error-free, but most of the students who accepted the offers of admission were subsequently found to have the characteristics sought.

II

The Courses

4 Western Civilization Courses

Louis Greenspan

Editors' Preface

The courses that were first called Western Thought I and II were later named Western Civilization and Modern Western Civilization. The change of name reflected the wish to pay more attention to the cultural as well as the intellectual history of Western Civilization and to bring them into relation with one another. Two generations of instructors have taught these courses, but only the author of this chapter, Louis Greenspan, has been, in different years, responsible for both courses. With the agreement of the other instructors he undertook to provide an account, based in part on discussions with each of them, of common and distinctive features of their approaches to the teaching of these foundation courses.

Context

In 1979 the Planning Council of Arts and Science proposed Western Thought as one of the core courses of the Programme, directing that it be compulsory for all students in first and second year. They proposed that Western Thought I cover materials from ancient Greece to the eighteenth century, addressing issues in philosophy, religion and the rise of the scientific outlook, and that Western Thought II cover materials in the literature of the nineteenth and twentieth centuries (including materials in the social sciences), addressing issues such as the structure of society, contending visions of political order, and divergent theories of human nature. The proposals were circulated throughout the university and met with enthusiasm from some and with skepticism from others. The skeptics, mainly from the humanities, argued that, however well-meaning, the proposed courses were merely a token gesture towards the liberal arts in a programme that was top-heavy in sciences and social sciences (p.33) comparable to a designer's notion that adding a precious piece of antique furniture to a room filled with high-tech devices would give the room some "class." These criticisms notwithstanding, the Programme was approved, and with it the emphasis on Western Thought. As the Programme proceeded the criticism evaporated, and it is now widely agreed that the Western Thought courses as conceived for the Arts and Science Programme have been a success.

In part, this is because of the enthusiasm of those who agreed to become the instructors. We knew from the beginning that Western Thought in the Arts and Science Programme would be different from Western Thought as it had been traditionally taught, that there would have to be a great deal of improvisation. But we were convinced that the Planning Council had taken the right decision in reviving the study of the basic concepts of the West in an environment where that study had been largely forgotten, or denigrated without any serious consideration of its value.

For the better part of the modern period, Western Thought courses had flourished in liberal arts colleges and in such larger institutions as Columbia University and the University of Chicago, where the mission was understood to be bearing the wisdom of the past to each new generation of students; that is, serving old wine in new bottles. However, the transformation of the universities that took place after World War II dislodged Western Thought from its role as a key component in the education of many undergraduates. Les King has described this transformation in the first chapter of this book. The refurbished university looked forward, not backward, and looked with suspicion on the succession of global visions that had comprised Western Thought. The new disciplines took only marginal interest in the history of their enterprise, and conveyed little to students about how they had arrived at the present state of that enterprise. Even the old humanities subjects transformed themselves under the influence of this paradigm. Philosophers and political scientists, for example, were reinventing their disciplines. Philosophy proclaimed a revolution based on linguistic analysis, mathematical logic and the philosophy of science. Political science focused on quantitative analyses in such matters as voting patterns and demographic trends. In this new culture of specialization, the once celebrated courses in Western Thought were increasingly marginalized and, in many places, even jettisoned. This was the fate of the programmes I knew best at three universities, Dalhousie, Columbia, and Brandeis. In the last, a promising History of Ideas Department was simply disbanded.

Any interest in reviving Western Thought courses later in the twentieth century confronted a new challenge: the so-called cultural wars. An account of the details, the issues, and the intellectual ammunition that sustained these wars would be too complex to provide here. Suffice it to say that a cry arose that the traditional approach to teaching Western Thought and the Western Canon had promoted an account of rationality that marginalized and excluded identifiable groups: women, and people of non-Western cultures. Those who rejected these claims dug in to protect the core of Western Thought and its texts as the canon of universal rationality. Hence the term "cultural wars." McMaster University housed some departments that were outposts in these wars, but for the most part they did not spill over into the Arts and Science Programme (in spite of the large number of women in the Programme as well as its ethnic diversity). Nevertheless, this episode did affect Western Thought in the Arts and Science Programme by promoting greater sensitivity to the claims of feminism, and by the readiness of the instructors to abjure western triumphalism and the temptation to present Western Thought as a sacred catechism.

Other issues that the instructors had to take into consideration were the backgrounds and ambitions of the students. They were the products of high school curricula that had undergone multiple reforms from the older arts curriculum. Whether the clarion call of educational reform insisted on "Socratic dialogue" or "back-to-the-basics," history had lost its pre-war preeminence. By the time the McMaster Arts and Science Programme was being planned, Ontario high school students, who constituted the majority of likely applicants, were required to take only Canadian history—and not necessarily those aspects of Canadian history that connect Canada to its European past. In spite of the earlier celebration of the Socratic method, optional courses in philosophy have been introduced into high school curricula only in recent years. Thus, students came to the Western Thought courses as tabulae rasae, products of a culture and curriculum that had denigrated historical and philosophical learning. Moreover, most of those who were to enter the Arts and Science Programme were contemplating careers in other fields of graduate or professional study, and were unlikely to do further work in Western

Thought as a discipline. Thus, the concentrated exposure offered in Arts and Science was likely to be their last.

In summary, the instructors were challenged to create a meaningful set of courses that would give students whose aspirations lay in other directions an encounter with the fundamental values and ideas of Western Thought—a programme that would show the continuing power of seminal ideas from the past to address the dynamic world of the present.

On the other hand, we did not only, or even mainly, face an uphill challenge. There was much in the air that favoured experimental programmes such as Arts and Science, and much that favoured a revival of Western Thought. There was a great deal of unrest worldwide focused on the function of the university, which many saw as an institution that had rejected humanistic ideals.

In its earlier history McMaster had been a typical liberal arts college, under the stewardship of the Baptist Church. In the late fifties and early sixties it transformed itself rapidly into a much larger university with a greater emphasis on research, especially in the sciences—a development that traumatized some departments in the humanities. But, fortunately for the Arts and Science Programme, many of the administrators and scientists who had created this research university backed the new experiment and were especially hospitable to Western Thought.

Finally, the unrest in the air and the support of the majority in the university for the inclusion of courses in Western Thought fed into the most important source of strength for the instructors, namely the enthusiasm of the students for studying such a subject. Despite deficiencies in their background and despite the fact that many students conceived of their futures as lying in such professions fields as medicine and law, most welcomed courses in Western Thought as an important part of their education.

Common Approaches

There remains then the question of which approaches the instructors found most suitable. Though they came from different backgrounds and had different perspectives on the material, they quickly came to a number of common understandings. First, although they were aware of any number of texts and course-outlines of Western Thought that had proven successful elsewhere, they decided unanimously to reject, as the frame for their curricula, any of a variety of surveys, such as the "Plato to Nato" quickie, or traditional narratives and meta-narratives of nineteenth-century Western Thought as a story of progress, or the more recent, postmodern narratives of Western Thought as tottering on its last legs. Instead of such surveys, the instructors intuitively elected to adopt a method which prodded students to engage with individual thinkers and texts. They believed that the students could achieve philosophical depth by exploring limited topics rather than by attempting to achieve a global perspective on the entire field. The method can be understood by the analogy of a voyage to a continent called Western Thought in which the voyagers weigh anchor at selected points, then probe, engage, and study the local surroundings in depth, believing that such discrete forays will teach more about the continent than grand but rapid tours of the whole land-mass.

Second, the instructors could draw on a toolbox of accepted approaches that were being used for the study of Western Thought, in some cases focusing on texts, in others on individual thinkers, and in still others on the relation of ideas to their historical context. But they drew on these approaches in an eclectic fashion. In general, they all acknowledged the value of analyzing ideas in their historical context, but they conceived of this approach in different ways. The problem that frames any course on the history of ideas is whether ideas can be understood independently of their historical milieu. We would not, for example, try to understand the axioms of Euclid's geometry by connecting them to conditions in the Hellenic world. On the other hand, while we might try to understand Shakespeare's *King Henry V* as a timeless statement on power, we could also analyze it as a manifestation of Shakespeare's support for the Tudor kingship. This latter approach, however, if applied exclusively, would bring us to the extreme position that ideas make no sense except within the context of their historical milieus. I shall say more about this when we examine the approaches of individual instructors.

Whether the Western Civilization courses in Arts and Science have produced philosopher kings or even philosopher CEO's cannot be known, but a comparison with Plato's academy would not be altogether far-fetched. In Plato's academy philosophy was meant to be of value to all students— the few who were destined to be philosophers and could devote their lives to contemplation, as well as the many who chose to make their mark in practical life. Philosophy was a humanizing force, one that oriented its students morally and metaphysically; but however compelling the rewards of contemplation, the majority were obliged to return to the everyday world to become leaders. Similarly, in the Arts and Science Programme's courses in Western Civilization, the exposure to its most significant figures and texts was designed with the knowledge that many would go into other professional pursuits. Each instructor knows a student who struggled with a decision between proceeding to graduate work in topics suggested by Western Civilization or accepting an offer of admission to medical, law, or business school.

In keeping with the metaphor of exploring a continent by selecting restricted locales, the courses, as I have made clear, emphasize local exploration and discussion, not comprehensiveness. Each instructor directs the attention of the students to specific components of Western Civilization: particular works, authors, or issues. But though the instructors have come to a number of common decisions, when they appear in the classroom there are significant differences in their approaches and in what they wish to convey. One pair of instructors, the Mendelsons, give high priority to encounters with the timeless issues that have been put forward in Western Thought. Another pair, Ahmad and Jenkins, have explored the role played in social sciences by assumptions about human nature. Another instructor, Levitt, has focused on the thinkers' relation to one another, while I have focused on the central ideas as guiding lights to modernity. Each of these approaches dictates different strategies of explanation and elucidation. One will seek greater philosophical depth to uncover the timelessness of the ideas, another will seek a richer temporal context to uncover how they are historically situated and conditioned.

The Courses

It will be remembered that the mandate of the Planning Council called for two courses: Western Thought I was to consider materials from ancient Greece until the eighteenth century; Western Thought II, materials from the nineteenth century to the present. (In practice, the chronological and conceptual borders turned out to be porous.)

When the Programme began, Alan Mendelson and I were responsible for Western Thought I. Both of us had taken courses in Western Thought as undergraduates; both were pleased to accept an opportunity to create courses for the Arts and Science Programme. Mendelson is a scholar in the field of Alexandrian Judaism, with emphasis on Philo, a subject that keeps him in contact with ancient Greece, and I work on modern political thought with emphasis on Bertrand Russell, having published an essay on Russell's *History of Western Philosophy*. We taught two separate but equal segments on related topics. Following the Planning Council's scheme, we covered materials from ancient Greece to early modern times, including discussions relating to Plato, the Bible, and founders of early modern science such as Descartes and Bacon. I delivered two-hour plenary lectures designed to give an overview of the subject, while Mendelson split the class into two groups and conducted two one-hour seminars per week. Though Mendelson and I were in constant contact, our sections functioned independently. My lectures focused on three themes. The first involved questions related to the nature of the state. These questions drew on the trial and conviction of Socrates and on Plato's relevant writings. The second series of topics dealt with writing concerning the tensions between reason and religious belief, featuring the work of Descartes, Bacon, and other commentators on the scientific revolution. Finally, the theme of history and individualism featured the writings of Luther, Calvin, John Stuart Mill, and Nietzsche. These topics were selected as constituting landmarks of Western Thought, introducing concepts that are still influential today.

Mendelson's seminar served different pedagogical functions. His earlier texts were from Plato, but he was less interested in the survey than in the details of the argument, the logic, and the rhetorical structure of each work. This meant that he would dwell upon one text for several weeks. The aims of the seminar were threefold. First, the texts were intended to serve as springboards for discussions about grammar, syntax, and composition. Second, the texts furnished models for teaching the craft of constructing an argument. For example, Plato's *Phaedo* is a series of arguments for the immortality of the soul. As such, it provided excellent examples of philosophical arguments that could be analyzed and imitated. Third and finally, Mendelson's intention was to engage texts that raised issues of permanent significance—ones that transcend the time and place that gave them birth—but he also insisted on the crucial importance of historical context for the interpretation of texts, and for that reason he welcomed the change in course title from Western Thought to Western Civilization. The apparent paradox is perhaps resolved by noting that every interpretation of the human condition, including of course the most contemporary, is grounded in its time and place, and is in that sense contingent. By taking into account the influence of historical context, our insight into the meaning of a text is deepened, a fact which, without robbing it of contemporary relevance, enhances our understanding of its enduring value.

Dr. Sara Mendelson replaced me in the early nineteen nineties and continues to teach Western Civilization along with Dr. Alan Mendelson. Dr. S. Mendelson is an historian and the author of books and articles on women's history in the seventeenth century. She too was exposed to liberal arts as an undergraduate, and was for a time attracted to the study of physics. She is certainly versatile enough to feel at home in the Arts and Science Programme.

Her course outline follows the outline of the Planning Council in spirit and in deed. She begins with the study of Greek historians, continues with readings concerning the world views current in mediaeval and early modern society, and concludes with readings from critics of the Enlightenment.

A close reading of her course outline and sub-topics indicates her immersion in history and historiography, but much of the outline provides material for an extended reflection on the uses of history for a liberal education. For example, almost all of her material from the ancient world is drawn from the work of Greek historians, and the topic is introduced as historiography. In this section she treats historical works as philosophical texts, that is, as possessing continuing relevance to our thinking about history. Accordingly, in treating Thucydides, she focuses on an episode known as the Delian Dialogue, which features a debate within Athens regarding the fate of the city of Delos, hinging on the question whether Athens should show its might by slaughtering the population. The episode is acted out in a theatrical performance by students, a teaching technique which brings the ethical conflict between justice and the use of brute force into sharp focus. In this case, history is treated in much the same way as it is treated in the texts selected by Alan Mendelson—as the bearer of timeless moral issues.

Other sections of the course illustrate some of the skepticism which, despite the Programme's relative insulation from the cultural wars, has still managed to make its presence felt. This skepticism attempts to demonstrate the opposite of what was shown in the Delian debates; namely that truths sometimes considered timeless are in fact framed and bound by history. This is the case with mediaeval world views, which are shown to be products of their time. Similarly, the debates between Locke and Filmer about human nature hinge on the issue of whether the natures of women or of different races, as understood in that period, are historically determined. A similar atmosphere of skepticism infuses the section on the Enlightenment, which focuses on the work of its critics, Rousseau and Wollstonecraft.

The founders of the second-year course, Modern Western Civilization, which began as Western Thought II, are Dr. Syed Ahmad and Dr. Herb Jenkins, the first Director of the Arts and Science Programme. Dr. Ahmad is an economist who has studied theories of capital formation, and Dr. Jenkins is one of the founders of a very empirically oriented Psychology Department. Both had an interest in the history and philosophy of their disciplines.

The topics they explored with the students included assumptions about human nature, focusing on authors such as Machiavelli, Hobbes, Marx, and Veblen; capitalism, socialism and democracy, focusing on authors such as Marx, Schumpeter, and Milton Friedman; and finally human motivation, which focused on the works of Freud and Skinner. All of these topics engaged fundamental questions about the extent to which the social sciences can provide stable theoretical approaches to the subjects of political order, social and economic structure, and human nature.

When Ahmad and Jenkins stepped down, Dr. Cyril Levitt took over the second-year course, and he also taught fundamental texts of the social sciences, as part of the history of ideas. Levitt had completed his degree at the University of Berlin, where the social sciences were still influenced by the tradition of Hegel and Marx, a tradition that was not disposed to regard the boundaries that separated the social sciences from one another, or for that matter from history and philosophy, as ontologically binding. In his dissertation, a study of Marxist texts, Levitt's methods were closer to those of the critical literary scholar than to those of the empirical social scientist, though he was trained to work with both. In the context of the Arts and Science Programme, Levitt was more concerned to elevate the students into a realm of ideas than to immerse them in a realm of praxis.

The topics that Levitt selected for his course are similar to those established by Ahmad and Jenkins. They, too, included modern views of human nature, capitalism, socialism, and democracy, and modern theories of human motivation. The material that he selected included many of the texts also used by Ahmad and Jenkins.

Levitt's approach to the material rejects the promotion of any particular ideology, either political or academic. He holds to the older notion that it is best that the students not be able to guess the teacher's views. This means that he adopts the views and the passions of each thinker in turn, and encourages students to relate to each work according to their own lights.

He believes that the adequacy of the historical and philosophical depth of the course can be assured by treating the entire syllabus as a debate, in which all the thinkers argue back and forth over the centuries. He pays careful attention to historical context, showing for example that when Rousseau and Hobbes speak of human nature, the phrase has different contexts and meanings for each. Levitt treats his class meetings as foci for extended forums on these subjects, providing students with opportunities to participate in the debate.

In the year 2000, following Levitt's resignation, I was asked to teach the second-year course, now called Modern Western Civilization, and to try my hand at finding the right combination of historical contexts and philosophical thought. Like the others, I too had had background courses in the older liberal arts curriculum, and had even completed my PhD at Brandeis in the History of Ideas. My focus, however, had become the social and political thought of Bertrand Russell, and I had worked extensively in the Bertrand Russell Archives at McMaster.

My course was modelled on the traditional History of Ideas programmes. However, I avoided the sort of chronological, book-after-book sequence of thinkers and movements that is given in many texts that have appeared in recent years. I began with the Reformation in the sixteenth century, covering first the reformers, then the thinkers of the Enlightenment, writers on the modern state, and contemporary writers on feminism and multiculturalism. Keeping in the spirit of our endeavour, I attempted, like the others, to construct the course in such a way as to provide philosophical and historical depth.

As I have noted, my approach was to begin with major turning points that lay in the background of modern thought, to examine the basic ideas that emerged from them, and finally to trace the themes that have persisted right through to the present time. For example, my lectures provide a vivid sketch of the Protestant Reformation and its course from 1519-1648; I then select the theme of Christian liberty as found in the work of Luther and Calvin, and explain its role in creating modern individualism. Following this I interrupt the historical narrative to discuss the different views of individualism from the sixteenth to the twentieth century, treating individualism as a philosophical issue for debate. Then I return to the historical narrative and take up the scientific revolution and the emergence of the scientific account of reason. My aim, as I tell the students, is to provide a map of modernity, of the seminal ideas that form the modern outlook in the West.

In all of these courses an effort was made to engage the students in the critical evaluation of the material. A typical arrangement would have students, when preparing an essay, present their ideas in a tutorial and only after discussion submit their final paper. Through this process the students gained experience in oral presentation and in writing. Their essays were sometimes spin-offs of lecture topics. For example, if the lecture topic was Adam Smith, the student was asked to identify and describe the position of a contemporary writer who either supported or argued against his views. In this way the students were led to see Smith's ideas as still worthy of reflection.

The question that can be fairly asked is whether we have succeeded in providing a meaningful exposure to these basic ideas, and indeed brought the culture of the humanities to the students in a programme as diverse as the Arts and Science Programme. There is, of course, no way to determine this in a precise fashion. What we can say is that some students have gone on to do graduate work in subjects for which the Western Civilization courses have provided a solid foundation, and they have been found to be well prepared. Their success is one fair test of our achievement. We have also found that other students have become so engrossed in the material that they have seriously considered abandoning plans to take up careers in professions such as medicine and law. Finally, we know that there are students who, after many years, believe that the two years in Western Civilization courses were crucial to their development as human beings. It is hard to imagine any better indication of the achievement of the Arts and Science Programme in this field.

5   Writing and Informal Logic

Editors' Preface

The Programme planners believed that among the essential skills to develop in students were those needed to read, write, and think clearly and critically. It therefore appeared to make sense to combine writing and logic in one course to be called Writing and Verbal Reasoning. The name was later changed to Writing and Informal Logic. As this course evolved, the various instructors made different links between the two components and with other courses.

Writing

Sylvia Bowerbank

From Lectures to Workshops: Evolution of the Course

During the early 1980s, when the Arts and Science Programme emerged as an innovative option for McMaster undergraduates, I was working on my PhD dissertation in the English Department. As I had had some experience teaching writing, I had been appointed to instruct the one writing course the English Department offered in those days. I had inherited the teacher-centred lecture format and the course's emphasis on improving basic skills in grammar, organization, and revision. One day in class, I got lucky and learned something new about teaching writing. A student spoke up in class to say that she felt paralysed, unable to write her essay; she was labouring over every word and phrase; she was worried that the course might be making her writing worse instead of better. How was a writing teacher to respond to such comments? I was still learning to think on my feet. I said something that I knew from my own experience: such a loss of confidence is a temporary part of the process; it often happens when a writer is struggling to take her skills to a new level. I was stumbling around trying to find the right words to support the unlikely narrative of "getting worse before you get better." I remember comparing the experience to being stage-struck; if a person becomes overly analytical while she is on stage, she might not be able to perform the moves she knows so well. At this point, a young man raised his hand and gave me a valuable teaching.

His gift to me was a corresponding narrative that clarified the process of integrating new understanding into one's own substance. The young man told the class that he held a black belt in the martial arts; his sensei was Dan Inosanto of California, who had learned the art from Bruce Lee. The teaching was this:

> Before you learn the martial art, you fight naturally, going with the flow of your body: A kick is just a kick; a punch is just a punch. When you begin to study the art, you take notice of your technique, you second-guess yourself, and judge as you learn new moves. You think too much perhaps; you are acutely self-conscious and unnatural: A kick is not just a kick; a punch is not just a punch. After you have mastered the art it becomes part of who you are. Once more you fight with the flow of your own body: A kick is just a kick; a punch is just a punch.

I tell this story of a classroom encounter here partly because it embeds some of the ideas that I began to cultivate as a teacher of the writing component of this course: Listen to what students say about their realities as writers. Think in front of the students. Adapt what I know about writing to their immediate circumstances. Speak to students not primarily as a critic of their work, but as another writer, one who strives to master the same art. Miss Thistlebottom enforces the rules, but doesn't do any writing herself. Create an interactive environment in which students collaborate to think more deeply about their diverse practices as writers.

In the second year of the Arts and Science Programme, I was hired by Herb Jenkins, the first Director, as a sessional instructor to teach the writing course for one year only, and I've been here ever since. Teaching the writing course has become second nature to me, so in writing this essay, I feel as if I am regressing to a self-conscious stage of analyzing what I now do almost effortlessly. I am not able to describe the course separate from the sort of teacher I have become, developing in relationship to the generations of students who have participated in the ongoing writing community of Arts and Science. My reconstruction here is necessarily selective and even idiosyncratic. Let it be.

In the early days of teaching the course, I gave two-hour lectures to half the class (about thirty students in each session); the format was conversational, but I was at the front of the room doing most of the talking. It is worth pointing out that, whatever changes have occurred, the general course description has remained constant:

> The writing component of Arts and Science 1B6 is an advanced course in the theories and practices of expository prose. Areas of study include: strategies for writing creative and authoritative prose; the processes of revision and evaluation; methods for analyzing prose style; writing about science; collaborative learning and writing; appropriate pedagogy for teaching writing.

In my lectures, I taught grammar rules—the conventions and the exceptions. I talked about good writing habits and time management. I mapped the various stages of the research paper—from note-taking to proofreading—by going through the sections of Sue Hubbuch's *Writing Research Papers Across the Curriculum.*[1] I made the students practise standard essay structures; my favourites were the extended definition, the comparison strategy, and the précis. I assessed the advantages and disadvantages of different opening strategies, from the funnel method of Sheridan Baker (so favoured by high school teachers) to the setting up of the substantial opponent (rather than the straw man) and the opening hook (start with a startling fact, great quotation, key statistic …). I sometimes pointed out the rhetorical techniques used by great stylists.

Even in the early years, there was plenty of student discussion in class. When I was a new teacher, I read lots and lots of books on how to write and how to teach writing. I was writing every day myself, getting the habit, and learning the art. Early on, I asked the students to write reviews of writing books, and then together we would debate various ideas about language and writing in class. Last year (2002), when I was doing a major clean-up of my office, I realised that I had not assigned the book review for some years, so I decided to get rid of the old books by having a give-way. Some of my books looked very well-read; they had dog-eared pages and interesting comments in the margins; loose papers and post-it notes were stuck in here and there. One student told me something interesting: his way of selecting from the give-away books for his own library was to look through for any signs that others had read the book—a pencil line or comment in the margin—or even that I had taken time to put my name in the book.

In those early days of the Programme, I learned how to teach by giving interactive lectures, but what did the students learn? After all, you learn writing, not by reading books about writing or listening to teachers, but by writing. I decoded the body language of my students this way: so the professor knows her stuff; she displays her expertise in all the official topics; she holds the authority to decide what merits a high mark; even her little stories about the struggles of the writer are about the work of some published writer. I began to encourage students to interrogate everything they heard with the question: "What is this to me?" I wanted them to become more self-conscious about the objectives, interests, and values that they brought to their work; unexamined intentions were often present in their work, undermining the coherence and grace of their writing. It took me a while to embrace structural change, but after several years of lectures, I changed the format so that the sixty (or so) students were scheduled to meet in four workshops of about fifteen students each. The new structure permitted all the students to speak more readily and to learn from each other about their needs, their habits, their struggles, their desires, and their discoveries about how to write well. And I was sitting in a circle with the students, bringing whatever I knew as a writer and teacher to bear on their present realities.

One last word about the legacy of those early days. At the time, the philosopher David Hitchcock was the instructor of the logic component of the course, and we used to attend each other's classes. As we were experimenting with the design, we were very receptive to receiving ongoing student commentary. Dr. Hitchcock devised a simple questionnaire to be used for midterm course evaluation: 1) what works, 2) what needs refining, and 3) suggestions. This system was effective because the form was divided equally into three parts, and thus not only balanced the positive and negative feedback, but also invited the students to share in creating ways to teach the course. We liked having our work evaluated in this way, with the negativity kept within one-third of the bounds, while positive energy prevailed. It took me a while to realize that the students might prefer me to use a similar evaluation sheet for their work, ensuring that my comments would be mostly constructive and productive.

Writing is a Social Practice

One of my aims as a writing teacher is to demystify certain lofty (and often debilitating) notions about "the writer" and "the intellectual" in order to instil the idea in students that, as citizens, we all have the freedom and responsibility to use our time and talent: i) to critique existing knowledge; ii) to preserve and refresh what is good in our language and culture; and iii) to create appropriate knowledge for our generation. As writers, we are implicated in and responsible for the knowledge we are reproducing, resisting, or creating. The beauty of the workshop format is that, over the course of the year, groups of fifteen (or so) students begin to form small unique communities of writers. Feedback on their writing is more plentiful and frequent; and over time, they tend to know each other's strengths and problems. The process of discussing their writing fosters a collective determination and increased capacity to acquire higher standards of research, revision, and proofreading. And in their small communities, they begin to understand how powerful and persuasive good writing can be.

Most Arts and Science students are already competent writers when they enter the Programme. Many of them have been able to pull off decent grades writing at the last minute, so they resist one of the chief lessons that a writing teacher can teach: the crucial importance of leaving time for revision. The myth still prevails that good writing is a natural, spontaneous gift rather than the product of practice and reconsideration. Some students claim they can only write well (or authentically) when the mood is right or when the muse inspires them. Under the pressure of having so many assignments, students often write their essays at the last minute, using the adrenaline rush of a looming deadline to overcome doubts and any desire to think deeply about the subject. It is a challenge for the writing teacher to convince students of "the pleasure of taking pains," as the adage goes.

Some students find the disciplined labour of writing academic essays joyless and (some say) soul-destroying. They tell me that, when they first select a topic, whether for Western Civilization or Inquiry, they are excited by the prospect of making new discoveries; they often enjoy the process of research and thinking about difficult issues. Yet, somehow, there is a discrepancy between what they learn in the process and the

72 WRITING AND INFORMAL LOGIC

products they hand in. This is how Louis-Philippe Plante, one of my students, described his alienation and doubts about the conventions of academic writing:

> The first thing that strikes me about my professional (read: University assignment) writing is that it sounds very accurate, authoritarian, and complete. This is not always reflective of the state of mind I am in while I write these papers. ... [My second Inquiry paper] will (hopefully) fetch me a good mark, but I'm sure that the utter frustration and confusion about the entire situation was completely lost during the writing process. Relative to what there is to know about the situation in the Brazilian Amazon rain forest, I know nothing. I spent hours upon hours compiling information, sifting through it, and explaining the situation to the best of my abilities. However, the fact remains that my paper sounds as though it knows what it is talking about, but more questions have been found than answers. This phenomenon of professional-sounding papers is great from my academic point of view, but the end product is still not reflective of the thought process that occurs as I am writing. (*Timber* 2000, see p.76)

Louis-Philippe's words remind me of an ironic comment that was written on the back of a postcard sent from India by Andrew Ide, an Arts and Science student from an earlier generation: "India proves harder to save than we thought."

In teaching writing, I aim to break my students' dependency on the school system and the writing teacher; I aim to put myself out of work, as I used to say. In class workshops and short exercises, I try to stimulate a shrewd awareness of the protean power and play of words and to find fresh ways to introduce students to a range of rhetorical practices that they might adapt to their own purposes. I also aim to instil a respect for the integrity of English as a rich, varied and historically changing language (coupled with a disdain for and resistance to the reduction of English merely to a serviceable tool of global communication, capitalism, and colonialism). From the first day, I say to the students that I will not emphasize finding faults in their writing, but will strive to get to know them and to help them to develop as individual writers and young intellectuals. In return, I expect my students to strive to be good writers; this means they are not just to learn the rules of correct punctuation and to master the stylistic devices of successful prose; they are to take the risk to do research on topics that matter to them, to write courageously about their ideas, and to be accountable for what they choose to write. Despite the hard realities of the first-year workload, I find most students do strive to stop thinking only in terms of "assigned" writing and to identify with their own intellectual work.

As a teacher and writer, I aim to instil a sense of our collective responsibility for being attentive, active citizens in an emerging democracy. For me, this means learning to use our intelligence and disciplined skills to assess and, if need be, to transform existing power structures, as well as to develop and to put into practice shared values of social justice and ecological wellbeing. Not only is the classroom a microcosm of the larger community, it also provides a vital site for coming to understand the present conditions by which knowledge, privilege, and power are acquired and produced, and at the same time, for studying the historical contexts and forces that have shaped the "reality" in which we now live. I am not so much interested in converting students to my own political commitments as I am in imbuing them with the democratic ideal that they have both the right and responsibility to produce appropriate knowledge and practices for their generation.

As the programme is uniquely interdisciplinary, I devise various assignments in which the students can dwell in the boundary zones between disciplines, studying the ways in which different departments of the university formulate methods of knowing and interpreting reality. This long commitment to interdisciplinary learning is evidenced by certain assignments that that have been shared with other first-year Arts and Science courses and instructors over the years: i) the persuasive essay, with the Informal Logic component of this course (in collaboration with David Hitchcock, Hans Hanson, and Darcy Otto); ii) the historical essay on ideas in Western Civilization (with Louis Greenspan and Sara Mendelson); and iii) the "math essay" on the cultural meanings of mathematics or science (with Brad Hart and now Miroslav Lovric).

Until recently, when the Local Environments Report took its place, the best example of using the writing workshops to inculcate the practice of revision was the Western Civilization essay, which historian Sara Mendelson and I used to assign together. The essay would be primarily written to meet the requirements of the Western Civilization Course, but would be handed in first to me and discussed in the writing workshops of my course. The process worked this way: Sara Mendelson and I would formulate a series of topics regarding the early modern period, which is the area of expertise for both of us. For my course, the papers were due according to a staggered schedule; three (or four) students handed in their papers one week before their workshop;

all other workshop participants read the three papers and wrote comments during the week; I also prepared written assessments according to the pattern: what works, what needs refining, suggestions. Then, a week later, in class, we discussed the three papers, in turn, for about fifteen minutes each. The public process of learning from each other's perceptions, mistakes and strategies went on for a month or so. A week after all the workshops were finished, all the revised papers were due in the Western Civilization course. Thus, the very structure of the assignment provided the students with a direct incentive for undertaking suggested revisions. From reading course evaluations, I know that the majority of the students found the revision workshops stimulating and invaluable. Admittedly, despite all attempts to be respectful and tactful, the process of peer-editing did create anxiety and dread in the classroom. Let Christine Palmay's words explain why this may be so:

> The Western Civilization essay workshops were a tortuous experience, despite the helpful intentions of all the critiques and suggestions offered. I equated all comments with failure and immediately became defensive instead of contemplative. Never before was I forced to face the reader. (*Timber* 1999)

Peer-editing workshops are effective because they break the pattern of silence by which the teacher is the only reader of the student's paper before it is forgotten and assigned to a drawer. Ideally, students begin to think about how different kinds of readers might respond to their ideas and how they might best present their work in public.

Another assignment that is exceptionally well suited to the concerns of Arts and Science students is "the math essay," an interdisciplinary assignment, given by the calculus and the writing instructors of the first-year Arts and Science Programme. Some years ago, Brad Hart and I took a big risk; we appeared together—as the mathematician and the cultural critic—in front of the students to talk not only about possible topics for an essay on "the cultural meanings of mathematics and science," but also about the ways of knowing that characterize and limit our disciplinary training. It was the beginning of an edgy assignment that took on a new vitality and direction several years ago, when Miroslav Lovric became the calculus instructor. The "math essay" lets the two instructors and the students experiment and enjoy the pleasures of thinking about the big questions that cut across the disciplines; we talk about a range of topics from the historical origins of scientific discoveries to the ethical responsibilities of scientists and of the agencies that grant their research funding. Several years ago, with the inspired help of Nadine Ijaz (our teaching assistant at the time), we arrived at the present structure that includes three stages. First, small groups of students formulate controversial (but researchable) questions (shades of Inquiry!); together they read and discuss important articles or chapters of books on the topic; lots of e-mail discussion takes place among students, teaching assistants and instructors. For stage two, the students write individual essays, addressing their key questions. After the essays are assessed in both courses, for the third stage, we meet outside class (in evening sessions of about twenty students) for open discussion. The three-stage process has created a wonderfully diverse exchange of ideas for the students, the teaching assistants, and the instructors.

The Local Environments Report is another appropriate assignment for Arts and Science students because it requires them to identify and do research on pressing issues in their own home communities. For this assignment, I have an agreement with *Alternatives*[2] (a professional journal on environmental issues and policy) that some of their reports will be considered for publication. This agreement, which frames the assignment, helps me to encourage the students to overcome the perennial problem of "writing for the teacher," that is, of producing commendable work that, after being read by the marker, ends up in a drawer. Their completed reports are not only given detailed written assessments by me and one other student; they are also read and discussed in workshops. Finally, at the end of a long process of discussion, refining the proposals, writing and revision, I submit a summary of all sixty student reports to *Alternatives Journal* for consideration. Over the years, a small number of the students have subsequently been invited by *Alternatives* to undertake more rigorous revisions in order to be published in the journal. And I am proud to say that a few reports by first-year students have been published in *Alternatives*. Although the success of individual students is sweet and inspires the new students, the main attraction of the Local Environments Report for me is that it is unsurpassed in creating a lively research climate in the classroom and in overcoming student alienation from their own academic work. The students get to know a lot about the places from which their classmates come and about the kinds of community concerns faced in other parts of the province and country. A spin-off effect is that students often comment that they are motivated to go on a country- or province-wide tour to visit the places they learn about. Exciting work that matters to the students is produced.

The Legacy of Timber, or Discoveries

When I abandoned the book review assignment, I began to ask the students to read a courseware collection[3] of excerpts and short pieces about writing, which I entitled *Timber, or Discoveries*, after a commonplace book, once kept by the seventeenth-century author Ben Jonson, one of the architects of the ideals of modern prose. Here is an excerpt from the first edition of *Timber* (1641):

> A strict and succinct style is that where you can take away nothing without loss, and that loss to be manifest. The brief style is that which expresseth much in little; the concise style, which expresseth not enough, but leaves somewhat to be understood; the abrupt style, which hath many breaches, and doth not seem to end, but fall. The congruent and harmonious filling of parts in a sentence hath almost the fastening, and force of knitting, and connection; as in stones well-squared, which will rise strong a great way without mortar.

Timber is used in the classroom as a starting point for discussing and writing about writing. I encourage students to write in the margins and to talk-back to the various ideas found there. Recurrent topics include: practical issues such as editing, documentation, and plagiarism; good and bad ways to evaluate writing; the politics of the English language; and the uses of a writer's journal.

I'm not sure when it dawned on me that *Timber* should include student ideas about writing as well as published opinions. Probably it was in 1994, when I read the dazzling words of Anita Wong, writing about cultivating her own voice:

> "You're just like a typical Chinese," my father said with his usual complacency. "You don't know how to express yourself forcefully, with bravado." These were his words in his critique of my resumé after I had slaved over its composition for a whole three days to get it just right. In my mind, I believed it made a clear statement about me. I had even balked at some of the words I had used to describe my qualifications. To me, they bordered on downright lying. But he was encouraging me to use those very words, those power-words that embodied *self-confidence, pride* and *"Don Cherry arrogance."* ... For a while, I mourned over my own fate. ... I felt trapped by my culture, by my background, and by my inborn tendency to mince words. Even though I was born in Canada and educated in the same school system as all my outspoken Western colleagues, I couldn't escape this influence of Chinese

thinking and Chinese language use on my modes of expression....
What lies! I had actually convinced myself that the stereotypes
were true! But they are blatantly false. Shame on my dad ...
(*Timber* 1994)

The piece goes on to present a brilliant account of the subtle ways in
which the strong women of Anita's family use the Chinese language. Anita
Wong's essay was so well received by the next year's students and fostered
so much creative energy, there was no going back. *Timber* grew and grew
to include a wide range of published and student pieces, often in direct
conversation with each other. *Timber* focuses student attention on how
rhetoric works, whether one's goal is to produce successful prose (that is,
clear, concise, useful prose) or to understand the discursive structures by
which identity, community, gender, ethnicity, class and race and nature
are constructed in texts. One of the set pieces that I include is a selection
of Raymond Queneau's *Exercises in Style*. Using a range of about a
hundred modes from "awkward" and "passive" to "exclamatory," and
"mathematical," Queneau repeats the same nonsensical narrative about a
guy who gets on a bus and encounters a man with a long neck, wearing a
hat .... The point is to show that "voice," however personal it may sound,
is at the same time an effect of rhetoric. The students enjoy inventing
alternative or updated versions of Queneau's exercise, as can be seen in
this Gangsta RAP version by Tim Ho:

> I was chillaxin' wit my homies, goin' places on the S BUS,
> Some punk thinkin he's all dat starts a ruck-US
> Got some big pimpin' hat on his head,
> And a frickin long neck, I said.
> Word up. (*Timber* 2001)

Timber gets the students thinking about themselves as writers and about
the role writing plays in people's lives. Sarah Senecal wrote a superb
piece about her discovering (and secretly reading) the letters her parents
wrote to each other before they were married, when they were attending
two different universities:

> ... The letters were so powerful, I thought about them constantly
> for weeks afterwards. I knew that during the sixteen years spent
> with my parents I had spoken with them often and even had
> moments of deep conversation. But there was some aspect of them
> that was never visible in conversation. This aspect had managed to
> transfer itself onto the page, into each bravely written word. ...

For two years of their lives, they had imagined, dreamed, thought
about the world and their place in it, and wrote these things down
for each other. (*Timber* 2002)

Timber has become a mixed bag of stuff, including student pieces on
everything from graffiti to gay English, changing each year as the students
change. The *Timber* of today is described here by Courtney Chasin:

> A stack of one hundred and seventy-four leaves of paper ... this
> monstrosity is appropriately named. I imagine a woodcutter calling
> out as the trees fall, one by one, and become bleached paper. I
> wonder if every page upon which my words are sprawled, awkward
> arrangements of black ink blotches upon white, can justify their
> existence. (*Timber* 2003)

Perhaps because there is so much cultural diversity among the Arts
and Science students, the section in *Timber* on language and identity
provokes a broad range of responses. What follows is a few passages in
which students describe the place and power of English in their lives.
Aruna Dhara addresses a direct challenge to "English" to say that, although
her mastery of the language is growing, English has its limits: "you can't
begin to understand how I think." Aruna's first language is telugu:

> very few canadians, and even very few indian canadians, have ever
> even heard of it. the women of my mother's family speak very
> quickly; when my grandmother converses, every sentence sounds
> like a statement, as if her age had made her a reluctant authority ...
> on everything. telugu is round, ending in vowels and flowing in a
> circular pattern. the roundness of it envelops me in a bubble. ...
> broken telugu does not work. there is no such thing as a charming
> accent, which English speakers seem to love so well. (Timber 1999)

Some students have experienced either the loss of the language they knew
as children or cannot speak to their grandparents in their family's traditional
language. Melissa Phillips regrets that, once they came to Canada, her
parents decided not to teach her and her brothers Afrikaans, the language
of their homeland, as it was the "language of the oppressor":

> ... Afrikaans is also the language of our relatives. In not teaching
> us the language, my parents also did not pass on any sense of a
> real "culture" to which we belong. As a result I always feel like
> I'm missing something, especially when I'm with my relatives (and

when they're speaking Afrikaans to each other). Yes, Afrikaans is
the language of the oppressor, but it was the people who spoke the
language, not the language itself, that were at fault. Now I'm still
left with a piece of my cultural identity missing. (*Timber* 2000)

Lucille Chan points out that her parents understood the power of English
and made sure that she "lived and breathed quite naturally in the world of
English." Yet, Lucille's proficiency in English came at a cost:

When I came to Hong Kong for a two-year stay when I was 3, my
cousins laughed because I spoke Chinese like a white person. But
they saw what I had traded for this when I helped them on their
English spelling tests. ... I still remember the inner derision I felt
when I stared at the outrageously simple words [my cousins] Alan
and Maggie were learning. ... And now I wonder at myself, that
while I secretly ridiculed them, I never once marvelled at my
inability to write my name in Chinese. (*Timber* 2000)

When Hinal Sheth came to live in Carleton Place, near Ottawa, in Canada
in 1989, her native tongue was Gujarati; soon she and her brother became
fluent in English, but were determined to speak Gujarati at home and to
keep up their reading and writing knowledge of the language. At present,
however, "our parents speak Gujarati to us and we understand it perfectly
but unfortunately we answer back in English. Carleton Place is a white
community. The other Indian family was my aunt's family." Once Hinal
came to McMaster and began to meet different types of people, including
many Indians, she started to feel the loss and now plans to learn how to
read and write Gujarati: "I remember meeting a guy during frosh week
who was also Jain and also spoke Gujarati. I had a great time sitting at the
bar with him—having a conversation with him in Gujarati!" (*Timber* 2001).

As young writers faced with numerous compulsory assignments,
many of the students are concerned with keeping and developing their
own styles. Everyone wants to have "a voice" of one's own. One reason I
always require a writer's journal, in some form or other, is to ensure that
the students will be able to write whatever they want in at least one case.
Here Alex Avila explains why the writer's journal works for him:

The words of my journal are my words, for me, by me, and part of
me. ... I wonder a lot about the person who I am, who I have been,
and who I am becoming. I wonder what my real goals are, what
my purpose may be (if one exists at all) ... (*Timber* 1999)

In contrast, Ying Ying Li protests that the schools use journal assignments too much; the very freedom of the journals undermines the necessary role of the teacher in pointing out "logical inconsistencies and unsubstantiated claims":

> Both teacher and the student accept the the premise that it is a "personal" journal where one gets to write whatever one wants to. The teacher, then, must accept everything a student writes. She has thrown away her authority to evaluate critically. She is reduced to a series of check marks and comments such as, "on the short side" or "very interesting!" ... The emphasis shifts from quality to quantity. (*Timber* 1999)

Yet, it is the very suspension of self-criticism and the marker's red pen that makes the journal a desirable place to write. Sarah Dobson uses the journal to find the right words to describe "the luminous things" of everyday life:

> It's my brain on the page ... a tattered notebook that houses my soul. It is a rainbow of multicoloured pen and a mosaic of ideas. I grab my pen when I hear a beautiful song, or come back from a lecture that has fascinated me. I am never sure what it is that inspires me to write, but there is always something in me that I need to expel. I won't stop writing until the desire to create has risen and disappeared, whether it is a pleasant experience of not. I am playful: the words tease and tickle me while they crawl onto the page and leave their mark. (*Timber* 2000)

Let Julia Croome have the last word here on the creative potential of keeping a journal. One night, she used her journal to pour out raw feelings and chaotic thoughts on the page. The next morning, she found this passage:

> My lips crack and bleed
> My eyes sting and weep
> My skin is stretching
> I cannot contain my heart.

The passage may be or may not be poetry, writes Julia, but it "seems to be the exact translation of what I felt last night. I am startled by its presence in my journal, a small gift I unknowingly left myself" (*Timber* 2001).

As part of the *Timber* legacy, one of the most enjoyable topics we explore is the gap between what is taught about writing and the actual experience of the process of writing. These discussions are useful not only in getting students familiar with the conventional stages and guidelines for writing academic papers, but in helping students to internalise and to experiment with the ideas and strategies other writers have used. One year, one of the workshops prepared a Night Writing event to explore their individual writing habits and rituals. With the generous help of Jonathan Chan as the photographer (he was my teaching assistant that year), the students transformed the common room of Wallingford Hall into an art gallery of photographs of themselves writing in their favourite spaces, whether in their personally designed study areas in residence rooms or in their hideouts in the library or in the woods. To cite one example, Dan Milisavljevic appeared in his study with the clutter of his desk and his bust of Elvis-as-writing-muse (*Timber* 2000). We had a marvellous discussion that night about the conditions that make our best writing possible.

By way of conclusion, I let Moira Hare explain how *Timber* works to make students more discerning writers. At first, writes Moira, the individual pieces of *Timber* appear to be merely "a collection of random anecdotes, excerpts, and drawings":

> ... taken together as a whole, [however,] the material begins to entwine, overlap, interest and entice, forming a foundation for a series of discussions on theory, technique, and unintentionally revealed, random yet interesting aspects of my classmates' lives. All writers face the many issues covered in *Timber*, whether they be social science professors, starving auteurs or first-year arts and science students. Like cutting wood, writing is a conscious and concerted effort. It can be messy and painful. Most of the time you end up with a pile of wood shavings under your desk—the "darlings" you have had to sacrifice for the good of the piece. (*Timber* 2003)

Even Moira Hare's last line recalls the words "kill your darlings," which I am apt to quote as the favourite editing advice of Dwayne Hodgson, (a former 1B06 teaching assistant). So I close this brief account of the writing course with the words of Adriana Brook, a student who wrote a piece this year to celebrate the "legacy of *Timber*" and thus gave me the title for this section: "*Timber* is the inside story on Arts and Science. ... I have the secrets of second year soon to be third year, from the perspective of first year soon to be second year" (*Timber* 2003). The community of writers lives on.

Informal Logic: Listening is the Beginning of Peace

Mark Vorobej

The so-called "Informal Logic" section of the Arts and Science course is really a course in the human practice of argumentation. Pretty well everyone engages in this practice on a daily basis. That is, most of us, including all my students, are critical thinkers already. My principal aim in teaching this course is to enhance my students' critical thinking skills while engendering within them a love for the subject matter. It's helpful, in achieving this end, to do two things. First, make the learning fun. Second, encourage the students to recognize, without directly telling them, that logic matters.

The study of logic can be fun if the instructor possesses a genuine passion for the subject (students will inevitably pick up on this), if she can use humour effectively and establish a relationship of trust within the classroom, and if she can involve the students directly in every stage of the learning process. I don't claim to have any special talent or expertise in any of these areas and so, with the exception of some few remarks about enhancing student participation, my remaining comments will focus on pedagogical issues which arise out of my conception of argumentation as an inherently *political* enterprise.

Argumentation is the practice of attempting to convince someone (either yourself or others) to do or believe something by an appeal to reasons. The goal of argumentation, therefore, is interpersonal rational persuasion. Accordingly, at least two parties, playing functionally distinct roles, are involved in every argumentative exchange: an *author* who constructs and presents the argument, and an *audience member* to whom the argument is directed. The author's aim is to rationally persuade the audience member to adopt the conclusion of her argument, on the basis of the evidence cited in the argument's premises.

This simple model has two important implications. First, arguments are offered by, and directed towards persons who, for a variety of reasons, typically care a great deal about what other persons do and believe. Second, those who participate in the practice of argumentation have, in some fashion, elected to attempt to influence the beliefs and actions of others through rational (i.e. evidence-based) means, rather than through the exercise of countless available non-rational means of persuasion (e.g. intimidation, coercion, violence, indoctrination, etc.). Logic matters, therefore, if we generally have reason to care about what others believe and how they behave, to prefer the social practice of argumentation over non-rational means of persuasion, and to promote strong critical thinking skills within our community. (For the purposes of this particular exercise, I unabashedly invoke reason to promote reason.)

Throughout the course I drop hints to the effect that, in my opinion, rationality is the best guide to the pursuit of truth and the realization of the good life. I call this (deliberately stodgy) claim my "Rationalist Commitment." But the term "rationality" is really just shorthand here for the homely practice of being *reflective* about your beliefs, i.e. paying attention to what you believe and why you believe it, attempting to judge wisely whether your existing beliefs and practices are well-supported by the existing body of evidence, and being open to the ever-present possibility that your beliefs may be in error and so may stand in need of revision. Each of us is already rational in this sense, to some extent. But it's also true, of each of us, that there is room for improvement. A more skilled critical thinker is, according to my rationalist commitment, more likely to arrive at true beliefs and to behave in a judicious fashion.

Since the pursuit of truth and the good life is a collective (i.e. political) undertaking, we're more likely to realize these goods if, within limits, we encourage each other to be (more) reflective about our beliefs, and if we allow our beliefs to be subjected to public critical appraisal through the interpersonal practice of rational persuasion. Therefore, how well we live our lives—both individually and collectively—depends, to a considerable extent, upon how skilled we are in the practice of argumentation. Or so I believe. I rarely talk to my students in precisely these terms, since they're more likely to adopt something like this position if they come to it on their own. What I *can* do in class is set the stage for this "awakening."

It's astonishing, however, how few logic texts make systematic reference to persons as the participants within argumentative discourse. In an effort to ensure that my students never lose sight of the role which they personally play as *arguers* in the practice of argumentation, I have come, over the years, to give prominence throughout the course to the two non-standard notions of a *normal* argument and an individual's *epistemic state*. To motivate the introduction of these terms, I first need to say something about the more familiar notion of argument cogency.

Cogency is perhaps the central concept around which any course on argumentation is structured. Crudely, cogent arguments are good arguments, arguments that don't commit logical errors or fallacies, arguments by which we ought to be persuaded. Conversely, non-cogent arguments are bad arguments, arguments that are fallacious, arguments of which we ought to steer clear. Logic courses are typically framed as exercises designed to enhance a student's ability to differentiate between cogent and non-cogent arguments, and in so doing to promote the flourishing of rational belief. So construed, logic clearly plays a central role in all forms of inquiry, regardless of the topic under investigation.

There is much about this standard understanding of cogency which is attractive and correct. Unfortunately, however, cogency is most often treated as pretty much a fixed, context-invariant property which a given argument either possesses or does not possess *simpliciter*. Persons, therefore, drop out as irrelevant. If an argument A just *is* cogent, then it doesn't matter either who is presenting A or who is evaluating it. Our job, as critical thinkers, is simply to recognize that A is cogent, and explain why the argument bears this "objective" property.

This approach ignores the fact that rational belief formation is a process that is inextricably embedded within a rich epistemic context. That is, whether it's rational for someone to adopt an argument's conclusion on the basis of the evidence cited in the premises, very frequently depends upon *what else* that person rationally believes. Suppose, for example, that someone argues that the practice of slavery is never morally permissible because it's a violation of our shared human dignity for any person ever to be treated as chattel. Whether it's rational for you to believe the conclusion of this argument, on the basis of the evidence cited, will depend, amongst other things, on how you define the practice of slavery; how you conceive of the moral point of view and the notion of human dignity; your position on the substantive restrictions which morality may reasonably impose on our interactions with others; your understanding of the empirical conditions under which slavery is, or can be, practiced; and whether you're willing to allow for the possibility that it may be morally permissible for humans to engage in morally reprehensible practices within certain tragic or particularly desperate circumstances.

Accordingly, I prefer to define cogency, more controversially, as a person-relative, context-dependent property of arguments. More precisely, an argument A is cogent *for person P* in context C if, and only if, it's rational for P in C to accept the conclusion of A on the basis of the evidence cited in the premises. More succinctly, A is cogent for P if, and only if, it's rational for P to be persuaded by A.

Working within this framework, it soon becomes apparent that it's not only possible, but very common in fact, for a single argument A to be cogent for one person, while failing to be cogent for someone else. Since cogency is defined in terms of rational belief, it follows that it's not only possible, but very common in fact, for two individuals to rationally disagree over any number of issues. As worthwhile a practice as it is, argumentation cannot rationally resolve all disagreements.

Pluralism, therefore, reigns within the classroom. Very often, "the right answer" to a problem in logic cannot be found in the solutions at the back of the textbook. Radically opposing viewpoints may equally well withstand critical scrutiny. Logic cannot settle all disagreements for the very simple reason that many disputes turn on non-logical issues, about which we can each, often defensibly, form competing judgments.

The possibility of rational disagreement arises, therefore, because each participant within an argumentative exchange approaches that argument from a particular and often highly idiosyncratic epistemic state. I use the (deliberately nebulous) term "epistemic state" to refer to each arguer's (huge and ill-defined) set of background beliefs, desires, practical commitments, value judgments, and emotional engagements,—the elements of which together capture both how that person views the world and how they see themselves as an agent of change within their environment. My epistemic state, therefore, includes everything which I may in principle bring to bear upon my personal understanding and evaluation of any argumentative exchange. In my lectures, I try to demonstrate how the author's project of rational persuasion, as well as the audience's reception of the author's argument, are systematically shaped by each arguer's respective epistemic state. It's fundamentally mistaken, therefore, to view arguments in isolation from the identities of the persons involved in an argumentative exchange. It's always relevant to ask: *Who* is arguing with *whom*?

I now want to move away from these abstract, theoretical considerations to a discussion of how students react in the classroom to this model of argumentation. Many students enter an introductory logic course feeling somewhat timid and apprehensive, suspecting that they will be required to master voluminous amounts of complicated technical material, and to memorize clever tricks and formulas needed to solve intricate puzzles involving issues that are of no relevance whatsoever to their personal lives. Logic, they imagine, is going to be a little bit like some of their (more dreary) high school math courses. And these expectations are not entirely unreasonable. There certainly are many (especially formal) logic courses that fit this description. So to counteract these concerns, I try to present logic to my Arts and Science students, not as something which they should either fear or idolize, or feel awed or intimidated by, but simply as an extremely useful and utterly prosaic tool which, if employed wisely, can have a profound and positive effect on their entire world-view, and on how they interact with others. To begin with, my students are surprised to learn—even on the first day of class if I can pull it off—that the solution to a logic problem very often lies within, i.e. within their own epistemic state.

Whether an argument is cogent, remember, hinges on whether it's rational for *you* to be persuaded by it. And whether it's rational for you to be persuaded often hinges on what else *you* rationally believe. So, when students are discussing whether a particular argument is cogent, they're forced to delve into their own epistemic state. This focus on personal epistemic states almost immediately accomplishes four things.

First, the study of logic becomes, in part, a journey of self-discovery. It's best to introduce students to logic by asking them to respond to the arguments of others, rather than requiring at the outset that they construct arguments of their own. But even in this relatively less demanding, apparently more passive exercise, students need to ask themselves what they believe on a wide variety of topics, and whether those beliefs are rationally defensible.

Second, and this is obviously a related point, students can become deeply engaged with the material once they recognize that, in a sense, their own identity is at stake. The problem for the student is not simply whether the argument of some stranger X on topic Y appearing on page Z of the textbook is cogent, but whether she can clearly articulate her own relevant beliefs on Y, and rationally defend them in a public forum—both against X's claims in the text, and in response to questions and criticisms from her fellow students. A student's motivation to study logic can increase dramatically once she's called upon, within a supportive and encouraging class environment, to struggle with the difficult and often frustrating task of stating clearly and precisely what she believes, and why she believes it.

Third, these exercises have a wonderfully liberating effect on student behaviour within the classroom. Once they realize that the answers do not appear at the back of the textbook or in an instructor's manual, students tend to lose that fear of speaking out in class which feeds on the concern that they might give a wrong or even stupid answer. Rather, they come to realize that, insofar as each person is an authority on her own epistemic state, they can each offer a certain perspective on the argument at hand which perhaps no one else can provide. So, once again, they're encouraged to share publicly their own personal engagement with the argument. They're encouraged to speak out about where they're coming from.

Finally, through these sorts of exercises, students learn to appreciate the importance of listening. This is not an easy lesson to learn, but it's so important that I usually tell the students very early on about the course motto – "Listening is the beginning of peace"—a quotation from the sociologist and peace researcher Elise Boulding. I'm sure this puzzles them at first. How can a logic course be about listening, never mind peace? But since I want them to take these questions seriously, I also tell them (truthfully) that this quotation captures, better than any other with which I am familiar, my main reason for wanting to teach this course year in and year out. This quotation explains a great deal about my own personal commitment to, and enthusiasm for, the study of logic.

Listening is a difficult task. Humans aren't programmed particularly well for it. When first presented with arguments, beginning logic students often enthusiastically jump right into the work of evaluation and criticism, assuming from the outset that they've understood what they're analyzing, i.e. what was said to them. Yet it's remarkably difficult to understand clearly what another person is saying, whether in speech or in writing. This is shown by the remarkable frequency with which we misunderstand one another. By encouraging each student to speak at length about their own epistemic state and their own personal engagement with particular arguments, the class gets into the habit of listening to each other. They learn more about each other, and they learn that even beliefs which may initially appear strange and peculiar to them can usually be provided with some sort of rationale. Most beliefs "make sense" at some level. Seeing this, they're a little less inclined to automatically dismiss altogether those beliefs (or those people) with which (or with whom) they disagree. And so they learn to respect each other more, and to become more open to their own fallibility, and to the possibility that they can perhaps learn something *from*, and not simply *about*, almost any person they encounter.

Here's an example of a simple listening exercise which we work through as a class early on in the course. Consider the following two statements: "May begins on Monday. Mary should get married in May." Initially, the juxtaposition of these statements (containing no so-called indicator words signalling the presence of premises or a conclusion) doesn't make a whole lot of sense. Nonetheless, I ask the class to consider under what conditions could these two statements constitute an argument. This question prompts them first to focus on the person who could be offering the argument, and then to imagine scenarios within which that person could see themselves as offering evidence aimed at rationally persuading someone, perhaps Mary, to get married in May, for example.

Usually, lots of bizarre, "crazy" scenarios are suggested. But it also usually doesn't take too long before someone arrives at a fairly sensible interpretation of the passage. This typically involves an appeal to background conditions and beliefs—epistemic states!—and provides a nice first illustration of an enthymematic argument, i.e. an argument in which an author employs one or more claims, as either premises or a conclusion, without explicitly asserting those claims. By next asking students to consider scenarios within which this argument could actually be cogent for them, one can make the point that listening—attending carefully both to the words of another and to the context within which those words are expressed—creates often unexpected opportunities for instructive dialogue. It's then but a small step for them to appreciate the power and significance of the concept of a normal argument.

An argument *A* is *normal* if, and only if, its author believes *A* to be cogent both for herself and her intended audience. (Normality is defined in terms of belief rather than rational belief, since it's a descriptive rather than a normative concept, and we want to allow for the possibility of error and irrationality within the actual practice of argumentation.) Throughout the course we explicitly adopt the methodological stance of assuming, of any new argument which we consider, that it is normal. Of course, this assumption is defeasible. Evidence of abnormality should not be ignored. But in the absence of any such evidence, we assume that the author of any argument we encounter believes that it's rational both for herself and her intended audience to believe the argument's conclusion on the basis of the evidence cited.

The normality assumption invokes a kind of sincerity condition. It assumes that someone ostensibly engaged in the social practice of rational persuasion will participate in that practice in good faith, and will not deliberately attempt to manipulate others by offering arguments which, in their own personal estimation, fail to be cogent either for themselves or their intended audience. Normal arguers present arguments which they themselves sincerely believe to be cogent for all relevant parties.

The normality assumption, therefore, ensures that we take *the author's* argument seriously by making a sincere and deliberate effort ourselves to understand how the normality condition could be satisfied. This means probing into the author's epistemic state, including her beliefs about our (i.e. the audience members') beliefs. It means listening to the author, and being open to the possibility that we may be able to learn from her. Note that we don't assume that the argument *is* cogent for us; only that the author believes it to be cogent for us. The presumption of normality, therefore, is one of the principal means, within an argumentative context, of showing respect for your interlocutor. We respect her by assuming that she herself is behaving in a transparent, respectful, non-manipulative manner towards us. Again, listening is the beginning of peace.

At the same time, I concede that it can be difficult to know for sure whether the particular argument before you actually is normal; never mind whether most arguments are normal. The normality assumption, therefore, can lead us astray by propagating false beliefs. Its adoption is certainly not justified by statistical considerations. However, communication of any sort is a difficult hermeneutical exercise which simply cannot be undertaken without making a host of fallible working assumptions. Attempting to understand what another person is saying to us is, in an important sense, guesswork. To be sure, we try to make reasonable, well-informed, "educated" guesses. But we're bound to get things wrong much of the time, especially when our epistemic access to authors is limited, as it is when dealing, say, exclusively with a printed text. All things considered, however, the benefits of the normality assumption, principally in fostering a climate of mutual respect, outweigh the inevitable risks.

There are other, more serious dangers to guard against in promoting this general approach to the study and practice of argumentation. The discipline of logic presupposes that some arguments are better than others. A good critical thinker is adept at differentiating between those arguments she should and those arguments she should not be persuaded by. The fact that the cogency of arguments is assessed relative to an individual's particular epistemic state complicates, but in no way undermines, these general claims.

Nonetheless, I recognize that my Arts and Science students are frequently tempted to adopt a fashionable, but severely mistaken form of epistemological relativism according to which each of us is justified in believing whatever we want, so long as we can relate it in some way to our own seemingly privileged epistemic state. Encouraging students to speak from the perspective of their own personal subjectivity can simultaneously delude them into thinking that it's not possible to commit a mistake in logic, and that it's never necessary to accommodate one's beliefs to the critical judgments of others, so long as one is quick enough on one's feet to tell a clever and compelling narrative about one's favoured epistemological standpoint.

Since this attitude is so deeply antithetical to the very concept of argumentation as a normative exercise—the possibility of rational persuasion presupposes the possibility of *irrational* persuasion—it may

be useful to offer a few concrete illustrations which will help to explain
how relativistic temptations of this sort can forcefully arise in a logic
class.

Traditionally, a fallacy is a mistake in logical reasoning which
people often fail to recognize as erroneous. Many texts identify various
very simple argument forms as logical fallacies, regardless of the context
within which they arise (analogously to the way in which cogency is
typically presented). The *ad hominem* fallacy, for example, is said to occur
when someone attempts to discredit another person's claim by appealing
to some personal characteristic of that individual, rather than assessing
the evidence for that claim. One kind of *ad populum* fallacy is said to
occur when someone presents the popularity of a belief as evidence for
the truth of that belief. And arguing for the truth of a claim on the basis of
a lack of evidence against that claim is said to involve an *ad ignorantium*,
a fallacy of arguing from ignorance.

I argue in class that none of these patterns of reasoning *as such* is
fallacious. That is, it is possible to identify many commonplace arguments,
exemplifying one or other of these forms, which are cogent for particular
individuals within particular epistemic contexts. Once again, it's best to
design exercises which allow students to discover this for themselves.
For example, I sometimes give students a short list of possible personal
characteristics of individuals and ask them to work through the list
constructing, in each case, (a) a normal, non-cogent *ad hominem* argument
involving an appeal to that characteristic, and (b) a parallel normal, cogent
ad hominem argument. I claim, in advance, that this exercise can be
completed for any personal characteristic which anyone in the class can
propose. The assumption of normality running throughout the exercise
creates an opportunity for students to explore, possibly in a more
sympathetic and less judgmental fashion than they may be used to, the
nature of, and motivation behind a variety of common human prejudices.
Hopefully, they learn that compartmentalization is a dangerous
hermeneutical practice. Beliefs, including seemingly prejudicial,
superstitious, or offensive beliefs, rarely function in isolation.
Understanding is enhanced as we situate those beliefs within their broader
epistemic context. And understanding can, on occasion, lead to respectful
appreciation, if not acceptance, of the views and identity of another.

Exactly the same issues arise in our discussion of argumentative
appeals to popularity. In my opinion, nothing whatsoever follows about
the truth value of a belief B merely from the fact that B is widely held
within a certain epistemic community C. Whether an appeal to popularity

has probative force for you will depend on (a) the topic T that B is about, (b) the composition of C, (c) how widespread B is within C, (d) how confidently B is held within C and, most importantly, (e) whether it's reasonable for you to believe that the members of C can be relied upon to form reasonable beliefs about T. Different arguers ought to assess appeals to popularity differently, depending, once again, upon what else they believe. Therefore, in assessing the arguments of others, we shouldn't compartmentalize our own beliefs either. Whether, for example, the mere fact that most people believe in God constitutes evidence, for me, that God exists, depends in part upon what it's reasonable for me to believe about the competency of others to form reliable beliefs upon religious matters. (Whether I should buy Crest toothpaste because everyone else does obviously raises a whole different set of issues.)

God, not infrequently, also makes an appearance in discussions of argumentative appeals to ignorance. Suppose, to take just one case of this complex form of reasoning, that someone argues that God does not exist because we have no evidence of His existence. Clearly, it's just plain silly to make a general ruling on the cogency of this argument without asking a series of related difficult questions over which there is plenty of room for rational disagreement. What would count as evidence of God's existence? Have we conducted a competent search for evidence of the relevant sort? What would count as a competent search in this case? And if such a search has been conducted, do we have reason to believe that evidence of God's existence could nonetheless still elude us? Indeed, do we have reason to believe that God, should He exist, might have deliberately created the universe in such a way that evidence of His existence will remain elusive regardless of the nature and extent of our search? And so on.

I hope these illustrations allow for a better appreciation of why students might be tempted by forms of relativism which make problematic the notion of epistemic justification. My approach to argumentation might be characterized as a kind of *pluralistic holism*. It's pluralistic in the sense that argumentation creates a forum within which there is a great deal of latitude for idiosyncratic, independent, and creative critical thought on issues over which there can be deep and irresolvable rational disagreement. It's holistic in the sense that the justification of belief typically involves an appeal to a vast network of intricately related beliefs within an individual's epistemic state. So I can justify my belief in proposition P, for example, by appealing to my other beliefs in propositions Q, R, and S. None of this implies relativism, or scepticism about the very notion of epistemic justification. But one can understand the temptation to think so.

One thing some students may not immediately appreciate is that Q, R, and S too may subsequently become appropriate objects of rational scrutiny. Suppose, for example, that I challenge an argument from popularity by invoking a personal belief to the effect that most people aren't competent to form reliable beliefs about the (widely discredited) predictive value of astrology. Holism allows me to defend astrology in this manner. But holism doesn't let me off the hook that easily. With liberty comes responsibility. So if someone challenges the belief which I have just introduced into this argument, I am obliged to respond to her challenge by offering evidence in support of what I have in effect proposed as a rational belief. And she in turn is free to challenge the argument which I construct. In particular, I can't justify my belief in P, as a rational belief, merely by pointing to the fact that I also *believe* Q, R, and S. In order for these beliefs to do the justificatory work required, they must be related in an appropriate way to my belief in P, and they must themselves be rationally defensible. From a logical point of view, mere belief is never adequate to underpin cogency.

Pluralistic holism, therefore, does not vitiate the need for a coherent and workable notion of epistemic justification. It emphasizes, however, that the demand for justification is prompted and shaped by pragmatic concerns; specifically, by the contextually embedded interaction between the epistemic states of authors and audience members.

The most important thing, in class, is just to get the students to argue frequently and passionately, face-to-face with one another. There's no better way to convince them that they can indeed make mistakes in logic, and that they need to think very seriously about revising some of their beliefs. The specific manner in which they learn this will be influenced by the particular individuals with whom they are arguing. But arguing well is such an incredibly difficult task that, regardless of the skills or identity of their interlocutors, everyone who practices argumentation in good faith will discover it to be both a humbling and an empowering exercise. My job is to provide the class with a common logical vocabulary and set of logical skills which will enable them to better articulate, to themselves and to others, what they already believe; and to understand more fully the constraints which reason places on the process of inquiry, the construction of belief, and the evolution of our epistemic states.

I want to conclude by commenting very briefly upon some practical matters, relating to the design and running of the course, which help to promote this end.

Logic is a foreign subject for most first-year students, as it's usually not covered (in any depth) in Canadian high schools. Logic also has more to do with acquiring a set of skills than with memorizing facts. So, fortunately, each year I've been able to spend two full terms with my Arts and Science students. They need this kind of time span in order to appreciate the concerns that drive an unfamiliar discipline, and to practice the skills involved in arguing. At the same time, since the logic component is combined with "Writing," each week I limit our discussion to a single relatively small, discrete, well-defined topic, so that by the end of the course we've covered roughly what other students would have covered in just one term. This helps to keep the overall workload in the Writing and Logic course somewhat more manageable.

In an effort to involve them as much as possible in each stage of the learning process, students spend one hour per week in tutorial, working through problem sets or take-home assignments in small groups. In my experience, students much prefer to work in groups, and they're required to submit many of their assignments as a group, with each student receiving the same grade on the assignment. Since the assignments are worth 40% of the final grade, they're strongly motivated both to argue and to get along with one another.

The tutorials follow the single weekly one-hour lecture for the entire class by a couple of days. In the lecture I lay out the groundwork for a certain topic, which the students will then explore, in more depth, on their own in the tutorial. I've adopted four techniques in my logic lectures which, I believe, facilitate the learning experience. First, I lecture on a topic on the assumption that everyone has done the assigned reading on that topic beforehand. Of course, students are told about this in advance. Therefore, I don't have to waste a lot of time in class going over extremely elementary material. This allows me to focus more quickly on the interesting or controversial issues.

Second, at the beginning of each class I distribute a one-page handout covering the salient points of the lecture. I tell students that I do this so they won't have to frantically take notes throughout the hour, and will instead be free to listen carefully to what I have to say, and to pose and respond to questions.

Third, I try, whenever possible, to frame what I have to say as a critical response of some sort to the assigned reading. This requires finding a textbook which gets most of the elementary material basically right (for the reasons stated above), but which also makes many claims with which I (strongly) disagree. Fortunately, it's not been difficult to find texts of this sort. The lectures therefore set up an interesting three-way dialectic: the students know what the textbook says from having read it; in the lecture they hear where, how, and why I disagree with the text; and finally I ask them to make up their own mind on the material under discussion. They can agree with me, they can agree with the author of the text, or they can develop their own position.

This pedagogical style is admittedly difficult and confusing for many students. At first, many simply want to know who's right, what they should study, and what will be on the exam. But I honestly believe that it eventually works for the majority of them. I know of no better way to encourage students to respond critically and creatively to the material, to alert them to the possibility of rational disagreement, and, most importantly, to get them to speak out and argue in class. And that's my fourth technique. Keep the lecturing to a minimum. Use the traditional lecture format just to provide enough stage setting so as to enable students to articulate and respond to well-framed, critical, probing comments and questions. It's best if the students themselves, at that point, play a substantial role in controlling the direction of the classroom discussion. In fact, when things go well, I have difficulty finishing my prepared "lecture." Often, by the end of the class, I have to struggle to get a word in edgewise. Some students find the atmosphere too chaotic and unfocussed. And sometimes they're right. This approach to teaching is not risk-free. So if a classroom discussion becomes ridiculously unwieldy, I might reluctantly take over some tutorial time to introduce a bit of order and stability.

The topics which I cover in the course are very traditional, with perhaps three exceptions. First, I no longer teach any formal logic. One really needs a substantial amount of time to do anything philosophically interesting in formal logic. And I've found that spending, say, just two or three weeks on propositional or syllogistic reasoning results in a rather anomalous module, awkwardly detached from the main concerns of the rest of the course. Rather than spending time teaching technical material about truth tables and truth-functional connectives, for example, I find it more useful to concentrate, in a more philosophical vein and without any formal machinery, on the differences between deductive validity and inductive reliability—a distinction that serves the students well throughout the entire course. I also spend a very substantial portion of time on the topic of argument diagramming. The purpose of an argument diagram is to represent, in a perspicuous visual fashion, the evidential structure of an argument as it is conceived by its author. Diagrams, therefore, straightforwardly relate to our concern with argumentative listening; and particularly to explaining exactly how the author understands her argument's premises to be relevant to its conclusion (a condition of normality). In this regard, I introduce the distinction between convergent, linked, and hybrid arguments. The novel set of techniques for argument diagramming, which I have developed while teaching this course, also allows one to record precisely the points upon which there is rational disagreement between an author and her audience, thus dovetailing with another central theme. The expressive capacity of the resulting diagram can be quite powerful; allowing one, for example, to depict an argument's normal structure while simultaneously identifying its principal flaws.

Finally, the course concludes with what's proven to be a very enjoyable and successful "capstone experience." The class divides into groups of five or six students to work, on their own time, on developing an approximately four-page, single-spaced argumentative essay on any topic of mutual concern which is controversial enough to sustain this kind of relatively lengthy treatment. Their task is to compose a normal argument. Each group distributes a copy of their essay a few days in advance to roughly one-third of the class, and has one hour of class time to respond to questions and criticisms from those classmates, who then, along with me, grade the essay and its oral defence. Everyone in the group receives the same grade on this assignment, which is usually worth about 15% of their final grade. This exercise, which consumes anywhere from five to six weeks of precious class time, provides an entertaining and structured forum within which students can synthesize and showcase the entire package of logical skills which they have mastered over the year.

The students in the Arts and Science Programme are a wonderfully bright and talented bunch. It's been very, very gratifying for me to work with them over the years, and to witness what they're capable of. But what sets them apart, even more than their native intelligence, is their natural curiosity, their infectious enthusiasm for learning, and their exceptionally generous and forgiving nature. I've learned a great deal from them, and they've put up with a lot from me, unwittingly serving as guinea pigs in my various torturous pedagogical experiments. For whatever it's worth, my understanding of argumentation and my capacity to teach this stuff would be even more seriously impoverished, were it not for the unflagging support and encouragement of these kind souls.

Notes

1. Susan M. Hubbuch, *Writing Research Papers Across the Curriculum* (Fort Worth: Harcourt Brace, 1996).
2. Alternatives: *The Journal of the Environmental Studies Association of Canada* (Faculty of Environmental Studies: University of Waterloo, 1996).
3. Custom courseware is assembled and bound by McMaster University Bookstore for purchase by students.

6   Inquiry Courses

Editors' Preface

From the outset of planning the Programme it was agreed that giving students opportunities to develop the skills needed to address complex problems in the public domain would be an important component of the curriculum. The nature of the problems to be used would necessarily require that knowledge and methods from different disciplines would be applied to their analysis. While this kind of learning can occur in many courses, it was decided to develop a series of Inquiry courses in which the development of the relevant skills would be the central feature. Students are now required to take the first Inquiry course in the first year, and they must select at least one other from a small group of Inquiries offered in upper years. The themes of the latter group change fairly frequently and have included, in addition to those described, Culture: Censorship, Native Peoples and Northern Settlements, The Phenomenon of Work, Society in the Nuclear Age, Environment, Human Rights, Federalism, and Multiculturalism.

The terms "Inquiry" and "Problem Based Learning" are used to describe approaches to student-centred learning that have become widely discussed and applied. Although the approaches have much in common, the terms are not interchangeable. A course using problem based learning is usually a replacement for a conventional lecture course in which the students are expected to acquire specific knowledge. They seek this knowledge independently, but are guided to it by working to understand carefully constructed problems given to them by the instructor. In inquiry courses it is usual that students have to identify and formulate hypotheses

*or questions themselves within the overall context of a large theme, and
the emphasis is tilted more to the process of investigation than to the
acquisition of knowledge. Hudspith and Jenkins have discussed the two
methods' similarities and differences in greater depth.[1] We offer here
descriptions of three Inquiry courses that illustrate the variety of methods
used by different instructors.*

Introduction

Graham Knight and Jennifer Smith Maguire[2]

Although inquiry-based pedagogy has been growing in appeal for some
time, it has recently acquired particular prominence in North America as
a result of the publication and impact of the report of the Boyer
Commission on Educating Undergraduates in the Research University
(1998).[3] The report situates inquiry-based education in the context of the
research-intensive university, i.e. large universities with extensive graduate
programmes and a strong emphasis on active research programmes on
the part of faculty. The assumption of the report is that undergraduate
education gets short shrift in these institutions, where organizational
emphasis, faculty incentives, and rewards have normally been based on
research output rather than teaching.

According to the Boyer report, the problem has both objective and
subjective dimensions. On the one hand, the expansion of higher education
has diluted the relative market value of credentials at the same time that it
has enhanced the value of credentialism. The competitive logic of the
labour market has trickled down into the educational system and the real
effects of this are felt at the subjective, individual level. What is problematic
is not the student's education *per se*, but his or her educational experience.
It is not so much that students suffer in the sense that they are deficient
from the viewpoint of acquired knowledge, but that their educational
experience is lacking, spoiled by missing out on the opportunity to be
active participants in the production—as opposed to the "simple
transmission"—of knowledge. This is embodied for the Boyer
Commissioners in the figure of the bored undergraduate who feels estranged
from his/her surroundings and, by implication, lacking in motivation. The
principal source of this boredom lies in the shortcomings of conventional
practices of educational instruction that treat students as "passive receivers"
of their education rather than "active participants" in it.

The problem lies not in what is being taught and learned but in how it is being taught and learned. For the Boyer Commission, therefore, the solution lies in adopting pedagogical methods that will foster a more engaged and active subjectivity on the student's part. Inquiry-based approaches are seen as the key to the revision of pedagogy because they bridge the division between teaching and research by making use of the latter as a means to the former. The assumption is that involving students in the process of research will enhance motivation and active engagement in the learning process, and result ultimately in a more productive and responsible citizen (see p.127).[3]

Though the terms are often taken to be self-evident, the dichotomy between active and passive, student-centred and instructor-centred, and process-oriented and content-oriented pedagogy is a common way in which both the problem of undergraduate education and the distinction between conventional instructional techniques and inquiry-based approaches are characterized. Passive, instructor-centred, content-oriented teaching treats students as vessels into which knowledge and information are poured with the goal of maximizing the level of accumulation, at least for the duration of the course. Knowledge is transmitted in the form of received information, and the role of the student is to act as the vehicle of its reproduction rather than production. The student is rewarded for replicating what is already known rather than inquiring into the conditions and assumptions underlying this, or thinking creatively beyond its parameters. Education becomes a matter of training geared to conformity.

Inquiry-based approaches are seen to tip the balance to the other pole. They are active inasmuch as they involve students in the process of investigation, exploration, and discovery on the basis of a more self-directed determination of what are relevant and feasible questions to pose, how these questions imply different perspectives or frameworks of analysis, and how they can be answered. The student ceases to be the passive container, and becomes a producer of knowledge. At the same time, the role of teacher changes from one of information delivery to advising, guiding, mentoring, and challenging the student through critical feedback. The teacher no longer teaches in the conventional sense, but becomes someone who facilitates learning on the part of others .

The pedagogical argument for inquiry-based learning, such as that offered in the Boyer report, is compelling. However, education is not only a matter of the method and practice of giving or receiving instruction; education is deeply bound up with the social reproduction of ideals, practices, and ways of thinking. As such, the development and diffusion of inquiry-based learning needs to be understood in relation to the broader structural and ideological context in which particular values, attitudes, and logics are privileged over others. The growing interest in inquiry-based methods since the 1970s has to do with more than simply a recognition that students were bored with being lectured to (and at). A number of factors help explain why inquiry-based methods have become more popular and, conversely, why conventional instructional practices based on the lecture format are seen as problematic. In their endorsement of inquiry teaching, Postman and Weingarten draw a telling parallel between conventional instructional practices of knowledge transmission, with their differentiated, sequential structure determined and implemented from above, and the organizational structure of Fordist, assembly-line industrial production.[4] Just as the latter is being made increasingly redundant by newer, more flexible, decentralized systems of work organization, so assembly-line education is also being replaced by more flexible, student-centred pedagogical methods. Flexibility, the devolution of responsibility, risk, and uncertainty, and the transformation of authority holders from actors into facilitators are key aspects in the neo-liberal restructuring of workplaces generally, including universities.

In part, inquiry-based learning evolved within the late-twentieth-century context of an accelerating rate of technological change, and an intensification of market competition on both local and global scales. In such a milieu, what is needed are citizens who engage in ongoing training, employ flexible skills that can adapt to the pace of technological change, and are unlikely to be left behind. As post-industrial economies shift from producing material goods to producing information and images, an adaptable, flexible, and educated workforce becomes an increasingly important national resource. The challenge of teaching attitudes that favour ongoing training and flexibility is met not by emphasizing rote learning and the acquisition of specific and finite data, but by promoting skills that can be transferred and adapted across problems. Thus, the promise of inquiry-based learning to cultivate, as is said in the Boyer Commission Report, a more "productive and responsible citizen" is one that makes sense in an age in which productivity (of information as well as things) and responsibility (for keeping up with the rate of change) face new obstacles.

The concern of inquiry-based learning with the educational experience of students points to the growing importance of consumerism as the logic (as well as practice) in terms of which individuals see themselves—their identity—and orient their expectations and understanding of the social world. The consumer in post-industrial society is faced with an increasing variety of choices and a growing need for information about how to make those choices in a way that minimizes uncertainty and risk, and maximizes satisfaction and benefit. The situation is a paradoxical one: choice means insecurity in addition to freedom, as calculations have to be made and decisions taken whose outcomes remain to some extent contingent and unclear. The logic of consumerism—and the freedoms and risks it entails—applies more and more to post-secondary students, who are encouraged to see education as a crucial investment, yet to do so in a context where the substantive knowledge that they acquire can become quickly outdated. As the proportion of the cost of undergraduate education borne by students (or their families) has steadily increased, moreover, this instrumental outlook has become irresistible, and education, like any other service, is judged on the basis of value-for-money. Assembly-line-like pedagogy becomes less and less tenable from the viewpoint of either student satisfaction or the need for flexible, mutable skills. Consumers have the power to complain and discourage others from following in their footsteps, and universities have to pay heed to this power.

The structural and ideological pressure to make public institutions and professions more accountable can be seen as an impetus in the promotion of forms of learning that articulate the ideal of a self-directed, adaptable, enterprising student. Inquiry-based learning can thus be understood in relation to the broader neo-liberal discourses of social and economic accountability, an expanding logic of consumer choice and experience, and the intensifying need to keep pace with technological change in a knowledge economy. In addition, shifting responsibility for the process of education onto to the shoulders of students echoes calls, more generally, for individuals to assume responsibility for their actions and the outcomes these have, such as those found in post-1970s health promotion, which has emphasized the need (from the point of view of individuals and populations alike) for people to choose their lifestyles and goals appropriately. This devolution of responsibility opens up new risks as well as new opportunities, and helps to explain why, at least initially, students may be resistant to the challenges that inquiry-based teaching poses. As is often the case with a new experience, there is something comforting and reassuring about being told exactly what to think and do, about being able to hand over responsibility for oneself to the care and demands of another with authority and expertise. This is the reason why successful inquiry-based approaches should not be equated with the absence of structure but should be viewed and promoted as a methodology of thinking, questioning, and testing that enables students to develop structure for themselves. It is not structure *per se* but rather the art of structuring that inquiry-based pedagogy has to offer to the learner. The growth of new fields and perspectives as well as the changing demographics and size of the undergraduate population have created challenges for established academic disciplines. The development and adoption of inquiry-based pedagogy in traditionally male-dominated fields such as the natural sciences is probably not unrelated to growing pressures to attract women and other groups that have typically been excluded from higher education. Though the debate over the gendered nature of epistemology and pedagogy is still ongoing, it is plausible to assume that more innovative teaching methods incorporating greater self-direction and active engagement reflect a growing awareness of the need to respond positively to changing student backgrounds, interests, and aspirations. If inquiry-based education is about making students more responsible for their own learning, it is also about making teachers more responsive to the needs and expectations of an increasingly diverse body of students to enable them to take on this responsibility.

Discussions of inquiry-based education often emphasize that a central part of designing and developing a research framework is to specify what the expected results of the study are likely to be. This can be done formally by means of explicit hypotheses, or less systematically by drawing out from the literature review what the likely outcomes will be on the basis of past research. These expectations help to keep the focus of the research under control and help prevent digression from the central aims of the study. There is, however, a potential danger insofar as students may seek to confirm these expectations rather than keep an open mind. Research expectations should serve as guidelines and not become a Procrustean Bed. Rather, thinking against the grain should be encouraged. Students should be helped to understand that the purpose of doing research extends beyond simply accumulating knowledge in the form of factual details and involves the process of interpretation, critique, and revision. Knowledge, information, and facts are all, ultimately, about meaning, and meaning is relational and contextual.

Certain features in particular characterize inquiry-based learning. The ideal of the critical-minded, self-directed, and flexible student entails an emphasis on, on the one hand, inter-disciplinarity, and, on the other, collaboration. Inter-disciplinarity offers the individual the capacity to approach a problem from several perspectives, bringing multiple tools to bear on the issue at hand, and to do so in an interactive rather than simply additive fashion. Collaboration amplifies this flexibility by encouraging reciprocity—not only between disciplines, but also students—as an integral part of the research process. These two aspects, however, are grounded skills and attitudes; that is, they cannot be taught in the abstract, but must be acquired through "hands-on," "inquiry-based" learning. Learning through practice not only encourages students to be active participants in the educational process, but also promotes an attitude of ongoing training, as the research skills that can be "transported" between problems are also skills that are always augmented, reshaped, and refined through the process of research itself.

Interdisciplinarity and collaboration make inquiry-based teaching methods appealing and innovative, but also contentious. One of the characteristics of post-industrial society is that the principle of scepticism, which typifies the scientific attitude towards its object of study, has now become generalized and reflexive; it is science itself, as well as other forms of institutional and intellectual authority, that we are sceptical of and about. This scepticism is a result of increased awareness of the ways in which knowledge, when put to use to solve problems, often results in unforeseen side-effects that create new problems. Interdisciplinarity offers a way to incorporate the reflexivity of knowledge into the process of investigation and knowledge production by creating greater communication and interaction between specialized fields and disciplines that, in the final analysis, share an interest in common issues and topics that can only be pursued productively through collaborative endeavour.

The question of interdisciplinarity is the first of several aspects of inquiry-based learning that will be illustrated in the following descriptions of three inquiry courses taught in the Arts and Science Programme. Two other aspects are collaborative learning and practical or 'hands on' learning. Collaboration is implied in the emphasis on interdisciplinarity. The institutional structure of undergraduate and graduate education means that students are still typically qualified in disciplinary fields. Inter-disciplinarity does not eliminate these fields so much as create the conditions for interaction between them by bringing different areas of expertise to bear in a cooperative and reciprocally informing way. By practical or "hands on" learning, we do not mean that students necessarily get involved in the on-going research of faculty members; rather, we mean the ways in which an inquiry-based approach can enable students to undertake their own empirical research that draws from and is informed by existing work in the field, but is determined conceptually, methodologically, and analytically by the students themselves. Practical learning aims to introduce students not only to a set of procedures for inquiry, but also to an understanding of the rationale and assumptions on which those procedures are based, and the ways they can be opened up to creative revision. Further consideration of Interdisciplinarity, Collaborative Learning and Practical Learning will be found in the description of the Media Inquiry Course (p.109).

Third World Development : a First-year Inquiry Course

Barbara Ferrier and Herb Jenkins

Since it was first offered in 1981, this Inquiry has involved problems in the Developing World. In the first year it attempted to focus on problems of food supply and population growth, but it was immediately apparent that even at an introductory research level, students were faced with the reality that other social, economic and political problems had to be recognized, and the scope of this inquiry was subsequently broadened to include all aspects of development. In each subsequent year the desirability of changing the theme is considered, but the course-planning group, which includes students and considers student feedback, has suggested that the theme is one in which all students can find an interest, and it has been retained. Some students have already explored this area by the time they enter the Programme in specific high school courses on the subject, high school activities such as Model UN groups and fund raising campaigns to help in emergency situations, from having family members in the Developing World, from a wide range of volunteer activities and from general awareness. Even those who have spent little or no time thinking about the issues find that the theme is sufficiently urgent to engage their interest. Some changes have taken place in the structure of the course but they have been small. What is described here is its recent structure.

The course objective and the expectations of students are listed in Box 6.1. It can be seen that while skill development is emphasized, some knowledge acquisition is also expected. Although students are expected to acquire some common knowledge about issues of development, students differ in the particular issues that they explore in depth. They individually pose and address one question/hypothesis and submit a research paper on their findings each term. This is the major activity of the course and most of the other planned activities are arranged to support it. These include a small number of lectures by the course instructors, guest lectures, movies, simulation games, group preparation of an application for a development grant, and group and class presentations and discussions.

The course demands a lot of instructor time and it has been allotted three faculty members, each of whom attends all classes but is primarily responsible for the work of a third of the class. They function as guides and consultants to their students, for whom research of the level expected is usually a new undertaking.

The approach taken has been to expect the students to get into an individual inquiry on a question of their own choosing almost immediately. This has four stages each approximately two weeks in length. They must formulate a research hypothesis/question, prepare an outline of their

---

Box 6.1 Course Objective and Expectations of Students

Objective: to provide students with the knowledge and skills necessary to investigate a complex public issue.

Expectations of Students:
Students will be expected to develop and to demonstrate that they have developed:

- the background knowledge required for a general understanding of the major issues of development in Africa, Asia and Latin America
- detailed knowledge of selected issues of development, as determined by their choice of research projects
- skills in selecting appropriate aspects of the issue for individual inquiry and in formulating hypotheses or questions that permit effective investigation
- skills in identifying and collecting information to address the hypotheses or questions posed
- skills in assessing the value of the information collected
- the ability to present the results and conclusions of their inquiries clearly, both orally and in writing
- the ability to participate in discussions and group work
- the ability to manage time effectively
- the ability to evaluate their own performance honestly and effectively.

Students are guided by instructors about the level of these expectations.

research strategy, submit a summary of the arguments they will use and a list of their major sources, and finally submit a research paper. Each stage requires a written submission on which they get prompt written feedback. They find the demands daunting, even cruel, and some are angry. But they are assured that if they take the first steps there will be ready help and feedback available. Hudspith and Jenkins, in a detailed description of the method, have defined inquiry in the learning setting as "a self-directed, question-driven search for understanding," and they identify an essential feature as "the explicit formulation of a set of questions that provides a framework for research".[1] On this basis and our own experience, we have maintained the requirement that students find their own question (i.e. they do not select from a list given to them, a process that too often becomes a choice of the least of the evils). Once they have found their question students are much more likely to maintain their interest and engagement in the challenging undertaking of many weeks' duration.

How are they encouraged to start? The class is divided into three groups,—Africa, Asia and Latin America—and they are asked to confine their first question choice to their geographic area. This facilitates subsequent discussions both within and between groups as they compare research findings at the end of the term. If they have no particular interest to guide their choice, they are advised to think about the information provided in the introductory lectures and activities, or to scan current newspapers and news magazines to find an issue that catches their interest, and to follow this up promptly in the University Library. Part of the course's introduction includes orientation to this Library. We have tried various ways of doing this and have found that the most successful has been to have focused tours led by second year Arts and Science student volunteers who have successfully completed the course. The guides have vivid memories of what had helped them to find their feet. The tours include an introduction to the catalogues, the available on-line information search systems, abstracting services, key-word indices and some general search strategies. The course instructors also offer advice on the task of maintaining a record of what they have read in a way that allows them ready future access to specific publications, on the expected method of citing sources in their papers and creating a reference list, on the issue of integrity in acknowledging sources, and on the reliability of different sources.

An exercise that has proved useful is writing a précis of a paper which we select. Its purpose is to give experience in reading scholarly articles and identifying important points—a skill that they will need for their research projects. For most, this is a new task which they find more difficult than expected. Although the first précis they submit is often poorly done, they are given feedback and assigned a second, which almost always shows a marked improvement.

Several difficulties become apparent when the first hypotheses/ questions are submitted; the questions are often too ambitious or otherwise unmanageable, or they are worded in such a way that they give no obvious direction to the potential inquiry. Further, the emphasis high schools put on the importance of the thesis for an essay can make it difficult for a student to understand that a thesis in the matter of an inquiry is inappropriate. Rather, they have to think in terms of hypotheses or questions. They are fearful of outcomes in which they might have to say that their hypothesis was invalid, or that it was not proven, or their questions incompletely answered, and they see these as indicators of unsuccessful research. The course handout tells them the subject chosen for the Inquiry course is "very large and very complex and obviously important," and that "there are no simple answers to the problems presented.... and it is not expected that students look for solutions." The instructors find that they have to do a lot of reassurance on this point.

Once the students have worked to get a researchable question or testable hypothesis, the rest of the project goes more smoothly, even though it turns out to demand more time than they anticipated. The usual student tendency to procrastinate makes the preparation of the 3500- or 5000-word research paper (length of first and second term papers) stressful, but no extension of the due date is allowed. (Developing the skill of time-management is one of the course objectives!) The end products are often remarkably mature.

It is important to keep students thinking about the large set of development issues while they are immersed in the work for their own research on just one. Various class activities are planned to achieve this. These have included guest lectures, debates, discussions, movies, and simulation exercises. After the research papers have been submitted students realize that they have individually gathered a lot of information and understanding that would be worth sharing. Various ways have been tried to achieve this. There have been group reports to the class that have ranged from straightforward presentations from each student to mock TV news interviews and skits. While some of these have worked well, have been fun, and have given them experience in managing the task of group reporting, none has been notably successful in conveying new knowledge and understanding.

The exercise of preparing a research paper is repeated in the second term, with somewhat larger expectations. The student choice of a research question is no longer restricted to one geographic region; they may continue the question they addressed in the first term; they may choose to do a comparative study using their first term results; or they may start a new question. The same stages of preparation are followed and parallel activities continue, with guest lectures from people actively engaged in research on related issues. These lectures not only supply the students with information and insights relevant to their own research, but help them maintain a broader concern for development issues or get an introduction to newly surfacing ones.

Many students' choices of inquiry topics are predictable. For some years it seemed inevitable that some aspect of the social impact of China's one-child family policy would be chosen, and more recently the impact of AIDS in Sub-Saharan Africa has received a lot of attention. Some have been concerned with various aspects of world unrest and have examined such issues as the reasons for the militancy of the Muslim population in the Philippines and the use of children in combat roles in Sierra Leone. Many students have interest in environmental protection, and this is reflected in examinations such as the impact of pollution on the biodiversity of the Galapagos Islands. Some have been ambitious, such as an attempt to develop an alternative method of assessing the impact of technology transfer in Ghana. Overall, most of the inquiries carried out reflect their interest in health, education, and social well-being.

The evaluation of the research papers is initially done by the instructor responsible for the group. Evaluation is based on criteria known to the student: the effectiveness of the hypothesis/question in giving the research direction, the overall organization, the use of sources (depth and scope of research), interpretation of evidence and argument, summary and conclusions related to the question, quality of writing. To assure consistency of standards of grading, among the three instructors, they meet once they have completed grading, and sample papers and problem papers are read by the others and a consensus grade is given. This helps to calibrate the grading standard across instructors. The grades for the two research papers make up 70% of the students' course grades. The remaining 30% is for a series of individual exercises (e.g. précis, evaluation of published papers) and group exercises (preparation of a grant application) and for participation in class activities, as judged by instructors and students.

Students' evaluation of the course changes dramatically as the year proceeds. Early in the first term many are shocked by the expectations of them. Most find reassurance from their instructors and big siblings (p.195), and by the end of the year the course is very favourably evaluated. Their appreciation of it seems to increase over subsequent years in university and beyond. At the end of the course the students are remarkably adept at library research and confident in their ability to address questions in diverse areas by appropriate use of experts and other resources. In the view of many instructors they have already exceeded new graduate students in these abilities.

Many students are saddened by their increased awareness of the complexity and intransigence of the problems of the Developing World. But they are only briefly discouraged; many are on their way to becoming practical idealists (p.263). Many have had prior interest in working to reduce disparities among people, and this interest is usually reinforced by the course. Through their summer activities and in their subsequent careers, many have shown that they are willing to commit themselves to action in pursuit of this interest.

Media: an Upper Level Inquiry Course

Graham Knight and Jennifer Smith Maguire

The media are a particularly appropriate focus for inquiry-based learning. The very ephemerality of the content of news and entertainment media provides the rationale for a pedagogy that emphasizes the process of research over the findings, and the skills of questioning rather than the answers. At the same time, the sheer ubiquity of media images in everyday life highlights the need to interrogate the production of the seemingly benign taken-for-granted truths and commonplace assumptions that both enable and limit the ways we see the world. The Media Inquiry course combined both of these goals of inquiry-based learning: to foster research skills that transcend the specificity of a particular research problem, and to cultivate a critical attitude towards the often-unquestioned organizations and representations that shape our daily lives. It is through learning how to inquire and learning to be inquisitive that students take on the role of being self-directed, process-oriented, active participants in their own education.

This chapter provides an overview of Media Inquiry as it was taught over the 1990s. In general, the course introduced students to theoretical approaches to studying the media, as well as empirical analyses of the political economy of the media, the production of news, and popular culture and entertainment media. The classes themselves combined student-led seminar discussions with informal lectures by the instructor. The elements of the course are discussed in relation to their contribution to the different aspects of inquiry-based learning: interdisciplinarity, collaboration, and learning through practice.

Interdisciplinarity

Media studies is a fast-growing area of teaching and research in higher education, in part because it overlaps with existing disciplinary fields such as communication studies, political science, sociology, linguistics, and literary studies. All of these fields deal with media as means of representation and signification, registers of expression, and institutions that structure social interaction and exchange. The growing popularity of media studies also reflects the increasingly prominent role media such as the telephone, television and the Internet play in everyday life, where, again, their presence overlaps different spheres of activity from home life to education to work to consumerism to pleasure. We rely on the media for information about the world outside the sphere of our direct social experience, just as we rely on them for entertainment, relaxation, and distraction from that world. The media can be said to be interdisciplinary in a practical as well as scholarly sense: they cut across the differentiated zones of social reality as well as academic areas and fields of knowledge.

The pervasiveness of the media gives them a presence and immediacy which is both an advantage and drawback from a pedagogical viewpoint. Studying the media can be a way for students to interrelate and integrate other courses in the curriculum. The Arts and Science curriculum is clearly a *multi*disciplinary one, but this does not automatically mean that it is an *inter*disciplinary one. Interdisciplinarity has to be constructed by bringing together ideas and research from different fields and actively relating them in a context of critical inquiry, where the questioning never stops.

Interrelating and integrating ideas from distinct disciplinary fields can happen in different ways. It can happen firstly by allowing students to discover the common ground shared by ideas that may derive from separate fields of knowledge. One of the books that formed part of the core of required readings, Joshua Meyrowitz's *No Sense of Place* (1985),[5] does this explicitly by relating the theories of sociologist Erving Goffman, on the dynamics of face-to-face social interaction and the way in which we attempt to construct and convey a favourable impression of ourselves to others, to Marshall McLuhan's theories about the ways that different media extend and accentuate different aspects of our sensory apparatus—sight, hearing, taste, touch, smell—and thereby shape our experiences, perceptions, and knowledge. This synthesis allows us to see the sociologist in McLuhan and the media scholar in Goffman without reducing the views of either one of them to the other.

Interdisciplinarity can also happen by way of an antidote, that is, by providing alternative ways of looking at a shared aspect of reality. An important aspect of Media Inquiry was the impact of technology and economics on systems of communication and society generally. Here the course overlapped with other courses students were taking, often at the same time, such as Technology and Society. Much of the research on the social dimensions of technology and the nature of economic forces is based on a positivistic methodology, and arrives at a rather deterministic conception of how technology and economics make their impact. To offset the deterministic emphasis of this dominant paradigm, the course also examined approaches to media use and effects that stressed the importance of individual and group agency, choice, and values. This alternative approach, which has been developed primarily in the study of media messages and the ways audiences receive and interpret them, emphasizes the ways that the impact of large-scale technological and economic forces is socially negotiated, and their meanings socially constructed and contested.

The growing pervasiveness and immediacy of the media may foster interdisciplinarity, but it can also be a drawback. On the one hand, the media are now so commonplace that we simply take them for granted. The messages and meanings they disseminate seem normal and natural, and this can militate against the development of a critical, questioning attitude towards them. It seems perfectly natural, for example, that when public sector workers go on strike the news media focus on the inconvenience and disruption caused by their actions, just as it seems natural that when violence occurs the news media focus on the emotions, feelings, and suffering of its victims. But what the media choose to focus on and how they choose to focus on it are the result of social, political, economic, and cultural factors. The task of inquiry-based education is to demonstrate this by enabling students to discover and understand for themselves the biased, selective nature of any representation of reality. Many of the seminar readings and at least one of the three main assignments in the course were oriented towards deconstructing the naturalness of representation, and demonstrating how meaning and pleasure are constructed through the juxtaposition of language and images in ways that always accentuate some aspects of reality while playing down or occluding others. The way the news media tend to focus on the emotions of striking workers, for example, means that they tend to ignore the motives of management; focussing on the inconvenience and disruption caused by strikes means overlooking the way that they can also create solidarity between workers and those sympathetic to their cause among the general public.

On the other hand, the presence of the media in people's lives means that students enter the course with their own unquestioned prejudices and convictions about the media. Perhaps the most common is the widely held view that the media are some kind of shadowy force that manipulates people behind their backs, and results in harmful social effects. To subject this kind of prejudice to critical inquiry means not only looking at existing empirical research that might suggest otherwise, but also enabling students to recognise that the relationship between media messages and their effects in the outside world is layered in complex ways. The relationship between, for example, violent media images and violent behaviour involves several disciplinary approaches: sociology is relevant to examine the structure and incidence of real world violence and understand how images are socially valued (how some, but not all, violence is socially condemned or sanctioned); political science is necessary to understand how social concern with violence may be the result of political ideology (how conservative political parties routinely emphasize violent crime as an issue in their election campaigns); linguistics is relevant to understand how messages are structured discursively to predispose the audience in the direction of certain interpretations over others (how representations of violence are organized to promote or discourage imitation); and psychology plays a part in understanding how cognition is related to emotions and behavioural responses (how knowledge of violence may translate into violent behaviour, or into fear of violence from others).

The interdisciplinary focus of the course was substantive as well as perspectival. The structure of the course followed a similar outline over the period it was taught, opening with a section on theoretical approaches to the study of media, followed by a section on the politics and economics of the media, a section on the news media, and concluding with a section dealing with media, popular culture, and entertainment. Within each section the specific topics examined in weekly seminars changed to some degree over the period the course was taught, and the readings for each topic were updated regularly to reflect new ideas and research in the field. The overarching theme that connected these sections and topics was the interactive nature of the media. What was stressed throughout the course was that not only do the media act upon and influence society, but society also acts upon and influences the media. The question posed by the course was not only how do the media—and the plural nature of that term was emphasised throughout—affect society, but how does society affect the media: why do we have the media we have and what does this tell us about society more generally? While each section drew on interdisciplinary sources, the complexion of these shifted as the course progressed. Social science disciplines figured more heavily in the sections on the politics and economics of the media as well as the news media, while the final section on entertainment media drew more from the fields of cultural studies and its roots in literary analysis, the study of theatre, and the analysis of visual culture in the fine arts.

Drawing on interdisciplinary sources can create difficulties in the sense that students may find the different assumptions, theories, and methodologies they encounter confusing and lacking in consistency. To offset this, it is important firstly to stress that these differences are not in competition with one another for intellectual ascendancy. It is not a question of discovering which discipline has the truth and which other ones don't. While testing different hypotheses or ideas is a central part of research, the results of any study are conditional on the way that the variables are measured, the data gathered, and the findings interpreted. Knowledge-building is an incremental process in which discovery often works by process of elimination. At the same time, however, interdisciplinarity is not a euphemism for unconditional relativism. Inquiry-based teaching is oriented first and foremost to demonstrating how to formulate problems and raise meaningful and insightful questions about these problems. To do this well means taking account at every step of the inquiry process of the issue of adequacy—logical adequacy, conceptual adequacy, analytical adequacy, and methodological adequacy. Adequacy is, in the final analysis, a practical matter. Interdisciplinarity is a resource to be used—a kind of toolbox in which different instruments are taken up because they are deemed best suited for the task at hand, i.e. the particular facet of the overall problem being studied—and not as an ideological imperative. Trying out different tools also becomes a process of testing their adequacy for the problem at hand.

The potential "Babel" effect of interdisciplinarity was also addressed by blending inquiry-based methods of teaching with more conventional techniques, the principal one of which was the use of a reading list and schedule of discussion topics assigned by the instructor for each week's seminar. The initial, theoretical section of the course most closely approximated the conventional model of instruction, with the instructor managing and moderating the seminar discussion of the assigned readings. Once this initial section was complete (after about five weeks), students took responsibility for presenting the assigned reading for the topic. However, as everyone in the class was expected to have read the assigned material—usually a journal article or book chapter—the presenters were asked to critique and apply the reading rather than summarize it. Presenters were also asked to supplement the reading with their own illustrative material pertinent to the topic—a newspaper or magazine article, a video clip, or still photographs, for example. They were asked to finish the presentation—about twenty minutes—by posing two or three questions to the rest of the class as the basis on which to generate discussion. The presenter then assumed the role of moderator and commentator, with occasional input from the instructor when the opportunity for provocation arose or the general discussion flagged.

Classes were normally organized on the basis of a three-hour time slot, and the student-led seminar took up approximately the first hour and three-quarters. After a ten-minute break, the class resumed in the form of an informal lecture in which the instructor provided some background context for the following week's topic and reading. It was here particularly that linkages and contrasts could be made between different disciplinary approaches, assumptions, and perspectives. Students were encouraged to ask questions and offer comments, particularly in the form of comparisons with or connections to material and ideas already discussed in previous seminars. Stressing connections between different topics and readings over the span of the course was a way of encouraging students to produce interdisciplinarity for themselves.

Collaboration

If the essence of inquiry-based education is the integration of teaching and research, then one dimension of research that becomes a crucial part of the method is teamwork. For all that it is still associated with the figure of the lone, heroic scientist battling against the forces of superstition and reaction, scholarly research has become increasingly a collaborative enterprise. The model here is natural science, where the research team is the organizational norm. The obvious advantage of teamwork is that it can bring together different areas of expertise and experience in a mutually beneficial and productive way.

One of the implications of inquiry-based approaches to education is that rather than confronting one another in a struggle over competing interests, student and teacher become more akin to collaborators. Clearly, this is not a collaboration of equals: teachers possess not only formal authority but also superior resources in terms of knowledge, experience, and expertise. The teacher's role, nonetheless, can become something of a *primus inter pares*. This role is nowhere more important than in generating a collaborative, supportive, and motivating atmosphere in the weekly seminar—the one time and place where everyone comes together to ask questions, share views and opinions, and listen to others.

In a more practical sense, the principal ways in which collaboration was incorporated into the Media Inquiry course were the grading system and the research assignments. The overall grade had four components. Ten percent of the student's final mark was based on his/her seminar presentation and general participation in seminar discussions. Although in earlier years this grade had been assigned by the instructor, it later became the responsibility of the class itself. We normally think of evaluation as a privilege that instructors enjoy, and a major part of the power they exercise. Allowing students to grade themselves and their peers enables them to experience the responsibility involved in evaluating and the decision-making it entails. Peer review is, after all, a central tenet of evaluation for all stages of the research process, from funding grant applications to publication. The class was given the option of grading each person individually, or the class as a whole collectively.

The remainder of the grade was divided up evenly between three major assignments. The first of these dealt with the initial theoretical section of the course. Students were required to write a critical analysis of three of the five readings that were covered in the section, with one of these readings, chosen by the instructor, required for everyone. The other two readings were at the discretion of students to choose for themselves on the basis of their own preferences and interests. This assignment was undertaken on a conventional, individual basis. For the two remaining assignments, both of which entailed empirical research, students were given the option of working collaboratively in teams of two or three. Collaboration was strongly encouraged by the instructor but was not made mandatory. Some students prefer to work on a solo basis. Over the years the course was taught, however, the vast majority of students chose to do their projects collaboratively. The suggested length of the two assignments was adjusted according to whether the work was done individually or collectively, and according to the size of the team.

For those working in teams, the finished project was given a single grade which all the members of the team received. Some instructors require team members to divide the grade up according to individual merit and contributions, giving some a higher mark than others. This method of grading teamwork was rejected on the grounds that it undermines the purpose of collaboration, which is to foster cooperation and coordination. Teamwork does not mean that everyone does the same thing. One important benefit of collaboration, the reason why it can be more productive, is that it enables a division of labour between team members. Students were given full choice in deciding with whom to form teams (and the composition of teams did vary to some extent between the first and second assignments), and how to work out a division of labour and responsibility for the various tasks. These tasks included deciding on a research topic; conducting a background review and assessment of existing scholarly research on the topic (or, if none was readily available, on a related topic); developing a set of research questions or hypotheses and a theoretical or analytical framework in which to situate them; identifying feasible data sources; gathering, processing and analysing the data; and interpreting them in light of the guiding research questions and framework.

Later in the years that the course was taught, the second half of the class was given over to informal reports on the research projects that comprised the second and third assignments. Each week two groups and/ or individuals would give a progress report on their respective project, focussing particularly on practical problems they were encountering such as establishing a literature review, formulating practicable research questions, tracking down desired data sources, and analysing the data in light of the theoretical framework they were using. The point of stressing these problems was to elicit advice and suggestions from not only the instructor, but also the other students in the class who were likely encountering the same or related problems. In this way, the class as a whole became self-collaborating; students were able to use one another as resources regardless of whether they were part of the same research team. Students were discouraged from seeing the research process as a competitive one (though this is an unavoidable aspect of professional scholarship) and the emphasis was put on sharing information, reactions, misgivings, and advice. To motivate students to view the process in a co-operative way, the instructor began to allow any project receiving less than an "A-" to be re-written and re-graded (to a maximum of "A-").

Learning through practice

The most straightforward way to integrate teaching and research is, of course, to have students undertake their own original research projects and learn through practical, hands-on experience of how knowledge— and its limitations—are produced. This is much easier to undertake with smaller classes, and Media Inquiry averaged fourteen to twenty students per year—an ideal number.

The second and third written assignments for the course were both research based, and structured in a way that encouraged students to make use of different methods for gathering and analysing empirical data. In the early years, the second assignment involved composing an organizational profile of a major media company to be chosen at the students' discretion. A summary history of the company had to be included in all profiles, but each research team could then focus on two or three other aspects of the company, such as its market position and prospects, product development, organizational structure and management strategy, corporate image and identity, or political and cultural impact and influence (including controversy about the company or conflicts in which it was embroiled). Students were directed to use different data sources, such as company reports and other internal documents that were available (at this time the Internet was in its nascent stage): news coverage, government data, academic studies, and alternative information sources such as activist or advocacy groups that were—usually—in some kind of critical or adversarial relationship with the company. Using multiple data sources is a good way to illustrate the principle of triangulation that is the measure of methodological adequacy: to what extent do different sources converge or diverge in the story they tell?

In later years this second assignment was revised and students were asked to undertake research on news coverage of a particular topic, issue, or event, such as homelessness, violence, crime, election campaigning, social or political protest, or international conflict. The principal reason for making this revision was to engage students more fully in the process of data analysis. The corporate profile project introduced students to the skill of gathering and triangulating data from different sources, but the data *per se* were employed illustratively rather than analytically; they were used to support an argument or thesis rather than being unpacked, as it were, to discover their underlying structure and composition. The news analysis project involved a different methodology, closer in form to the third assignment, an analysis of a television show. This methodology drew not only from the social science traditions of content analysis but also, and perhaps more heavily, from research techniques in linguistics and the varieties of discourse and textual analysis found in the humanities. At the same time, the project was sufficiently different from the television analysis inasmuch as the focus on news coverage meant that students were analysing representations of real world events and issues rather than purely fictional constructs such as soap operas or sitcoms. Analysing news coverage meant dealing with the realm of social, political, and economic reality, and the theoretical and analytical backdrop for this project continued to be social science fields such as political science and sociology.

Some of the seminar readings for the third and fourth sections of the course dealing with the news media and entertainment television were explicitly chosen because they served as paradigms of analysis for fictional and non-fictional representation, and students were encouraged to use at least one reading from each section as part of the background literature for the two research projects. Using the readings in this way also helped to integrate the seminars and the research projects more closely. The instructor also acted as a resource person by providing suggestions for relevant journals and books in which existing research and analysis might be found. In the case of the news analysis project students were advised to pick a topic that was feasible in that it was neither too specific nor too general. It is essential to pick a topic on which there is sufficient news coverage and which fits into one of the established genres of news, such as crime, social problems or politics, about which there is a sufficient body of existing research literature to serve as a background resource for developing theoretically informed research questions and analytical techniques.

Using existing research as a point of comparison as well as inspiration for research questions and analytical techniques points to the way that comparative analysis plays a central role in scientific research, particularly when the experimental method (and the kind of control it affords over the research process) is inapplicable. In the news analysis project students were asked to build a comparative dimension into their research, not only via a literature review but also empirically, through the design for data gathering. Two ways of organizing this were suggested: comparing how different media outlets, such as two newspapers, covered the same event or issue, or comparing how the same outlet covered different instances of the same topic at different points in time. The final determination of which type of comparison was left up to the students, but their decision had to have a logic or rationale to it, and this had to be shaped by their review of the literature. Comparisons could be made between similarities or differences. When comparing similarities, students were encouraged to focus on the search for differences in their findings, and when comparing differences to look for similarities. This sharpens the research framework and strengthens the overall analysis by making the findings and interpretation more challenging and interesting.

In the case of the television project, students were advised to focus only on one show and to incorporate the comparative dimension via the literature review and by examining at least two episodes from different seasons. The principal reason for limiting the comparative focus was a practical one. Analysing television is more time-consuming inasmuch as a transcript (verbatim or annotated) has to be made of both the audio and visual dimensions as the working basis for the actual analysis. In view of this, it seemed unreasonable to ask students to undertake a comparative analysis on the same scale as the news project, where they normally worked with print sources. To offset this limitation in the data base, the analysis had to include an examination of the interaction between the audio and the visual images to demonstrate how the overall meaning or effect is produced. Although the data base was narrower, the scope of the analysis was larger and richer in this respect.

One of the main points stressed in the course was that, regardless of expectations, the research findings are the central feature of the whole endeavour; these are always the focal point, the object to be pondered, discussed, and explained. To impress this point as much as possible, students were urged to look actively for paradoxes and anomalies in their findings, and to take these not as an irritant or obstacle but as a challenge to creative, original thinking. One of the most important qualities a researcher can have is the desire and ability to think against the grain of received wisdom.

For both of the research assignments students were encouraged to keep the broader context of their projects in view throughout the whole process. Studying the structure and behaviour of media corporations, the ways the news media represent reality, and the ways that television entertainment produces meaning and evokes emotions only makes sense in light of a broader interest in and concern with the way power works in society. Whether it is through organizational structure, the definition of social reality, or the inducement of pleasure, power is always implicated in the process of communication. It is implicated, that is, in the structuring and diffusion of what will be seen and heard and in how it will be seen and heard, and will reflect the decisions and actions of some rather than others.

For the transformation of students from passive recipients of other people's knowledge into active producers in their own right to succeed, they need to be able to communicate their findings and interpretations clearly and cogently to experts and lay people alike. In this view, communication is all about clarity and effectiveness of voice. But communication is bilateral; it requires an audience as well as a speaker, and the roles should be interchangeable. To be an audience is also to possess a communicative skill, that of listening in an active, reflective, and critical way. The seminar—as a forum in which students can not only voice their views but also listen to others—was one way in which Media Inquiry attempted to strike this communicative balance. The other was the assigned reading for seminar discussion, which was deliberately chosen to balance scholarly research that addressed the objective, structural aspects of the media, with research that focussed on the subjective, experiential dimension of how people use and interpret the media, and are affected by them. Listening to the subjects of research, as well as other researchers, is an integral part of any inquiry.

Conclusion

Viewed from the perspective of pedagogical theory, Media Inquiry was taught as a hybrid course. Inquiry-based techniques were used in conjunction with more conventional practices such as informal lecturing and seminar topics and readings assigned by the instructor. Over the period that the course was taught, the ratio between the inquiry-based and more conventional instructional elements shifted toward the former, but only to a modest extent. While there are doubtless many reasons for this, what is more important is what this hybrid character signifies. If the objective of inquiry-based education is to foster intellectual independence, skill, and creativity on the part of students and teachers alike, then the methods used to achieve this must themselves be subject to the same kind of critical, reflexive scrutiny one applies to the content of knowledge. Creativity is re-combinative, the result of re-connecting what is already known or already practised in novel and productive ways. Pedagogical practices should be assessed not on the basis of whether they conform or not to a particular definition or classification, but on the basis of what they achieve and the kind of experience they impart. Teaching inquiry—imparting inquisitiveness—is a hybrid process.

Discovery—the Context of Scientific Research: an Upper Level Inquiry Course

P.K. Rangachari

Reflections of NOW and THEN

NOW: September 6ᵗʰ 2001, I am meeting my "new"class. They are chattering amongst themselves. I distribute my outline for the course. The course is listed in the University Calendar as an Inquiry course, and labelled "Discovery: The Context of Scientific Research." The Calendar description is brief and not very informative. There is a rustling of paper as they read through the more detailed outline. We then engage in a brief period of discussion. The tenets of the course, the marking scheme, their expectations of the course and mine. I explain to them what is meant by problem-based learning (which, as will be evident, shares many features of inquiry-based learning) and how the standard small group format has been altered to suit a larger class size. Then I suggest that it is time to stop discussion and simply plunge in to see how it would go. They agree. I distribute the first "problem," "case," scenario or what you will and another class, another year begins anew.

THEN: My involvement with the programme began in the spring of 1989. At that time, my major teaching involvement was with the medical undergraduate programme. Although I had been profoundly sceptical of its small group variant of problem-based learning (PBL), I had become a convert when I saw it in practice in small groups of five or six highly motivated students. So when I was asked to organize an Inquiry course, I saw it as a PBL course that could deal with our culture's concepts of health and illness and their economic and political consequences. The course was called "The Curing Society," a name suggested by an anthropologist. Since I anticipated that I would get about five or six students interested in taking my course, such a PBL approach seemed quite reasonable.

Before the term began, I heard from Dr. Jenkins that eighteen students had registered. This posed a problem since I had not signed on anyone else to teach the course, and, given my other teaching commitments, it was difficult to deal with three groups in the standard small group format. However, I was quite reluctant to abandon the PBL approach, so I decided to modify it to suit my needs.

The term "problem-based" is ambiguous and has been variously interpreted by different teachers and programmes. Shorn of all rhetoric, it is a format that encourages active participation by the students by plunging them into a situation that requires them to define their own learning needs within broad goals set by their teachers. The students are presented with problem situations that serve as springboards for learning. This is in sharp contrast to subject-based approaches that teach a body of knowledge prior to the application of that knowledge to specific problems, and differs from inquiry-based learning by providing previously formulated problems for exploration.

Problem-based learning seeks to meld process and content.[6] Thus what is learned is inextricably linked to how it is learned. With regard to content, the "what" of any course has two elements, instructional and expressive. Instructional elements refer to the items of information that the student is expected to obtain by the end of a course. This is usually what teachers and particularly administrators mean by course content. Expressive elements are not easily defined. In a sense, they offer the student an invitation to explore issues of particular relevance to them. As such, these cannot be rigorously prescribed.

Although not strictly necessary, PBL has come to be practised largely in the small group format, with five to eight students meeting in groups with a tutor. They use a variety of stimuli (paper problems, real cases, videotapes, even simulated patients) to generate issues that are then refined into learning tasks. Depending on the course objectives, their own objectives and their prior knowledge, the students may all undertake the exploration of the same area of knowledge or may take on different areas. The learning tasks provide the scaffolding to enable them to seek out information individually which they validate and/or share with their peers at a subsequent session. This self-directed learning requires continuous evaluation and monitoring of progress in the tutorials. Thus, active participation of the students in the process of self- and peer-evaluation is a crucial component. The process that was designed for small groups had to be modified to suit the needs of a larger class.

Now: The students have read the first part of the problem (see Box 6.2). A number of questions arise. What is beri-beri? What have chickens got to do with it? What is polyneuritis? They attempt to "solve" the problem. The larger context is very difficult to grasp. There is speculation as to the transferability of the diseases. Issues of genetics are raised. Clearly they are seeing the problem with the hindsight of a century. It is very difficult to imagine what the state of knowledge was towards the

---

Box 6.2

Problem 1   Chickens—Highly Prized

Part 1:

July 10th, 1886, a mysterious illness breaks out in the chicken house attached to a small laboratory in Batavia in the Dutch East Indies. The lab has been set up to investigate the causes of beri-beri, an illness that is causing concern to the Dutch government. They are battling guerillas in the Malaysian archipelago and their troops have been ravaged by the disease. A team from Utrecht attempting to define the causative organism had not made much progress. The neurologist on the team has established that the disease is some form of polyneuritis. The senior investigators have returned to Europe, leaving Christiann Eijkman, a military medical doctor in charge of a small unit.

Eijkman is intrigued. The disease amongst the chickens appears similar to the human condition. The birds become unsteady, have difficulty in perching and frequently fall over while walking. The wing muscles become weak and the paralysis continues. Attempts to transmit the disease from an affected bird to another fail. Mysteriously the disease disappears by the end of November. The affected chickens recover.

Part 2:

The laboratory has been housed provisionally at the military hospital, although it had been administered by the civilian authorities. Eijkman discovers that for a period, the laboratory keeper, for reasons of economy, had been feeding the chickens with cooked rice from the hospital kitchen. But a new cook refuses to allow civilian chickens to eat military rations and so the normal chicken diet had resumed by the end of November. The suspicion that something in the food was responsible leads Eijkman to undertake feeding experiments. Chickens fed cooked rice develop the disease, whereas controls fed unpolished rice do not. The condition seems easily treatable by altering the diet.

Part 3:

In 1929, Eijkman is awarded a share of the Nobel Prize in Physiology and Medicine. He is unable to attend the ceremony due to illness, but his co-recipient, Sir Frederick Gowland Hopkins, does. They are recognised for their contributions to the role of accessory food factors (now known as vitamins). Casimir Funk, who has coined the term and has isolated the active principle that cured beri-beri, does not get a share of the Prize.

---

end of the nineteenth century. Once I feel that the discussions are beginning to falter, I distribute part 2. This raises another set of issues. The role of dietary factors becomes more evident. When part 3 is given, the discussions range around Nobel Prizes and the reward systems in science. Based on the issues raised, five learning tasks are defined. Then begins a period of discussion as to who wants to select which task. The rules are simple; each student can opt for one task. Some tasks get more takers than others.

There is a bit of shopping around, but finally a roughly equivalent number are found for each task. I leave the room, the students are discussing meeting times. They need to get organized, since they are expected to present the information they have gathered in two weeks' time. I know they will.

Flow Chart 6.1

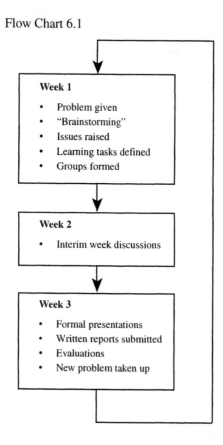

THEN: Given the larger size of the initial class, I had to modify the process (See Flow Chart 6.1). All students participated in the initial brainstorming phase where all ideas, however bizarre, were entertained. Once the students were either satisfied or exhausted, the issues that had been raised were refined into learning tasks. These tasks then served as a focus for the formation of study groups consisting of three to five students. Each student had to join one group. They then established a loose contract with the rest of the class to obtain the required information and communicate it effectively two weeks later. The interim week was used to obtain the information.

For the Curing Society, the instructional elements were loosely defined. Students were told that the course would permit them to explore the dimensions of health and sickness in our society. The first group met in September, 1989. I presented them with the scenario that dealt with the issues of a smoke-free hospital. Other problems that were written for that first class dealt with topics such as drug development, the role of midwives, toxic dump sites. Their performance during the discussions was evaluated by their peers, and the written reports submitted were graded by me. Each student got the mark allotted for the group. To permit students to explore issues of particular interest to them, they were asked to write an individual paper and give an oral presentation. Each student was required to identify an individual area for exploration, summarize their findings and conclusions in a paper, and present a summary of it to the class in an allotted time. The presentations worked extremely well, and the issues investigated ranged widely from health education in the school curriculum to the role of cosmetic surgery and the impact of proposed free trade agreements on health care (Canada's Prime Minister in this era, Brian Mulroney, led the move to ratify the North American Free Trade Agreement).

The course ran in the same fashion for seven years. I made a number of minor changes that were suggested by the participants. In subsequent years, I began with a session where I tried to extract from each class the major themes that they felt should be explored. Following again an intense discussion, a "wish" list was created that helped me write problems. Although many themes remained common throughout the years, the emphasis varied each year and I never had to use a given problem more than once. Given the wide scope of the course, there was never a dearth of issues or problems to be discussed. I used a variety of sources as starting points for the problems and tried for a judicious mix of current topics and more settled, stable ones. In the interim phases while students were seeking out the information required for their group tasks, I organized guest lectures and/or site visits to complement their learning. The site visits, though few (for example to the Anishnawbe Health Centre in Toronto, the Easy Street venture at St. Peter's Hospital), sparked much discussion in subsequent classes.[7]

In 1997, I was away on sabbatical so the course was not offered in the 96-97 cycle. When I returned from sabbatical, I refashioned the course to deal with another theme, the context of research. Many Arts and Science students hope to have a career in medicine. Not surprisingly, they tended to cluster in The Curing Society Inquiry course. This led over time to a sense that this was a "pre-med" course, with all the strengths and weaknesses implicit in that term. It was thought that this narrowed the students' view of what it tried to achieve, and a deliberately broader theme was introduced. The process remained the same, but the course was now termed "Discovery: The Context of Research," and students were asked to explore the antecedents and consequences of scientific discoveries. They sought to examine the interplay between individuals, institutions, investments, and ideals that characterises modern research enterprises. A full description has been recently published.[8] In contrast to the previous course, where I had used a number of hypothetical situations, I used real cases or data as triggers for discussion. The problems used included, amongst others, the early studies on the Pill, the discovery of the transmission of malaria by the Anopheles mosquito, the early studies on nitric oxide, the issue of water memory, and the studies on the Habakusha, victims of the A-bomb attacks on Japan. For their individual investigations, students ranged far and wide, exploring areas as disparate as DNA fingerprinting, Cryonics, space exploration, and pharmacogenomics. Guest lectures and visits to laboratories complemented their learning.

Now: September 20th. The students have done their work and are preparing to present their information to their peers. The first group presents their explorations into the nature of beri-beri. They have partitioned their tasks. Jerome presents the clinical picture, Nikki discusses the context in which that information emerged, and Amanda describes the process of discovery. When they finish, a brief discussion occurs before the next group takes over.

THEN AND NOW: My experiences as an instructor in this course have been very rewarding. The students have been extremely enthusiastic and eager. The arguments in the class have been exciting, and I have been often amazed at their resourcefulness in seeking out information. One student, for instance, explored the role of Médecins sans Frontières in Somalia and, given the paucity of information, got access to their files to read the transcripts of memoranda. The students were also imaginative in their presentations, some submitting their final papers as plays rather than as straight essays, to deal with multiple points of view. However, on occasion, theatricality overwhelmed the presentations in the class and the content seemed trivial in comparison. Nevertheless, the spirit was exemplary.

In the last cycle (2001-2002), I introduced the notion of a targeted oral. Students were expected to choose a particular issue for further exploration. They submitted a brief abstract along with key references. Based on that information, I conducted an old-fashioned oral examination. Each student was given a few minutes to summarise what they had learned and then the questioning began. The tenor was conversational. Each session was strictly timed. The sessions were held in a room with a one-way mirror, so that the exam could be witnessed by the other students. Initially, I had proposed that the marks be partitioned between the oral and the written essay. However, the majority of the students chose to have all the marks for individual explorations be allotted to the oral exams. The experience was quite exhilarating. The students seemed to relish the opportunity to demonstrate their learning, and I was delighted with the depth of their knowledge.

It is difficult for me to be entirely objective about the course. The experience of being involved with a dynamic, exuberant bunch of students year after year has added immensely to the quality of my life. I hope that I, in turn, have added something to theirs.

Notes

1. Bob Hudspith and Herb Jenkins, *Teaching the Art of Inquiry* (Halifax, NS: Society for Teaching and Learning in Higher Education, 2001).
2. Jennifer Smith Maguire was a student in this course and later successfully pursued Doctoral studies.
3. Boyer Commission on Educating Undergraduates in the Research University, *Re-Inventing Undergraduate Education: A Blueprint for America's Research Universities* (Princeton, N.J.: Carnegie Foundation for the Advancement of Teaching, 1997).
4. Neil Postman and Charles Weingartner, *Teaching as a Subversive Activity* (New York: Delacorte Press, 1969), 4.
5. Joshua Meyrowitz, *No Sense of Place: The Impact of Electronic Media on Social Behaviour* (New York: Oxford University Press,1985).
6. E.W. Eisner, *The Art of Educational Evaluation: A Personal View (London:* Falmer Press, 1985).
7. P.K. Rangachari, "Twenty Up: Problem-based Learning with a Large Group," in *Bringing Problem-Based -Learning to Higher Education: Theory and Practice*, ed. L. Wilkerson & W.H. Gijselars. *New Directions for Teaching and Learning* (San Francisco: Jossey-Bass Publishers, 1996), vol.68.
8. P.K. Rangachari, " Exploring the context of biomedical research through a problem-based course for undergraduate students." *Advances in Physiological Education* 23 (2000): 40-51.

7 Mathematics and Physics Courses

**The Role of Science and Mathematics in the Curriculum
and Links among the Courses**

Bill Harris

This section introduces three individual contributions dealing with the mathematics and physics courses taught in the Programme.

Modern science has exerted enormous impact on Western cultural history over the past three centuries and more, and a comprehensive view of that history can scarcely be achieved without examining that impact. Nor can advances in the sciences be fully appreciated outside their historical context. The regular science curricula in most departments are, however, focused on getting across to their students the vast range of techniques and content of their own disciplines, and rarely bring up this integrative historical element. On this basis, a new design of the science and mathematics courses for the core curriculum in Arts and Science was easily justified. The main practical questions to answer were, which sciences, and when in the four-year outline?

It was eventually decided that the broad education being planned should include some material from the physical sciences, biology, and mathematics, the first two being relevant to their consideration of major issues facing society, and the last to their ability to carry out quantitative reasoning and to appreciate the handling and reporting of numerical data that will confront most of them in their professional lives and all of them in their extra-professional lives. This education is intended to give them enough understanding of the basic concepts that they can participate in discussions that touch on these disciplines and know how to ask questions and seek clarification.

The sciences and mathematics courses in the Programme currently are a Biology and a Mathematics (Calculus) course in Level I, and Physics and a Probability and Statistics course in Level II. The Biology course may be postponed until Level II if the student wants to take a different course to test his/her interest in another subject or to meet some external requirement. Of the required courses, only the Biology course has not been newly designed for the Programme. The Faculty of Science offers a course with objectives that are congruent with those hoped for, and thus a new course could not be justified.

Many students take additional science courses as electives or as part of combined honours programmes or out of interest. Most of the choices made are to meet the prerequisites for application to medical schools, the intention of many Arts and Science students, particularly in their first two years at university. For most, this involves two full-year courses in Chemistry.

Science is really a way of thinking—a highly trained process which does not come naturally to most people—and learning a new way of thinking takes some time. But for courses in the physical sciences, an extra issue arises which is closely connected with the rather forbidding reputation such subjects carry with them. It helps here to bring up a student-body paradigm coined some years ago by American sociologist Sheila Tobias.[1]

Through a series of studies and interviews, Tobias found that the majority of students taking courses in the so-called "hard sciences" (math, physics, chemistry) fell into three rather distinct categories determined by how they reacted to the material. The smallest group (the "first tier") comprised bright students who easily accepted and adjusted to the traditional presentation style of these subjects—rigorous, quantitative lectures delivered by the professor from a remote intellectual height, with many mathematical derivations and worked examples on the blackboard, and not much class interaction except for an occasional question of clarification. Little reason is given for introducing any of the material ("Consider a ball held underwater. Now suppose it is released from rest..."), and little or no history or personal connection. These first-tier students have already made up their minds to pursue careers in the physical sciences, they adapt quickly to the prevailing style without questioning it, and (notably) they go through these courses relatively immune to the quality of teaching.

However, there is a "second tier" of students—often larger in number than the first tier—who are equally intelligent, often more extroverted and articulate, but less immediately in tune with this sort of material. Although they often start the course quite prepared to be interested, they may end up finding the style cold and forbidding, the concepts rather alien, and the social atmosphere primitive. They are not automatically ready to believe that this subject is worth their time. (Why is the ball underwater? Why should I visualize something like a force vector sprouting from its head, and why does this way of thinking seem so artificial? What about background, context, applications?) Their reaction to the subject depends quite a bit on the class atmosphere, level of discussion and interaction, quality of teaching, and other humanist elements.

Finally, most "hard science" classes also have a "third tier" of students who are less able or less motivated, and appear to have much more limited goals for themselves: passing the course is enough, and deeper understanding of the material is neither expected nor achieved. These students usually get just what they were aiming for.

In most physical sciences university classes, the mix of students consists of a majority of third-tier students, a dependable dose of first-tiers, and an uncertain proportion of second-tiers. The Arts and Science physics class is strikingly different. Both first and third tiers are conspicuously absent: the first-tier students have already put themselves into Science specialist or Engineering programmes right from the start, while the third-tiers do not have the academic standing to enter the Arts and Science Programme. We are left with the second tier—an entire classroom of intelligent, articulate, motivated students, but ones who need a fair amount of convincing about the worth of a subject which may seem alien, intimidating, or irrelevant to their personal goals. A few of them even dislike the prospect of taking university physics enough to drop out of the Programme entirely, sometimes because they have encountered unexpected difficulty in the Level I Mathematics course. Many others come into it with various degrees of fear, loathing, or uncertainty. In this situation a classroom atmosphere that is friendly and supportive is very much worth developing.

For many of the students in the Programme, their Level I course in Biology, Level II courses in Physics, Statistics, and, for those who elect to take it, Chemistry, will be their last direct contact with the natural sciences. This makes it all the more important to place the subjects in a wider context, drawing out links to as many other disciplines as possible.

Even so, many "second tier" students will find this material difficult in the end.

The opportunities for interdisciplinary study are enormously greater within Arts and Science than in most other programs in the University. Even so, genuine links are difficult to establish and maintain. On the instructor's side, the urge to explore and explain more of one's own discipline is extremely strong, and on the students' side, the tendency to compartmentalize knowledge into classifiable, non-overlapping boxes is similarly strong. Furthermore, interdisciplinary work may be most effective if it arises from deep-seated understanding of the disciplines themselves. All this notwithstanding, there is every reason to build links of various sizes at all stages in the Programme.

An immediately available avenue for actively connecting two of the courses is between Level II physics and statistics, which almost all the students take simultaneously. The conceptual approach of measurement and modeling which modern science builds on (describe real-world phenomena, measure them as accurately and completely as possible, then build either descriptive or mathematical models which isolate the important influences on the process) finds a natural home in statistical methods and overlaps extremely well with the natural sciences. Linking these two courses through their lab components is an obvious avenue: either the in-house physics labs or the independent projects can often be adapted to generate well defined databases in which two or three parameters are varying. The data can then be fitted and analyzed within the context of rigorous statistical models. Some initial steps in this direction have been taken, but there is much room for future development.

History is another obvious point of overlap. Key figures such as Galileo, Descartes, and Newton who deeply influenced the course of Western culture come up in Physics as well as in Western Civilization. Opportunities to develop this sort of link through joint essays or projects certainly exist but have not yet been pursued.

Calculus (Arts and Science Mathematics Course)

Miroslav Lovric

Mathematics rarely leaves us cold and emotionless. We find it amazing and fascinating; or we are terrified of it. We play with numbers, enjoy discovering patterns everywhere, absent-mindedly sketch geometric configurations while talking on the phone; or we hate every moment we need to spend learning mathematical theorems, definitions and algorithms. Some appreciate the inner beauty and elegance of a mathematics proof, while for the others, struggle with mathematical symbols and computations brings nothing but pain, frustration and misery. Inadequate and unimaginative teaching in elementary school, and later, in secondary and tertiary institutions, is partly to blame for the negative emotions many of us harbour towards anything that relates to mathematics.

The Arts and Science Programme provides an ideal environment for learning mathematics the way it should be learnt. It exposes students to all aspects of mathematics, from its "rigid" and "abstract" sides (axioms, theorems and definitions) to its applied sides (applications and modeling). The Arts and Science Mathematics course (called, somewhat inappropriately, Calculus) reveals mathematics at its foundations, presents its theoretic aspects, and investigates its meaning and purpose in social and cultural contexts.

Topics

A course in mathematics has always been an essential part of the Arts and Science Programme curriculum. The course is offered in the first year; its content is primarily structured around material that is typically referred to as Calculus. However, the mathematics course has changed over the years, and its scope now extends beyond the ideas and concepts of traditional calculus. The most recent form of the ever-evolving curriculum includes the following material (roughly divided into core topics, applications, and additional topics):

Core topics

> Introduction to mathematics and mathematical language
> Definition of a function and introduction to mathematical modeling
> Concept of a limit and its algebraic foundations
> Continuity of functions of one variable
> Velocity and tangent problems, concept of the derivative of a function
> Definite and indefinite integrals
> Differential equations
> Sequences and infinite series
> Functions of several variables

Applications
> Basics of mathematical modeling
> Applications of derivatives (construction of graphs, Newton's method of solving equations by iterations)
> Applications of integrals (length, area, volume, probability, etc.)
> Differential equations (learning curve, population dynamics, spread of a disease, etc.)

Additional topics
> Selection of topics from other mathematics disciplines (coding theory, number theory, Euclidean and non-Euclidean geometry, chaos theory, etc.)
> History of mathematics
> Mathematics in social and cultural contexts

Objectives

All branches of mathematics teach how to formulate clear, precise, and logical arguments. The study of mathematics provides excellent training in the verbal articulation of abstract concepts, which generally improves a student's ability to communicate ideas. In particular, mathematical modeling is an invaluable tool for conveying the fundamentals of more complex concepts. The mathematics course exposes Arts and Science students to modeling, which is the relating of mathematical objects and results to concepts in other disciplines.

Faced with problems to be investigated, mathematicians construct models that approximate the given situation. It is not possible to fully describe a non-mathematical phenomenon using equations or other mathematical techniques. Therefore, the art of good modeling lies in highlighting the most relevant aspects of the problem, and neglecting extraneous components. For example, when studying global climate, scientists usually exclude the effects of cosmic radiation from their model. Although cosmic radiation influences climate, its inclusion makes the mathematical model more unwieldy and thus, perhaps paradoxically, less reliable. This mode of critical assessment, in which crafting useful models depends upon a sophisticated understanding of the given problem, is emphasized and practised throughout the course.

Another of the course's objectives is to give students experience in constructing and interpreting pictures and graphs. Our society, compared to that of previous generations, is becoming increasingly visually-based. We absorb more information in a visual form, which is evident in the modern trend of densely illustrated textbooks. Most pages in contemporary mathematics texts contain at least one graph, sketch, or some other type of visual learning aid. Thus, the course is geared to enable students to interpret various forms of pictorial data, not merely those found in textbooks, but also data from sources such as computers, reference manuals, instruments, and statistical reports.

Aside from useful applications such as modeling and pictorial interpretation, perhaps the most fundamental objective of the course is to address the very concept of learning mathematics. That is, how does one study mathematics creatively and efficiently? What does it mean to understand a mathematical idea? What does it mean to understand mathematics?

In my view, mathematics cannot be taught successfully without raising these types of questions. This line of inquiry reveals the approach of the mathematical discipline, with which students of mathematics should be familiar. Mathematical theories establish—through axioms, definitions, and theorems—a framework within which students must learn to operate. Every new definition, statement, or result necessarily relies on previously established mathematical "truths." Thus, new knowledge cannot be produced without the solid and rigorous justification of mathematical proofs. It is essential that students gain an understanding of mathematics' discursive strategies, which enable the discipline to generate new information and insight.

Learning mathematics is akin to learning a new language; it is not sufficient simply to know the alphabet of symbols and the vocabulary of concepts and formulae. Students must also learn the appropriate grammar in order to construct meaningful sentences which, in this analogy, are connections between mathematical objects, ideas, and concepts. In other words, just as one learns to think verbally, so too must one learn to think mathematically.

An example of the distinction between merely knowing the vocabulary and being able to "speak about" mathematics is found in the approach taken to learning and teaching differentiation. Calculus theory provides the definition of the derivative of a function and gives a number of formulae and algorithms that are used to compute it. However, this is only the vocabulary. Intelligent articulation of this idea is only achieved through an appreciation of how this concept relates to other mathematical concepts. That is, how is differentiation, the calculating of derivatives, connected to the idea of continuity? Furthermore, what are the geometric interpretations of the derivative? How is the derivative applied in physics through velocity and acceleration, and in other disciplines through rates of change? Is it possible to compute the derivatives of all functions?

Since mathematics is a multi-dimensional discipline, every new concept, theorem, and algorithm should be understood algebraically, numerically, and visually. Each added concept has implications in multiple, diverse areas, and thus a complete understanding relies on determining the concept's various impacts in different contexts. Of course, it is sometimes a practical hindrance to investigate multiple avenues of applicability. It is often necessary for one's purposes to forego an exhaustive conceptual understanding and simply memorize some facts without fully uncovering their significance. Thus, the learning of mathematics requires an optimal balance between understanding and memorization. Part of the learning process consists of deciding which facts should be committed to memory and which facts can be reconstructed or re-derived when needed. It is almost impossible for students to banish rote learning from their study of mathematics; one needs to solve (literally) hundreds of problems to gain a valuable feel for the material. The Arts and Science course makes students aware of this dynamic between understanding and memory, so as to best prepare them for the demands of the discipline.

Teaching the Course

The structure of the mathematics course is designed to meet the objectives discussed in the previous section. The course consists principally of lectures, tutorials held by teaching assistants, and an independent laboratory component. The following is a skeletal outline of the course's main teaching elements:

- lectures (three meetings per week, the whole class attends), tutorials (one meeting per week; students are divided in three groups of approximately same size)
- small group learning sessions (usually once a week)
- computer labs (seven-eight per year; no meetings; students complete during their own time)
- short essay (one per year, assigned in conjunction with the Arts and Science writing course)

One issue that perennially needs to be re-addressed in the teaching of the course is the students' high school mathematical preparation. Due to the fact that the students in the Programme come from a myriad of schools throughout Canada and elsewhere, their mathematics backgrounds vary considerably. In September 2001, to gain a better understanding of their skill levels, I asked the current class of students to answer the "Mathematics Background Questionnaire" that I designed. The data I obtained from the survey enabled me to identify precisely the gaps and problem areas in the students' knowledge, and thus I could tailor the course to meet their needs more closely.

Lectures

An inspirational, well-prepared, and enthusiastically delivered lecture is essential to engage the students with the material, and to motivate them to explore the topics further. My aim in teaching is to ensure that students gain a qualitative grasp of the concepts and ideas examined in the course. Only when they have a clear, intuitive picture do I introduce mathematical symbols, definitions, theories, and formulae. I try to avoid, as much as possible, complicated calculations that reveal little of importance or relevance. As I have said, one of the purposes of studying mathematics is to learn how to think logically. Despite the need for technical proficiency, the course emphasizes the importance of the conceptual fluency that leads to greater understanding. Clearly the beauty and joy of mathematics does not lie in finding the "correct" answer by diligently inserting numbers into formulae. Rather, much of the value of mathematics is found in its elegant applicability to problems encountered in everyday life.

Besides introducing new material and establishing connections with the previously taught mathematics material, lectures are used to broaden students' viewpoints by presenting historic and cultural elements and discussing related contexts. For example, the definition of the definite integral is motivated by the real-life question of how to compute the area of a plot of land. Ancient Egyptians paid taxes based on the amount of land they owned; the amount of material required to construct a temple, or a pyramid, was based on a similar calculation of volume. In lectures, students are shown how these ancient, often intuitive, methods of computation were formalized and made precise in the 19th century. When I teach techniques of integration, I discuss the topic's various applications, which range from computations of distances to probability and population problems.

Although teaching real world applications is highly enriching to the learning experience, I am careful to underscore the dangers inherent in this endeavor. First, whose real world is one really portraying? Almost every calculus textbook has a word problem describing the scenario of a person on a ladder. The base of the ladder is sliding away from the wall against which it is leaning (i.e. the unlucky person is in trouble!). The question typically asks the speed at which the top of the ladder is falling, or some variation on this theme. But is this a real world problem? To whom is it relevant, and how culturally-centric is this model? Second, the calculus textbook used in the Arts and Science course contains a primitive model of human blood flow, but gives no explanation of how the formula was derived. The issue here is that creating a meaningful real-life situation is quite difficult, since it requires a proficient and sometimes profound working knowledge of mathematical concepts. Usually, such techniques are inaccessible to first year students, and thus there is the danger that, in exploring these applications, students will be forced to memorize the surface of the problem, since a fuller understanding is beyond their present level. According to modern trends in mathematics education (powered by the political push for accountability in universities), the study of real world problems motivates students, providing them with a better understanding of mathematics. However, I am careful to make my students aware that applying mathematics to real situations often demands both cultural sensitivity and an unlikely familiarity with the situations' contingencies.

An area of mathematics that is less prone to such logistical dangers is number theory. It is one of the most fascinating mathematical fields and, fortunately, one that is among the easiest to discuss. The yet unproven Goldbach conjecture, stating that every even number greater than two can be expressed as a sum of two prime numbers, uses concepts studied at the high school level. I use this conjecture in the Arts and Science course to illustrate the process of creating mathematical theory. By playing with numbers, we are actually performing an investigation, an experiment. If a pattern emerges, the pattern is formulated as a conjecture, which will become a mathematical theorem once it is proven or rejected. Also during the course this year, I showed a videotape history of Fermat's Last Theorem, which narrates the fascinating history of this famous mathematics problem. The discussion that followed did not focus solely on the mathematics technicalities, but also inspired a debate on a variety of issues, such as media representation of science, and the stereotyping of mathematicians. By introducing these elements into lectures, I hope to broaden the students' perspectives on mathematics, and situate mathematics within a larger cultural context.

Tutorials

Tutorials are small-group sessions (about twenty students per group), devoted mostly to the discussion of the material presented in lectures. In order to review the material, teaching assistants discuss a number of relevant examples. A large part of each tutorial is devoted to solving exercises, so as to give students an opportunity to gain familiarity in dealing with mathematical symbols, techniques, and algorithms. Short, reinforcing quizzes, held bi-weekly, are written during a portion of the tutorial. In 2000, the Arts and Science teaching assistants and I initiated even smaller group sessions for students who performed poorly on the mid-year examination. Each section was run by either an assistant or me, and contained at most three students. Meetings were conducted weekly, outside regularly scheduled lecture time, tutorials, or office hours, and were individually modified to the demands of the group. The success of the sessions motivated us to plan similar sessions in the future.

Since 1998, upper-level undergraduate students in the Arts and Science Programme have replaced mathematics graduate students as tutorial leaders. Surveys conducted by the Centre for Leadership and Learning at McMaster University have shown this practice to be quite successful. Arts and Science students know the background and mathematical needs of their younger peers better than an older student who, most likely, would not have taken the same course. These assistants are strongly motivated and enthusiastic about teaching, and are willing to involve themselves in other aspects of the course such as the extra-help sessions described above. In addition, they have provided valuable input in the planning of the course, and in the analysis of course evaluations. Thus, Arts and Science students have proven to be a valuable resource once they complete the Arts and Science mathematics course. Their mathematical proficiency is well-supported by their independence, and by their skills in communication and leadership which are fostered in the Arts and Science environment.

Computer Lab Component

When teaching mathematics, one realizes that a significant part of relevant material cannot be presented in a typical blackboard-and-chalk lecture before an audience of students. Numerous examples such as numeric algorithms or visualizations of graphs of functions in a three-dimensional coordinate system, and especially real-life applications such as population modeling, ecological systems modeling, and predator-prey equations, require not only sophisticated routines and calculations, but also considerable amounts of time. In searching for a suitable solution to this problem, I decided to use the "Maple" software (developed at the University of Waterloo), which is capable of performing symbolic computations, numeric calculations, and graphing. My idea was to develop computer labs that would complement my lectures by expanding the number of related examples and exploring material that would otherwise have to be neglected. The purpose of the computer lab component of the course is:

- to develop independent analytical thinking by combining logical argument, intuition and generalization
- to build the skills to mathematically model a situation by defining variables and establishing relations between them
- to learn how to work deductively to arrive at an answer
- to cultivate an appreciation of mathematics as an evolving entity created and discovered by human enterprise.

Due to space limitations, it was impossible to schedule the computer component during lectures or tutorials. The only option was to organize it so that students could do the labs in their own time, either in a computer lab or at home. Knowing that good learning, like good work, is collaborative and social, I opted to make the labs a team effort. Students are encouraged to collaborate at all stages of the project, and the final report can be signed by as many as three students.

It is my feeling that "Maple" labs are beneficial to students through increasing both their technological proficiency and their perspective on the course material. The "Maple" introductory self-study tutorial that I developed uses the approach of learning by example. This method I found to be most suited to the purpose, and it is more generally endorsed by researchers in teaching mathematics. The tutorial takes about two hours to complete and, through its completion, students attain sufficient experience to work on the labs. The questions in the lab assignments are formulated in such a way that the computer is unable to generate answers without student involvement. Thus, students must plan a strategy, distinguishing those parts to be done on paper from those elements suited to the computer program. Encouragingly, I have found that those students who work diligently with "Maple" software gain an added dimension in understanding the mathematics presented in lectures.

Essay Project

In order to investigate and discuss mathematics (and more generally, science) in contexts of society, history and culture, the Arts and Science mathematics course requires that students complete a project, called the Cultural Meaning of Science or Mathematics. In the past several years, this component of the course has evolved significantly.

The aim of the project is to investigate one scientific or mathematical issue and explore its cultural significance. In groups of three, students are asked to formulate a directed question within the following three categories:

-   assess popular myths about science or mathematics or competing histories of the origins and/or models of the development of science or mathematics
-   assess science/mathematics as an authoritative and powerful institution controlling knowledge production
-   to what extent is science value-free? Consider gender, class, race, non-Western approaches and contributions, etc.

Each group communicates their question to the instructors of both the Arts and Science Writing course and the Mathematics course, and to a group of four to six upper-year students who are selected for the purpose of assisting with the project and evaluating students' final oral and written reports. After receiving the feedback, group members revisit their question, and reformulate it or narrow it down, if necessary.

Each group member identifies a reference (could be several pages, or a chapter from a book) that they will use. They may use the references other group members are using. Several references are listed here, to show the variety of students' interests and the topics they investigated:

-   Marcia Ascher, *Code of the quipu: A study in Media, Mathematics, and Culture* (cultural history and sociological aspects of scientific discovery)
-   Jan Golinski, *Making Natural Knowledge: Constructivism and the History of Science* (a study of the recent history of science and its connections to culture)
-   J.A. Paulos, *A Mathematician Reads the Newspaper* (use and abuse of mathematics and mathematical reasoning in media)
-   Bruno LaTour and Steve Woolgar, *Laboratory Life: The Social Construction of Scientific Facts* (a classic in sociology of science)
-   G.H. Hardy, *A Mathematician's Apology* (why mathematics?, by one of the most famous 20th century mathematicians)
-   K. Menninger, *Number Worlds and Number Systems* (cultural history of numbers)
-   E. Rothstein, *Emblems of Mind* (among other topics, explores the relation between music and mathematics)
-   Ann B. Shteir, *Cultivating Women, Cultivating Science: Flora's Daughters and Botany in England 1760-1860* (is botany a "woman's science"?)

- Claudia Henrion, *Women in Mathematics: the Addition of Difference.* (profiles of professional mathematicians)

Each student is asked to write a critique of the reference they chose. Their work should not be merely a summary, apology, defence, or celebration of science or mathematics. Rather, it should interrogate and assess the role of science or mathematics in relation to society. The question that a student formulated helps her/him focus on one issue. The final part of the project consists of oral presentations: each group introduces the topic/focus of their interest, and then each member reports on her/his work. Oral reports are followed by a question-and-answer and discussion period. Due to the interest they generate, oral presentations are quite long, comprising several three-hour sessions, usually scheduled in the evenings.

Linking Arts and Science

A talk I gave in the Arts and Science Winter Lecture Series focused on linking mathematics (and science) to other disciplines in the Programme. A presentation of several past and present developments in the sciences and the arts led to an important conclusion—arts and science have never developed independently of each other. On the contrary, developments in each enabled developments in the other.

The lecture could be appropriately described by its title: Story about mathematics and art and life with an emphasis on the process of iteration and its relation to Fibonacci numbers and tiger tails, followed by an investigation of chaotic systems such as stock markets, ant colonies, and weather (with an occasional digression into art and literature), illustrated with beautiful pictures and computer graphics and accompanied by music, dance, and a mildly toxic chemical reaction.

A few of my former Arts and Science students were involved in the lecture, providing a lively introduction—singing songs they had written for the occasion, helping with the experiments and acting as choreographers and dancers in a dance based on mathematical computations related to chaos.

Final Reflections

When I look at my audience in the classroom, I see young people with aspirations for the future. These students are generally energetic and excited about learning, and expect that their education will provide them with an opportunity to live fulfilling, productive lives. As a university teacher, I treasure my involvement in their academic experience.

Furthermore, I am conscious that my role in this experience is crucial to the efficacy of students' university endeavors. While many other things in life are replaceable, or even redeemable, education is a much more tenuous and precious entity. If someone is educated badly, it is difficult to surmount this abuse of their time and effort.

Probably because they realize the critical importance of their situation, students succumb to the stresses of constant evaluation by the often faceless monolith of the university. High school teachers, in an attempt to prepare students for university, embed a scary mantra of "in university you are just a number" into the minds of wide-eyed teenagers. I am aware that the move to higher education is daunting, and so I strive to make students more at ease. Sometimes in lectures I try to encourage them, if merely by a simple urging such as, "Have trust in yourself; you'll be okay." I answer all of my students' e-mails, knowing that receiving a personal e-mail from their instructor is encouraging.

I realize the extent of my dedication to my subject and my students when, at 2:00 a.m., I contemplate my upcoming 8:30 a.m. lecture. Will they be able to understand me? Will I be able to connect it to my previous lectures, and will the students grasp these connections?

When I lecture, I try to enter the minds of my students; I listen to myself speak, and try to feel the echo of my words in their brains. Was this explanation clear enough? Was that example convincing enough? Maybe I should do another one? During such moments, I am not guided by any theory of education, but by my audience's reactions. I am pleased by the outcome of a lecture when I sense that the students leave the classroom having learnt something new, having gone through a new experience. Contrastingly, lectures are torturous for me when I perceive that students are present in body only, with their minds occupied by an approaching chemistry test! On such occasions, my attempts to convey new knowledge typically fail; even excellent content cannot save a lack of engagement between professor and audience.

Not long ago I was a student myself. I was very excited about learning not only mathematics, but also other intellectually stimulating subjects. During this time, I decided that my life was going to be devoted, in some form, to teaching and learning. I still vividly remember my undergraduate lectures, and the professors who delivered them. More than that, I remember the good ones, and remember why they were good. I also remember the bad ones, and remember why they were bad. Those experiences still form a frame of reference for my own teaching.

I think of my students as colleagues, and involve them in almost every aspect of my teaching. When I was writing a textbook in vector calculus, I asked my teaching assistants to help me work on the solutions manual. Weekly meetings with six former students in the Second Cup coffee shop in the summer of 1998 ended up in the publication of the "Mathematics Review Manual."

What will my students remember ten years from now? What do I remember of my undergraduate years? I do not remember which professor taught me what theorem, or which professor had impossible exams. What I do remember is their human side: how they lectured, how they communicated to us, and how they inspired and motivated us. A motivated and inspired student acquires a new wealth—a desire to remain an active and excited learner. That is a gift for life—and to convey that is my most important mission.

I would like to add a big thank you to my former student and friend, Laurence Scott, who read, criticized, and edited this contribution with energy, dedication, and enthusiasm.

Statistics: Mathematical Models of Change, Chance and Error

Román Viveros-Aguilera

Introduction

A weather report from a local radio station stating that there is an 80% chance of rain today or a news release from Statistics Canada informing the public that the current national unemployment rate stands at 7.5% are typical expressions of statistical information in their most elementary form. The Bank of Canada prediction that the economy will grow this year between 2.5% and 3.5% is another example. I once heard somebody make the comment that the probability of winning a lottery is one-half because either you win it or you don't. Unfortunately for the bettor, the laws of probability are far less optimistic on the winning outcome of any lottery. Statements conveying greater accuracy in the results of a statistical study are often made when reporting polling information. A typical example could be: "based on a survey of 2400 adults, the support for the governing party stands at 44% with a margin of error of 2% valid nineteen-times-out-of-twenty." For the most part, a general education requiring no more than a high school level would be sufficient to understand the meaning of the above statements. This may be the reason why the statements are now widespread. They may have been arrived at after large, costly and often long-term studies were conducted by experienced organizations. In order to assess their merit, it is necessary to get satisfactory answers to a series of questions that relate to the methods of data collection and analysis used and the strength of the conclusions reached. The methods of analysis go far beyond the calculation of averages and standard deviations that we usually identify as the signatures of statistics. Since much of our interpretation of what goes on in the world depends on media reports based on statistical studies, and much of the academic world uses data analysis to support new knowledge, graduates are well served by having an understanding that alerts them to the statistical issues that lie behind reported conclusions.

In broad terms, the Arts and Science Statistics course provides a systematic study of a large number of probability models and statistical methods useful in the analysis of data anywhere they are collected. The knowledge acquired from the study of the methods not only provides students with the basic statistical literacy needed to understand the final conclusions of a study, but also empowers them to become active participants in the behind-the-scenes data processing and statistical analyses that can be expected to be part of many of their future careers.

Finite Mathematics and the current Mathematics for Data Management courses in high school provide early encounters with elementary probability concepts and statistical methods. A thorough understanding and appreciation of the methods in the introductory-level Statistics course we offer requires differential and integral calculus as background. This partly explains the course's position in the second year of the Programme. But the role it fulfills as a rich source of research methods for other disciplines demanding quantitative statistical analyses is perhaps the most compelling reason for its placement as early as possible. Physics, which is taken concurrently in second-year, is an example, but many of the subsequent required and elective courses can also benefit from the students' knowledge of statistical methods.

Course Objectives

The students will acquire an understanding of:
- the fundamental concepts and models of probability
- the most widely used statistical methods to draw inferences from observed data
- the technical mathematical details behind the models and methods

- strategies to model and quantify variability in observed data; and the ability to:
  summarize data numerically and graphically
  apply statistical methods to anlayze data from many sources
  handle data and carry out statistical analyses using computer statistical packages
  The approach emphasizes not only the technical aspects of the methods but also their use in the understanding of practical data. The latter is perhaps the more relevant legacy, for the course's long-term impact will be in the wisdom the students display in their subsequent encounters with many data sets. Sherlock Holmes in "The Copper Beeches" (1892) captures the relevance of data by saying,"Data! Data! Data! I can't make bricks without clay."

Curriculum Overview

The course uses a natural partitioning of the areas of probability and statistics, with the former providing an absolutely essential background for the latter. The two areas are covered in sequence in two twelve-week academic terms. The subject acquires life and relevance only when its practical implications are uncovered. Each topic listed below is discussed in relation to real data from a wealth of case studies.

Core probability topics discussed in Term I are: probability concepts, properties and formulas; conditional probability, Bayes Theorem and independence; discrete random variables and their probability distributions; continuous random variables and their probability distributions; means, variances and other expected values; joint probability distributions, covariance and correlation; the distribution of linear combinations of random variables; the Central Limit Theorem.

Core statistics topics discussed in Term II are: descriptive numerical and graphical statistical methods; concepts and methods of estimation: methods of moments and maximum likelihood; confidence intervals from single samples; tests of hypotheses based on single samples; estimation and confidence intervals from two samples; simple linear regression; goodness-of-fit tests; statistical analysis of categorical data (contingency tables).

Delivery, Evaluation, and the Project

For the most part, the course is delivered using traditional approaches with three weekly one-hour blackboard presentations of concepts, methods, and illustrations. Students participate in often quite lively discussions on special topics such as an in-depth analysis of lotteries and the winning probabilities for the various prizes, the design and analysis of polls, and a probabilistic account on the intriguing occurrence of matches in a group's birthdays, using the birthdays of the members of the class. In each term, the course is delivered in six two-week packs of material, with an assignment at the end of each pack.

A highlight of the course is the project. Performed in teams of two to three students, the project presents them with an opportunity to perform a complete data analysis and write a report of their results. They may elect to summarize, analyze and interpret the data they generate in experiments they carry out in the Physics course (p.151) or data they collect in addressing another topic of their choice. It is, in all senses, a research project, one grounded on real-life data and requiring statistical methods of analysis. Because of the above-average inquisitiveness of the students admitted to the Arts and Science Programme, the projects produced cover an impressively wide range of topics. A statistical analysis of reality-based television, smarties (a candy), a proportionate rainbow of fruit flavour, Poisson distribution of gamma ray absorption, sex distribution of riders on the McMaster shuttle bus, and looking at pictures differently: a study on the relationship of picture preference to handedness and gender, are a few examples.

One team conducted a careful study of the color proportions in smarties, the small round chocolate tablets that are favorites of many kids. Using a large sample of smarties, the team's data revealed a statistically significant disagreement with the proportions advertised by Mars, the maker of smarties. Another team analyzed their own physics experimental results on the absorption of gamma rays by wood. Gamma rays were passed through wood pieces of varying thickness and counts of the gamma rays before entering and after passing through the wood were made. The team found that a Poisson probability distribution described the data quite well. Further, through statistical estimation and testing, they established a linear relationship between the average number of gamma rays absorbed and the thickness of the wood.

Although the project work's timing is left open, most teams end up doing their projects in Term II. The cumulative knowledge and experience gained in the course makes the second term a natural choice. For this reason, only one midterm test is conducted in this term, while there are two in Term I. The project guidelines emphasize that it is essential the reports include numerical tables and plots, and a proper account and interpretation of these. The project is worth 10% of the year course's final mark.

For a statistics instructor, the ideal lasting legacy of the course is not the students' accurate recall of the many models and formulas discussed in the course, but the enhancement of their quantitative perspective. After taking the course, this perspective should generate in the students a desire to seek quantitative answers to many of the problems and situations they encounter, to look for the necessary data and to extract from them, through the use of statistical methods, the quantitative features needed for an objective and logical unraveling of the problem or situation. The course project provides the best opportunity for the students to experience this process. In the 1960s, when the use of statistical methods was beginning to gain widespread acceptance in industry, the pioneer industrial statisticians Walter A. Shewhart and William E. Deming stated that "the long-range contribution of statistics depends not so much upon getting a lot of highly trained statisticians into industry as it does in creating a statistically minded generation of physicists, chemists, engineers, and others who will in any way have a hand in developing and directing the production processes of tomorrow."[2] With the rapid expansion of statistical methods into every discipline involving quantitative studies seen since then, Shewhart and Deming's statement is not only equally true today but also much more widely applicable. It is relevant to Arts and Science students because it applies to every challenge of analysis or understanding they will face when they encounter problems involving quantitative data subject to variability of any sort.

Students—the Essential Component

As indicated elsewhere in this book, a carefully conducted student selection process is followed in the Arts and Science Programme. The process favours open-minded high achievers with reasonably balanced interests in arts and science disciplines. They are often well-rounded, self-assured and highly motivated individuals with a much wider variety of experiences than the average student. Nearly all have developed at least one artistic creative skill. Hardly any possesses the traits of the specialist. These personal elements inject distinctive features into the teaching of probability and statistics. Every lecture has an engaged audience eager to contribute and ask questions. The Arts and Science students show great motivation to understand every aspect of a statistical application. Their varied general knowledge facilitates their quick grasp of examples from diverse areas. They go the extra mile, focusing not only on the specific aspects of an illustration but also inquiring about how to answer the same question under variations of the context considered.

The project is the course activity that generates the highest level of enthusiasm among the students. The Arts and Science students' eagerness and confidence lead them to seize this opportunity. The freedom to choose a topic, gather the data and unravel the questions/issues posed, is the main motivating factor. The writing of the project report, normally a painful activity for most students outside the humanities and social sciences, is embraced with great spirit and competence by the Arts and Science students. An evidence of their writing skills this instructor has noted is the consistently higher quality of the Arts and Science statistics project reports among the statistics courses this instructor has taught over the past twelve years for a sizable cohort of programmes at McMaster University.

In the arena of student dislikes, the only stomach-discomfort causing course ingredient is the derivation of mathematical results. The activity entails the careful combination of definitions, axioms and derived properties about math objects to prove whether a new general probabilistic or statistical statement is valid or invalid through the use of logical mathematical reasoning. While Arts and Science students exhibit a sharp mind in constructing logical arguments when discussing a general interest situation, many find it difficult to extend the skill to abstract objects. Insufficient prior exposure to formal mathematical reasoning possibly explains the disjunction. It should be pointed out, however, that this reaction is common in students of practically every programme of study other than the specialized mathematics and statistics programmes.

Synergies with Calculus, Physics and Other Subjects

Although the majority of the statistical methods discussed in the course rely primarily on arithmetic for their application to real data, the understanding of concepts, the manipulation of models and the formal solution of many general questions require the use of calculus. For instance, the concept of distribution for counts and measurements relies on the use of functions. The probability that a random measurement falls in a given range of values is represented by the area under a function and thus requires integration for its calculation. Integration is also called upon to obtain expected values and variances of measurements. Maxima calculations, which involve derivatives of functions and the solution of equations, are needed in developing estimates for parameters. There is no doubt that a good background in differential and integral calculus is an essential ingredient for success in the course.

Touted as the most applied area among its math siblings, statistics finds points of synergy with practically every other scientific discipline and several social science disciplines. This interaction frequently renders mutual benefits. On the one hand, the subject area of application gains enlightenment from the solutions the statistical methods provide to some of its problems. On the other hand, the area of application often poses problems necessitating the development of new statistical methods, which in turn enrich the wealth of techniques the discipline of statistics offers. Understanding and appreciating this synergy demands sound, general background knowledge at a minimum. The typical Arts and Science student meets this requirement.

The course project provides the potential for dynamic interaction with other disciplines, particularly with those making quantitative data readily available. Concrete examples of this interaction have occurred with the concurrent Physics course. Working in teams, the students run physics experiments as part of that course's requirements. Some of the experiments yield a substantial amount of data. The use of a variety of statistical methods is needed to summarize and interpret these data. The team selects one of the substantive physics experiments and writes a report focusing on the description of the experiment's objectives, experimental methods used, ensuing data and results, and submits it as part of the Physics course requirements. If the team has chosen to analyze the results of this experiment as their Statistics project, they write a second report for that course, centering on the details of the statistical modeling, methods, tables, graphs and data interpretations. The Physics and Statistics instructors share the reports to ensure the team has addressed the issues separately and to prevent any possible credit duplication.

In summary, the students take away from the Statistics course a variety of concepts and tools that enable them to understand and unravel situations where quantitative information in the form of data is the main basis for analysis. Their feedback from later years in the program suggests that the course project has left a lasting impression, since the students had many opportunities to replicate their statistics project experience in a variety of research projects for subsequent courses.

Physics

Bill Harris

Quite a few reasons can be invoked for including Physics as a required course in the Arts and Science Programme, and for designing the course to meet the needs of its students

- to trace the especially important impact of Physics on Western thought.
- to develop quantitative physical reasoning skills.
- to develop scientific literacy through familiarity with the "great concepts" in physical science: Newton's laws of mechanics, conservation laws, gravitation, the analysis of motion, wave motion and the nature of light, Einstein's special and general relativity, quantum mechanics, modern cosmology, and nonlinear or chaotic phenomena.
- to gain experience with laboratory measurements and illustrate the way in which science depends on the experimental process.
- to connect Physics with related sciences, particularly Mathematics, Statistics, or Chemistry, and to draw out common themes which illustrate the way contemporary science works.

These are deeply interconnected goals, and each one by itself represents quite a large bite to chew. The item on the list which truly distinguishes the role of physics within the Programme is the first one. In the 1700s, the new world view called the Newtonian Synthesis invigorated the long rationalist movement in Western culture and was the starting point for the history of modern science. And in the twentieth century, the genuinely revolutionary concepts emerging from relativity, quantum mechanics, and chaos theory—continuing with such recent areas as string theory and cosmology—have had wide impact on academic, philosophical, and cultural thinking that is still being absorbed.

If Physics should be a part of the Arts and Science program, where should it be put? Somewhat by default, it was originally slotted into Level II because the design for Level I was already sufficiently packed with the necessary foundation of Mathematics, Inquiry, Writing and Informal Logic, Biology, and Western Civilization. Nevertheless, even with a completely free choice we would probably opt for second year anyway: by then, the students have a clearly higher level of maturity and familiarity with the university environment; they have the specific calculus background which is an essential part of its vocabulary; and most of them are also taking the

Level II course in Statistics which provides excellent chances for learning links. Later years are clearly less suitable: in Levels III and beyond, the students have started to move away into their own academic directions past the basic Programme core. As initially designed twenty years ago, the course was intended to be a wide sampling of "physical science" which, in addition to its main diet of core physics, would include material on the foundations of chemistry (such as the physical origin of the periodic table). However, this latter unit was dropped in order to preserve the entire course for Physics.

The course content has continued to evolve from its original outline. In the late 1990s the curriculum plan looked like this:

First term:

Newtonian mechanics I: kinematics; the analysis of motion

Newtonian mechanics II: forces, mechanical systems, Newton's laws and gravity

Newtonian mechanics III: energy and momentum; conservation laws

Newtonian mechanics IV: rotational motion, torque, angular momentum

Special relativity: time dilation, spacetime and the Lorentz transformation

Second term:

Fluid mechanics: hydrostatics and Archimedes' principle; Bernoulli's principle

Oscillatory motion: simple harmonic motion and wave motion

Light: interference and diffraction

Quantum mechanics: Models for atomic structure including Rutherford, Bohr, de Broglie, Schrodinger; Planck's hypothesis; wave/particle duality; the uncertainty principle

General relativity: Einstein's equivalence principle, gravity and curved space, observational tests of GR, black holes

Cosmology: Stellar structure and the ages and compositions of stars; galaxies and the expanding universe; the cosmic background radiation and the Big Bang; the early universe

Much of the material is at an introductory level, but it is always calculus-based and quantitative rather than merely descriptive. The sections on relativity, cosmology, and quantum mechanics are usually the most popular with the students, stretching and challenging their instinctive notions of physical reality. But what about Newtonian mechanics? Almost all the students have taken it before in some high school form, so why revisit it? One supremely important reason is not very different from why we return to a first-rank piece of literature or music. On the first encounter we see the "surface" of the subject; on repeated passages, we cut into it at successively deeper levels where there is vastly more to find. High school physics is often presented through sets of arbitrary-looking rules and formulae dealing with various phenomena like motion, force, and energy. By second-year university, a deeper level of mathematical sophistication can be put to work and the unifying general principles embedded in the subject can start to be emphasized. In addition, its influence on Western thought can be drawn out if we see how the subject developed in a historical sequence from Galileo through Descartes, Huygens, Newton, Laplace and others, into its eventual form as an integrated and powerfully predictive world view. Today, this scheme of thought is often looked on balefully as mechanistic, repressive, or even anti-human; but in Newton's day and after, it was pursued enthusiastically as liberating and energizing. Tracing the reasons for these shifting viewpoints requires understanding both the inner workings of the subject and the long-term historical trends they were part of.

Physics is fundamentally a way of viewing the outside world. Its mode of thinking has a well deserved reputation for being hard-edged, analytical, and relentlessly rational, but its process also relies on the very nonrational leaps of intuition that appear in the work of Newton, Einstein, and many others. It is not the same as mathematical thinking, or even pure logic, because in addition to these it requires developing a strong sense of what fits the real world (and in subjects like relativity or the quantum world, what "fits" can go against a conventional sense of logic).

Physics intuition does not really resemble our everyday instincts of "how things work" and in fact does not come naturally to most people. The same is true for mathematics, literature, philosophy, music, art, or any other major area of highly trained human thought: not everyone can genuinely absorb any one of these, regardless of their basic intelligence. It's worth realizing, however, that physics thinking is different because it is a relative newcomer in human history: it was methodically constructed by European scholars just 300 to 400 years ago, and in some sense, we are still getting used to it. Before Galileo, physics was a branch of philosophy. After Newton, less than a century later, it was a new and well defined entity of its own, and the practitioners of this new field were quite definitely not doing philosophy any longer. They were bent on finding out how things work with the powerful new team of organized measurement and model (or, if you like, experiment and theory).

How the Physics Course Works

Every week there are three scheduled hours with the class, which are the backbone of the course. For physics as well as for any other subject, it's possible to employ the inquiry-type techniques that are well established in the Programme (and campuses all across North America are now experimenting with a wide range of such approaches in physics teaching). At the same time, the curriculum has a highly structured flow, and the material is cumulative: once the term begins, there are no other "fresh start" points later on. An effective model has been to adopt a mix of traditional lecture days and assignments—which keep the course on track and provide an appropriate level of structure—with inquiry learning and independent outside-the-walls projects. On average, the three weekly contact hours for the course might break down like this:

- One hour for an organized lecture on the subject of the week (or sometimes two hours, if the material is quite new and unfamiliar to most of the class). No attempt is made to talk about all the material in detail: the students can read and fill in the gaps for themselves later. The time is also used for benchtop demonstrations, discussions of links to other sections of the curriculum, and brief biographies of prominent scientists whose work is being discussed. Questions and comments are strongly encouraged, and impromptu discussions are followed up without undue worry about "getting through" a certain fixed agenda.

- One hour for an "inquiry day". This time is used for a wide variety of purposes, including student project presentations, short experiments and measurements, or discussion problems assigned on the spot and worked on by everyone in the class. Examples of the latter include "Fermi problems," which may or may not be directly physics-related (How many piano tuners are there in your city? How big would a helium balloon need to be to support your weight?) but which encourage rough-estimation reasoning skills. The consistent message is to develop judgment about finding the main factors in a problem and discarding small issues. Many students, at this stage, need a lot of pushing to get rid of the notion that science is all about total certainty, and that if we don't know something exactly, it's worthless. Realizing that there are shades of gray, and that some uncertainties in a problem are much more important than others, is a major step toward maturity.

- One hour for a tutorial or testing period. Hour-long quizzes are run three or four times each term on small units of the material, preceded by weekly assigned problem sets (but only the quizzes are marked, not the problem sets). Frequent small-scale testing during the term is more effective than fewer major tests.

What about lab work? Ultimately science is about the real world, and you can't just talk about experimental measurement and modelling. You have to go out and do some.

The laboratory component of the Physics course originally comprised two or three of the standard Level I in-house experiments each term. At first, these had the conventional laborious follow-the-manual style which was viewed dimly by students everywhere. These labs have been strongly modified and adapted to reduce the "cookbook" features considerably. Also, new computer-based apparatus (installed by the Department of Physics and Astronomy starting in 2000/01) has allowed the development of a whole new and varied set of experiments which (among other things) tremendously speeds up the process of data taking and graph plotting. Annual changes in the assigned experiments are also useful for erasing any year-by-year "memory" and maintaining fresh momentum.

Independent project labs were introduced in the late 1990s and have evolved further each year. These experiments (different ones for each student or pair of students) are done outside the normal lab environment, and with everyday low-tech apparatus which the students build, buy, or borrow themselves. The project instructions they are given to start with, early in the year, are nothing more than a bare outline two or three sentences long. Most of the effort comes in learning how to design, from scratch, an experiment that actually works. Toward the end of second term, each project team gives a short presentation in class, and turns in a complete writeup.

In the end, is there an ideal way to present physics, or the physical sciences, to an Arts and Science audience? I don't think so. The student body is so diverse, and has so much energy, intelligence and initiative, that many approaches will work. They are a highly adaptable bunch, and enthusiasm and friendliness go a long way from both sides of the lecture bench (students and instructor alike) to build a positive learning atmosphere. My personal reflections on the Programme are on p. 249.

As far as fitting physics into the academic needs of the Programme is concerned, I think in the end the only really important principles to pay attention to are these:

- Respect the "second tier" nature of the students: all are intelligent, but few have their natural intellectual homes in physics or math;
- Experiment is important. Let them go out and do some things for themselves and start understanding at a gut level the complex, untidy, uncertain and often perverse nature of the business.
- Respect the fact that physics is a process, and a trained way of thinking that does not come naturally to most people. Learning it is a spiral sequence: they need to return to the same concept more than once, and each time they revisit it, they can take a deeper cut into it.
- Understanding and enjoying what they do is, for the these students, immensely more important than getting through a particular prescribed curriculum.

Notes

1. Sheila Tobias, *They're not Dumb, They're Different: Stalking the Second Tier* (Tucson: Research Corporation, 1990).
2. Walter A. Shewhart and William E. Deming, quoted in *Statistically Speaking*, eds., C.C. Gaither and A.E. Cavazos-Gaither (Bristol and Philadelphia: Institute of Physics Publishing, 1996).

8   Literature

Jean Wilson

Introduction

For reasons that students of the Arts and Science Literature course will readily understand, this was a difficult piece for me to write. Like many of these students, who attest to their experience in the course as profoundly transformative, I have been deeply affected, both personally and professionally, by my engagement in the decidedly student-centred teaching and learning process that occurs under the rubric *Lit*, as the course is commonly known. Faced with the task of describing a course that has become central to my developing sense of what literary study is all about, I decided to seek help from a number of former students, knowing that their insights could provide the focus and perspective necessary for the kind of overview the editors of the present volume had in mind. As is evident below,[1] the solicited contributions have enabled me to piece together an account of the course and its place in the curriculum of the Arts and Science Programme as a whole. I will not be so presumptuous as to claim that together we have "told the story" of *Lit*, for who indeed, as one of the Homeric characters asks rhetorically, could ever "tell the whole story"?[2] Moreover, as the texts studied in the course make abundantly clear, there is always more than one story to be told. This account, then, does not present itself as anything close to complete or definitive, but it offers at least an outline of what has been referred to as "a highly unusual course" (Letkemann).

The same student ends his reflection with the statement, "For all this, I am very grateful." Taking my cue from his expression of gratitude, I would like to record my heartfelt thanks to the students of *Lit* with whom I have worked, for they in many significant ways have made the course what it is. "Every person a teacher" has been suggested as a fitting slogan for it (Sin Yan Too), given its "heavy reliance on contributions from students to in-class discussion" (Mackenzie). The latter student elaborates on the pleasure that comes from "hearing a peer draw the class into a new way of looking at an idea or a whole text," and he speaks of the "moments of discovery" made possible in a course where his mind was "awake, active, busy making connections"; productive class discussions "frequently brought us to meaningful new ground." Indeed, *Lit* quickly becomes a shared enterprise, and the acceptance of mutual responsibility for the course is without doubt the key to what it is able to achieve. I offer thanks also to the exceptionally supportive Arts and Science directors, administrative colleagues, and faculty members with whom I have been associated, and to Dr. Michael Ross, who taught *Literature* in the years before I assumed responsibility for the course in 1992-93. Normally one would place such acknowledgements in an endnote rather than in the body of the text, but adherence to conventional form in this case would obscure the fact that the contributions of the various people mentioned above are integral to the identity of the Literature course.

That first year, unsure of just what *Lit* would/should/could be all about, I borrowed the short description of the "aims of the course" from Dr. Ross's 1991-92 outline: "[it] aims to show how literature is an indispensable means of thinking about human life and society. To make this point, it looks at works in various forms (epic, novel, poetry, drama) from a variety of cultures and historical periods." The description has never been changed, not—or so I like to think—because of laziness or complacency on the part of the instructor, but because the fundamentals of *Lit* have remained constant. Although some features have, of course, been altered even since I first taught the class, the following account is not a narrative of progress, but rather an exploration of the particular ways in which *Lit* has been shaped over the last ten years. As indicated above, input from former students helped me to write this chapter. First to be approached were teaching assistants from the last five years: a small number of Arts and Science students who took the course in their penultimate year of undergraduate study and then became TAs in their graduating year. Requests for contributions were subsequently extended on a quite informal basis—again, with three exceptions (Caryll, Essaji,

Shin), to students from the last five years—and primarily to those with whom I am still in regular contact, whether it be someone temporarily living next door (Matheson) or a pair of travellers corresponding from an internet café in Bangkok (Curran and Oberndorfer). I wish that it had been feasible to include the insights of a greater number of students, for I know that every graduate of the course has much of value to say. One of the chief objectives of *Lit* is to foster the development of each participant's critical voice, and I regret that logistics did not permit anything approaching the full range of voices to be recorded here.

The three broad objectives of the Arts and Science Programme are "to increase understanding of achievements and methods used in selected Arts and Science disciplines; to increase skills in writing, in speaking, and in critical and quantitative reasoning; to increase skills in the art of scholarly inquiry into issues of public concern."[3] "Students are also expected to be responsible and active university and community citizens."[4] While *Lit*, a course in Comparative Literature, most obviously addresses the first of these goals, its mandate extends well beyond this; with the exception of "quantitative reasoning," all of the above-mentioned skills are certainly honed in the course. It "stitches together the topics emerging from the first three levels of the Programme and provides a forum for deeper exploration. I consider *Lit* a crowning Arts and Science experience, where, for an engaged student, 'everything comes together'" (Dancey). Below I have provided an outline of the course, but first, to capture something of its spirit, I offer a selection of brief descriptions in the students' own words.

Students' Descriptions of the Course

Lit is a "different course each year, and the uniqueness of the course is dependent on the uniqueness of the class" (Macdougall). This is consistent with a student-centred approach, in which the classroom becomes a place of mutual discovery: "it was a powerful comment about learning to see that Dr. Wilson, who was rereading works she had already extensively studied, could still glean so much from our class discussions" (Shin). Students agree that although the course takes a different direction each year, what remains constant is the creation of "a learning environment that is inclusive, yet intellectually challenging" (Essaji). They also find that the class "sneaks up on you"; only well into the term do you realize how much you are learning (Mackenzie). "The lectures are not unidirectional in the traditional style, but are more interactive, peppered with questions and often spontaneous discussion by the class. There is no 'banking model' structure in which the expert professor makes periodic knowledge deposits in the minds of the students. Rather, the class is a dynamic mix of lectures, small group presentations, exploratory papers, and discussion. The course promotes critical skills and new ways of thinking; disabuses students of the notion that there is an absolute interpretation to a work of literature; acts as a vehicle for discussion of timely and timeless societal issues; explores literature as a means of envisioning alternative ways of being" (Curran and Oberndorfer).

"*Lit* reflects the philosophy of the Programme by emphasizing critical thinking and analysis. However, the course is unique in that it requires students to engage personally with the texts studied. I learned to read critically, to uncover layers of meaning in a work, and to examine the various voices at play and in tension in a text. In the process, I discovered a voice through which to express my thoughts. Perhaps the most significant analytical framework I learned in the course was that of literature as peace research. Literature encourages us to think creatively. It reveals to us not only what we are, but also what we can become" (Chen). The concept of "literature as peace research,"[5] articulated by the contemporary German writer Christa Wolf, is repeatedly cited as an inspiration: "My involvement with peacebuilding initiatives has been enriched by the notion of alternative visions, a theme that was emphasized throughout the course. The perspectives introduced . . . flowed into ideas that expanded beyond the classroom. We were challenged to imagine, question, articulate, and incorporate discoveries into our own lives" (Dutt).

"In many ways it is the counterpoint to the first-year *Inquiry* course focused on Third World development. Whereas that course challenges students to adopt a less self-centred world view, *Lit* challenges students to transform their individual conceptions of self. The cleanly delineated structure of the course permits the same array of possibilities that Margaret Atwood attributes to the Japanese haiku: 'a limited form, rigid in its perimeters, within which an astonishing freedom [is] possible'"[6] (Fertuck). "The structure of *Lit* is such that you are expected to do the readings on your own and then contribute in class, for both your own and the collective benefit. This approach challenges you to immerse yourself in literary waters for eight months. There is a lot of floating about and some surprises from the deep, but then there are the treasures (which abound)! What made *Lit* such an integral part of my Arts and Science education was the recurring theme of transformation. As we watched characters and plotlines grow and change, I noticed connections with other works and, eventually, my other courses. I started to feel I was an author of my life, and all of my experiences and knowledge were the tools for building my story" (Parizeau). While the introductory Inquiry course, as the first student cited in the above paragraph attests, encourages "a less self-centred world view," *Lit*, strikingly, allows students "to be really 'self-centred,'" as they struggle with "fears and doubts about their own personal journeys. Maybe by seeing bits of myself in so many of the characters, I'm like Don Quixote, who confuses fantasy with reality, and mistakenly sees himself as the hero in all the tales of chivalry he reads. But at least he had fun along the way" (Liu). "For the students whose brains do not reject the unfamiliar mixing of real and imaginative, of their own 'important' journeys and journeys whose existence is seemingly constituted only by ink on a page, the course is supremely rewarding. *Lit* places the individual student at the centre of the world of ideas. The Programme up until this point disrupts and casts doubt on one's intellectual sovereignty, forever revealing new complexities and dark corners on an increasingly expansive landscape. While *Lit* does not shy away from this vastness, it does illuminate internal, imaginative possibilities, shaping for the student a new creative agency 'which has peculiar reference to the life of the being possessing it'"[7] (Kilby).

"An awakening. That is how I can best describe what *Lit* was for me. Never before had a class explored texts so intimately. Never before had I been encouraged to interact with such dialogical engagement" (Milisavljevic). "A firm advocate of the power of texts for social and personal transformation," Dr. Wilson exposed us to texts that were "provocative and deeply moving" (Rothfels). Indeed, "students are encouraged to reflect on the connections between the texts as well as on the links to challenges faced in our world. Moreover, by fostering a creative environment, the course opens up a time and space for reflection on complex personal values and aspirations (What kind of person do I want to be? What kind of world do I want to live in? Do I contribute to achieving these ends?). This space is of great value to students in levels three and four,[8] as they contemplate specialized studies and future paths" (Dancey).

"The discussions in *Lit* caused me to question the texts in ways that I never had before, but also to question my life, and my position in the world in new ways" (Macdougall). "It was about opening our minds," for literary study "blurs the lines between old and new, between fiction and reality, between writer and reader, between ourselves and those around us. It connects us" (Mazer). Indeed, "a gradual infection subtly spreads through the class, perhaps reaching its most feverish pitch just following the mid-year break, when students appear almost drunk by the ideas and images that the course presents. For that is the great marvel of the selection of works. Somehow *Lit* consistently manages to smash through the designated space and time of the lecture period and become larger and louder. Suddenly, the texts studied transform into an archive of allusions and analogies, which are then so readily applicable to one's 'everyday' life. In this way, the course creates its own powerful discourse, whose effects are certainly pernicious, not always entering one's consciousness with permission, but invading and infiltrating, enlightening and elucidating" (Scott).

The last contribution in this section identifies some important consequences of being asked—in the context of the Arts and Science curriculum—to examine the often "complicated and messy" themes chronicled in world literature: "militarization, racism, the reach of law, gendered experiences, 'progress.'" This student reports that *Lit* provided "a welcome framework following the disenchanting view of the world that arose from courses such as first-year Inquiry and Environment. The purpose of those courses was to develop techniques of achieving awareness about our planet and its inhabitants; the purpose of *Lit*, in my view, was to face up to the things of which we had become aware, and work through what they meant, and what we ought to do with them. And it was right on time. 'Facing up,' as fostered by the course, was incomplete without also becoming familiar with the face we were turning to the world. Twice in the year we were asked to offer journal pieces to our peers, and many, if not most, of the submissions were intense and intimate. While navel-gazing is possibly the favoured Artsci vice, this order of considered, creative introspection was an academic endeavour. We had a responsibility to put ourselves into the picture of the world we were developing, and we had to be damn sure that our honest face showed up. And we still had to write papers and an exam; this was not an easy course, by academic or personal measures" (Kinch).

An Outline of the Course

Reading List

As the title indicates, Literature is not specifically an "English" course; the reading list includes texts originally written in a range of languages from ancient Greek to Latin, Italian, Spanish, English, German, and Russian. This means, of course, that we read a good number of the works in translation, since none of us has competence in all seven languages. While purists like to point to all that one is "missing" by reading in translation, the premise of *Lit* turns this commonplace on its head: look at all that one is missing by *not* reading in translation, by restricting oneself to works originally written in the language(s) one knows. Students generally welcome the wide range of literary works and the various "historical and social-scientific assumptions" such texts enable us to question (Lui). Class participants are often surprised both by the amount of reading they do in the course and by the "vigour and energy" with which they do it (Luyt).

The reading load is not light, especially given the expectation that students come to class prepared to enter into meaningful discussion about what they have read. One student writes of a classmate who "always seemed to want a lecture, wanted THE truth." She explains that "it is the freedom of the course that makes it frustrating to some and exhilarating to others. Blindfolded mountain climbing comes to mind" (Caryll). She mentions "the diversity of the reading list," and she identifies an "underlying giddiness" in the class, which speaks, I think, to the undeniably forbidding challenge of interpreting these texts in all their diversity. Such giddiness is born of "the process of facing and sometimes overcoming a lot of fear. Fear of being wrong, fear of the unknown, fear of the gap that as students we were encouraged/allowed/required to traverse." Confronted with great works of literature but not told, as in some ideal "Great Books" course, the truths they should be gleaning from these masterpieces, many students naturally experience some anxiety. But the response this particular student learned in and through the course, "dramatic" as it sounds, was to "have faith." Faith in the individual and collective ability truly "to *get* somewhere," as another student puts it, through engagement in "courageous, active reading" (Sandomierski).

The current reading list, in the order in which the works are studied, is as follows: Homer, *The Odyssey*; Margaret Atwood, "Significant Moments in the Life of My Mother," "The Sin Eater," "Loulou: or, the Domestic Life of the Language," "Bluebeard's Egg," "Spring Song of the Frogs"; Thomas King, "Trap Lines"; Homer, *The Iliad* (selections); Virgil, *The Aeneid* (selections); Irmtraud Morgner, "Shoes"; Christa Wolf, *Cassandra*; Dante, *Inferno*; Cervantes, *Don Quixote* (selections); Heinrich von Kleist, "The Marquise of O..."; Margot Schroeder, "I'm Doing Fine"; Mary Shelley, *Frankenstein*; Heinrich von Kleist, "Michael Kohlhaas"; Fedor Dostoevsky, *Crime and Punishment*; Franz Kafka, "The Metamorphosis"; Barbara Gowdy, "Disneyland"; Bertolt Brecht, *Life of Galileo*; Joy Kogawa, *Obasan*; Toni Morrison, *Beloved*; Gabriel García Márquez, *One Hundred Years of Solitude*. Over the years, there have been a few deletions from the original reading list, made very reluctantly, and only in order to accommodate a few additions—for instance, the Brecht, the Gowdy, and the Gabriel García Márquez. Recent students will likely find it hard to imagine the course without *Life of Galileo*, "Disneyland," and *One Hundred Years of Solitude*, for these are powerful texts, both on their own and in the context of the development of class discussion. It is therefore instructive to consider that the first student cited in the above paragraph, who speaks of *Lit* as an exhilarating experience, took the course before these particular works were added. This suggests that while the current required readings work remarkably well together, the syllabus can easily bear change. At the same time, the reading list *has* remained surprisingly stable, even if individual works are approached differently from year to year.

Although one of the required texts is the first volume of *The Norton Anthology of World Masterpieces*, students learn "to be wary of the term 'masterpiece'" and "to resist the dichotomy between a 'master' and minor work. A contemporary short story can be compared to the *Odyssey*, without contradiction" (Sandomierski). "The course helped to deconstruct the canon without jettisoning it. It showed us that we can come up with new interpretations, and that while these texts are not sacred, they are pretty damn good" (Mazer). "The course provides an opportunity to see connections between works of literature that are probably not often seen. It might seem unthinkable to read Atwood's *Bluebeard's Egg* and Dante's *Inferno* in one semester, but we do it and it works" (Rabinovitch). This accords with one of the basic principles underlying our approach to the study of literature, articulated by Northrop Frye (1912-91), the preeminent Canadian literary theorist and critic: "Creation includes criticism as a part of itself. . . . Critics have been deluded into thinking that their function is to judge works of art, but their judicial role does not go in this direction at all. They do not judge the writer, except incidentally: they work with the writer in judging the human condition."[9] Such critical work, moreover, is not accomplished by taking a book from the library, reading it in isolation, and then returning it to its proper place on the shelf. Once opened, these books, some decidedly canonical, others less so, stay open, as we read them in relation to one another and in relation to the myriad discourses that structure our lives.

Approach

Frye is the source of another of the key concepts that inform our work in *Lit*: "[This] made me say, a great many years ago, that the aim of education was to make people maladjusted, to destroy their notions that what society did made sense, and that they had only to conform to it to make sense of their own lives. . . . Continued study of literature and the arts brings us into an entirely new world, where creation and revelation have different meanings, where the experience of time and space is different. As its outlines take shape, our standards of reality and illusion get reversed. It is the illusions of literature that begin to seem real, and ordinary life, pervaded as it is with all the phony and lying myths that surround us, begins to look like the real hallucination, a parody of the genuine imaginative world."[10] Every work that we encounter in the course is powerfully subversive of conventional thinking. As I see it, the Arts and Science Programme facilitates the creation of a countercultural space, where it becomes possible to resist some of the dictates of the dominant culture and develop creative alternatives—nothing short of "new ways to live," to cite for a second time the German author Christa Wolf.[11] The Literature course participates in this, as the critical engagement of the class with such a rich collection of profoundly interrogative texts equips and inspires students to challenge "the way things are," using all their unsettling imaginative energy.

Indeed, energy—critical energy, creative power—abounds in *Lit*, where discussions are fuelled by dialogical vigour and the making of transformative connections. None of us reads any literary work in the same way, and a good deal of the class's energy is generated by the bringing together of individual perspectives and sometimes stunningly original insights. For instead of accepting the weary resignation that frequently characterizes attitudes toward the undergraduate classroom, in *Lit* there is every expectation of originality. As Timothy Findley says, in a statement to which students are introduced on the first day, "No reader needs to be convinced of the unique power of the book. No one who has opened the covers and stepped into the world contained within those pages can deny the wonder of linking your own imagination to the writer's imagination. What results is a world unlike any other—because its creation came, in part, from your own unique perceptions and images."[12] This explains in part why it has not been necessary to vary the reading list greatly from year to year; each time I teach the course, there is a new energy and a quite different trajectory.

"*Lit* is a learning process in which, little by little, each student discovers his or her own ability to provide insight into century-old texts. Suddenly, everyone sees, . . . everyone adding a little insight of their own, everyone learning from one another" (Jessup). "Most people get to enjoy a class once. I got to live through *Lit* twice. I'd like to be able to say that it was love of teaching, or the desire to inspire, or even pure monetary greed that pushed me to apply for a TAship in the course. But I would be lying. The simple reason was that I wanted to read those books again and, perhaps more importantly, to hear what a new crop of students would say about them." This contributor characterizes *Lit* in terms of "the community of readers and thinkers it created. And not just those whom you would expect to participate freely. I cannot count the number of times that I was positively amazed by a peer's comment or insight." Moreover, *Lit* "stays, it lingers, it surfaces. And while the course assembles one of the most challenging, diverse, and thoughtprovoking reading lists any undergraduate could hope to encounter, the real gift was in being brought together, to tease out the doubts, the ideas, and the images in our minds" (Goldenberg).

Since the role of the reader is considerable, and *how* one reads is arguably as important as *what* one reads, each different class's approach to the texts is bound to lead to fresh discovery. "Together, the class travels to a new place" (Neufeld). Given that "reading literature is relaxing, a pleasurable pastime," the same student acknowledges, "if asked about the benefit or value of literature, I once would have responded that reading provides an 'escape' from the world. However, after taking the course, this statement makes little sense to me." Her classmate also speaks of how she "came to understand the power of literature. Before *Lit*, I read differently. Books contained stories that were sometimes entertaining and sometimes had important things to say. But after the course, I saw literature as something that could change my way of thinking" (Matheson). "When I read, I now feel as though I am part of the writer's project. And when I talk to other people about books, I no longer feel that I am just talking to them about books. Rather I am talking to them about life" (Mazer).

A basic hermeneutic assumption in the course is that while the study of, say, the Homeric epics allows us to learn something about the ancient Greeks, it will undoubtedly teach us a good deal more about ourselves. Thus, *Lit* "encourages us to relate our personal experiences to the readings, and thereby eliminates the expectation that any given culture is being transmitted through contact with a work" (Matheson). The course is designed to allow students to explore their own variegated culture through an encounter with texts arising from a variety of social contexts. One of the key factors here—and perhaps the most valuable discovery for me—is the considerable diversity that exists even within the class. When I first meet the students at the beginning of term, I am now more aware than I used to be of significant differences in location, of the fact that we in the *Literature* class are in many ways coming from very different places.

The question this raises—"Just who are we and what are we doing together?"—is perhaps the central question underlying the teaching and learning process known as *Lit*, in and through which we do indeed, as the first student cited in the above paragraph attests, "travel to a new place," enjoying as we go a "sense of community that arises out of true participation and creativity" (Goldenberg).

Each year I find myself, a specialist in Comparative Literature, facing a class of exceptionally capable students, who are not, however, Literature majors, though some may be combining Arts and Science with a subject in the Humanities. In addition to notable divergence in scholarly direction and expertise, one finds religious, racial, ethnic, socio-economic, ideological, and sexual diversity. Altogether, there is a remarkable range of cultural and personal experience. Some degree of diversity exists in every classroom, of course, but it is often masked, on the part of both instructors and students, by false assumptions of homogeneity. I have had the privilege of teaching in the multidisciplinary Arts and Science Programme for ten years, and my experience of being caught off guard— disoriented or alienated (in the Brechtian sense), in the sense that I could not assume I knew who my students were—has been decisive. Triggered by the confrontation with students of diverse disciplinary allegiances, but not stopping there, this experience of disorientation has helped me to shed assumptions of familiarity in my other courses as well, to relinquish certain illusions of cultural conformity and cohesion, and to ask, as the protagonist of Christa Wolf's *Cassandra* is forced to, "How many realities [are] there in [this place] besides mine, which I had thought was the only one?"[13]

A bald expression of a conventionally dismissive attitude toward undergraduate education emerges in an interview conducted by journalist Jan Wong with well-known cultural commentator Margaret Visser, who taught at a Canadian university for eighteen years. Wong reports, "Bored with her job—she taught only undergraduates—she pitched herself to *Morningside*, the CBC's flagship morning radio show."[14] While I have never regarded undergraduate teaching as boring, my experience in the Literature course has nevertheless opened my eyes further to the extraordinary potential of this work. Arts and Science students, introduced to student-centred pedagogy in level one, somehow expect to encounter it throughout the Programme, even in an upper-level course with an enrollment of fifty or sixty. In *Lit*, this expectation is only partially addressed in our classroom meetings; the assignments also do much to create a community devoted to the process of inquiry. At the outset of the course, as I've suggested above, each of us—despite the close-knit nature of the Arts and Science community—has only a limited idea of where, exactly, the other participants in the class are coming from, but that is what opens up so much room for discovery. Because "we" who come together in the classroom are always linked to diverse positions, the first person plural is necessarily used with care, and to my mind one of the most rewarding challenges of teaching and learning in the "spirit of inquiry" (Chordiya) is to make this "we" ("we" who come together in the classroom) meaningful.

One student coined the term "we-vision" to express her sense of what binds such an adventurous and imaginative community of readers (Mulligan). The neologism plays on Adrienne Rich's term "re-vision," to which the class is introduced in one of the essays included in the coursepack. In "When We Dead Awaken: Writing as Re-Vision," the contemporary American writer defines "re-vision" as "the act of looking back, of seeing with fresh eyes, of entering an old text from a new critical direction," for "[u]ntil we can understand the assumptions in which we are drenched we cannot know ourselves."[15] The essay proposes an approach to literature that "would take the work first of all as a clue to how we live, how we have been living, how we have been led to imagine ourselves, how our language has trapped as well as liberated us, . . . and how we can begin to see and name—and therefore live—afresh." It is fair to say that all of the course requirements promote "re-vision," as students engage in a variety of eye-opening exercises. "The value of the course for students is directly proportional to their own engagement" (Dancey), and the assignments are designed to elicit such engagement. The final mark for the course includes 15% for class participation, which includes active listening as well as effective speaking, and is predicated on the understanding that all members of the class need to assume responsibility for the "collective journey" (Mulligan). Two major essays, each worth 25%, call for originality, careful textual analysis, critical insight, a well-developed argument, and good writing. Each student participates in two "Reflections" exercises (2.5% each), as described below, and in one group presentation (10%). There is a final examination (20%), which ensures that students do the kind of integrative work that is partly responsible, I think, for the underground feeling that *Lit* is something of a capstone course: "The Literature course is the quiet culmination of Arts and Science" (Kilby).

"Reflections" Exercise

The "Reflections" exercise, I confess, was not my idea, and at first there was no such component. In 1994-95, Karen Bakker, the wonderfully resourceful teaching assistant in *Lit* that year, suggested that we adapt for our own purposes an assignment used regularly in Dr. Hudspith's *Technology and Society* course. Adapt—shamelessly—we did, and the exercise has developed to the point where it is now a key component of *Lit*. The "Reflections" provide an opportunity for students to engage creatively with the course material—without the stress of a graded assignment—and to read and respond to the work of others in the class. Everyone who participates fully receives full marks. Participants are encouraged to put their critical and creative energies to work, and to give as much of themselves as possible. The reading of the work of others is as important as the actual writing of the short piece (two pages, double-spaced); the insights of their classmates allow students to connect more deeply with the course material, which comes together with new and unexpected meaning. After reading the "Reflections," I am often overwhelmed with a feeling of gratitude, as are the students, who find that the results of the exercise can be "quite dramatic. I feel I learned as much from reading the work of my classmates as I did from writing my own" (Goodwin). This is a particularly significant statement, given what the same student says about the value of writing his own piece: "I chose to reflect on a deeply personal issue. It was the most rewarding academic exercise I have ever undertaken. Knowing that my classmates would be reading my work put a different kind of pressure on me, one that encouraged me to put forth my best effort." He credits the "great deal of trust and respect" built up in the class for "the courage to write about an issue that meant so much to [him]," and he speaks of a "lasting end result," of having engaged with the course readings "in a way that [he] will not soon forget."

Some of the writing displays a disarming sense of humour: "Picture a student bursting out with laughter at the 'Reflection' of another. In the middle of class. That is what happens when you are given the opportunity to exchange in a warm and open atmosphere, with a deeply reflective professor and peers" (Munshi). Another student writes of how one of the challenges of *Lit* is to create such a welcoming atmosphere, "in order for all to be willing to express themselves. Can you imagine sixty artists at a round table exchanging their ideas on a given work? This is what the course hopes to attain" (Choi). The "Reflections" go a long way toward the goal of what this student identifies as "fostering the importance of individual voices without sacrificing the direction and continuity of the whole." In speaking "to the richness of human relations and interactions" (Mahajan), as the course as a whole essentially does, the "Reflections" help to focus "the quest for common themes," which "frequently integrates itself into out-of-class discussions" (Palmay). What the same student speaks of as "the opportunity to write in a less conventional fashion" has benefits for the in-class expression of creativity as well: "Every idea, however offbeat, is given due consideration and used as a building block to explore further avenues of thought. Even the quietest students find themselves wanting to contribute" (Sin Yan Too). In short, "not only is it interesting to read classmates' views on the literature, but this process leads to further cohesiveness, which only leads to more open, honest, and elucidating discussion" (Macdougall).

The writing is normally of a high quality, both because students know their peers will be reading what they write and because, freed of the often stifling expectations—real or imagined—that accompany traditional academic assignments, each participant begins to speak in her or his own voice. Suggested topics range from the challenge of reflecting "on parallels between any of the texts we have read and your own experience," to the opportunity to retell one of the stories from a different narrative perspective, to the simple invitation to reflect on any idea, problem or question raised by one or more of the works studied so far in the course. While some students offer very personal and intimate thoughts, others maintain a more scholarly tone, but virtually everyone makes interpretive connections that open up both the texts and people's lives to further critical engagement. Thus, a more meaningful "we," a community of scholars, is developed in part through a simple exercise, but one which the participants take very seriously. The effects of an assignment that makes up only a tiny fraction of the final grade (a total of 5%) are surprisingly far-reaching. The subsequent oral and written work stimulated by the exercise, which occurs midway through each term, provides abundant evidence of a widespread conviction that "words matter, people matter, and there is meaning everywhere" (Kinch).

Teaching Assistants

As I reflect on the evolution of *Lit*, I realize that much has remained constant in the objectives, requirements, methods, challenges, and achievements of the course. The reading list has been reshaped, but not dramatically so. Certain questions that preoccupied us in the early years have given way to other concerns, but an overwhelming number of central themes arising from the readings continue to intrigue, disturb, and reassure. The two most notable developments are the addition of the "Reflections" assignment and the introduction of teaching assistants. The first year I taught the course there was no TA. The second year I received marking assistance from a part-time TA, who would provide corrections and comments on the essays before giving them to me for grading. The third year, a full TAship allowed us to divide the sixty students into two groups for seminar presentations and occasional tutorials. We decided that the TA would not mark any of the written work, and this has been the practice ever since. Because *Lit* is a level three course, which students may take in their third or fourth year, it can become awkward, given the size and nature of the Arts and Science community, for TAs, themselves fourth-year students, to undertake the marking of the written work. Moreover, I find it necessary to assume this responsibility myself, for if I did not read the papers of the entire class, I would not be attending to the full range and expression of students' voices as they develop. Not only would I be missing some remarkably energizing reading, but I would surely be a less effective teacher.

Each year, the TAs have been subtly but powerfully influential in determining the shape of the course. They have assumed responsiblity for facilitating the classes in which students offer small group presentations, and they grade this work. They have also assisted me in refining the "Reflections" exercise. They help students improve their writing; they run occasional tutorials; and they organize events outside the classroom. For a number of years there was a single TA, but 1998-99 ushered in a more flexible job sharing, and the course has benefited from new kinds of teamwork. The innovative power of the TAs keeps us on the move, and helps ensure that each year really is unique. The role of the TA in *Lit* is thus significantly different from what it would be in most comparable courses in other university departments and programmes, where the marking of written work is normally one of the teaching assistant's primary responsibilities. In *Lit*, the TAs are free to enliven other aspects of our proceedings. Because of the nature of the Arts and Science community, the TAs know the students in the class more intimately than would be the case in courses elsewhere in the University. Like any community, to be sure, the Artsci culture is not ideal, and there are certain drawbacks and tensions with which one has to contend. But here too—in the fostering of a healthy academic community—the TAs have an important role to play, and as the course develops, I generally find I can count on a good deal of "homework" being done, without even having to assign it: "At the time, I lived with five other students who were also taking the class. We would have in-depth, enthralling talks about the books we were reading. These conversations were often sparked by a topic touched upon in class that week, and sometimes the topics were very contentious!" (Matheson).

Conclusion

It would be a massive undertaking to summarize the content of the *Lit* class discussions. A mere listing of the perennial themes would not make for very compelling reading, and a useful account of these themes, even if I were to leave aside the more unexpected topics that arise in any given year, would require more space than has been allotted in the present volume. So too would any sustained attempt to address the theoretical considerations that inform our approach to literary study. What I offer instead are further comments from former students, which not only help to fill in the picture I have sketched above, but also suggest something of the lasting effects of the course. I asked contributors to reflect on the significance of the Literature course in their lives, now that they have graduated: where have they have taken *Lit* and where has it taken them? At the end of the last class in the 2001-02 academic year, which had been devoted to the pooling of our resources, in the form of each participant articulating something of what she or he had learned in the course, a student remarked to me how reassuring it would be if students, on the first day of class, could be given a sense of this—could be informed as to just how much they would gain in and through our course of literary study. His clearly preposterous idea (which he acknowledged as such) speaks to the initially disconcerting experience in *Lit* of being on a journey with no clear destination in sight. Indeed, I as the guide am never entirely sure of where we will end up; I often wonder where this journey will take us. But like the student cited in the second paragraph of the above outline of the course, I too have learned to "have faith": faith in the community of readers with whom it is my privilege to "sally forth," like the two main characters in Cervantes' *Don Quixote*, sometimes to descend into the depths of hell, like the two main characters in Dante's *Inferno*, but always ultimately to reach those magical places where we rediscover, as Toni Morrison's *Beloved* puts it, "what language was made for."[16]

Where Have I Taken "Lit" and Where Has "Lit" Taken Me? Further Comments from the Students

"Discussions and experiences from that time continue to resonate. The essays I wrote for *Lit* I consider my best work in university. I received detailed and sensitive feedback, which helped me to clarify my ideas and refine my writing. These strengthened analytical and writing skills carried over into my Master's studies and, now, into the policy environment in which I work" (Dancey). "The course is structured in a way that facilitates dialogue; it promotes idea exchange rather than idea absorption. Personally, this 'obligation to contribute' taught me a lot. It taught me to take a position and defend it, to engage in thoughtful debate to achieve a higher level of understanding, and to read with a 'critical eye.' I used these skills extensively in business school, and continue to do so" (Ghai). "The class inspired me to restructure the way in which I conduct my research, forcing me to think about new ways in which texts may be linked across disciplines, and giving me a framework that allows important commonalities across differences to be seen" (Magnet). "While my classmates were discussing geo-political realities, all I could think of were the words from Brecht's *Life of Galileo*: 'Unhappy the land where heroes are needed.'[17] To me, this phrase provided the best summary of the situation, in a succinct way that no political analysis could match" (Rabinovitch).

"The course taught me to think differently about myself, my choices, and my surroundings. In a field like medicine, it is important to step back and question your own (inter)actions" (Davis). "Literature is a type of 'experiential education,' and the ideas of the course are foundational to my peace activism and current visions of a just society" (Curran). "When the terms terrorism and security and unity moved into monolithic currency, Christa Wolf and Barbara Gowdy were right there on my shelf" (Kinch). Many students speak of the course as "a true opening up" (Poysa), both of questions, in "its capacity to unsettle" (Rothfels), and of answers: "The meaning that I obtained from reading and discussing the literary works answered life questions that no philosophy course has ever been able to touch" (Colman). Indeed, when they enroll in *Lit*, students are often "unsure of [their] direction" (Tam), and the course assists them not only in working through decisions about what career they will pursue, but more generally in "evaluating and transforming" the lives that they lead (Wagg). "My final paper for the course was one of the most difficult things I have ever written. And one of the most fruitful: for my well-being, my sanity, and my outlook on life" (Oberndorfer).

"I think I learned more from my time in *Lit* than from any other course. I am a more creative, more curious, and more critical student as a result of the class. Those skills I take with me, useful not only in academia, but in all other areas of my life" (Murdock). "The course transformed both the way I read and the way I interpret life's events. The dialogical spoke to me as the lifeblood of human relations, and the course sent me in the direction of listening more to others, building upon others' ideas, interacting with others to truly create something" (Sandomierski). "The class has given me a toolbox of words that I use across disciplines and even outside of my studies here in law school. These words include: voice, narrative, contending, re-vision, memory, meaning, silence, naming. Of course I knew these words before, but after *Lit*, they became a precious part of my vocabulary. The new ideas connected to these words each have a story behind them. The course manages to show that it is possible to read a book and study a book at the same time, and that, properly negotiated, this is not a concussion between opposites, but a mutual reinforcement. Where has *Lit* taken me? I don't know . . . so many forces determine destiny. But what I do know is this: I have taken *it* everywhere" (Li).

Notes

1. Students' comments, edited where necessary and with their permission, are taken from letters received from the following individuals: Brianna Caryll, Melody Chen, Matthew Choi, Deepa Chordiya, Sarah Colman, Andrew Curran, Evelyn Dancey, Melinda Davis, Monika Dutt, Azim Essaji, Stephen Fertuck, Sacha Ghai, André Goldenberg, David Goodwin, Louise Jessup, Michael Kilby, Kathy Kinch, Jacob Letkemann, Ying Ying Li, Theresa Liu, Andrew Lui, Russell Luyt, Jocelyn Macdougall, David Mackenzie, Shoshana Magnet, Sharmi Mahajan, Clara Matheson, Alex Mazer, Dan Milisavljevic, Kate Mulligan, Alpna Munshi, Karen Murdock, Robin Neufeld, Erica Oberndorfer, Christine Palmay, Kate Parizeau, Sven Poysa, Nina Rabinovitch, Carl Rothfels, David Sandomierski, Laurence Scott, Karen Shin, Debbie Sin Yan Too, Eric Tam, Allison Wagg.
2. Homer, *The Odyssey*, trans., Robert Fitzgerald, *The Norton Anthology of World Masterpieces*, gen. ed., Sarah Lawall, 7th ed., vol. 1 (New York: Norton, 1999), 233; bk. 3, l. 120.
3. This statement appears annually in the *McMaster University Undergraduate Calendar*.
4. Dr. Gary Warner, current Director of the Arts and Science Programme, in e-mail correspondence with the author, 11 June 2002.
5. Christa Wolf, "Speaking of Büchner," *The Author's Dimension: Selected Essays*, ed., Alexander Stephan, trans., Jan van Heurck (New York: Farrar, Straus and Giroux, 1993), 185.
6. Margaret Atwood, "Significant Moments in the Life of My Mother," *Bluebeard's Egg* (Toronto: McClelland and Stewart-Bantam, 1983), 8.
7. A.N. Whitehead, qtd. in the *McMaster University Undergraduate Calendar* to describe the philosophy of the Arts and Science Programme.
8. Although it is a level-three course, the Arts and Science Literature course, typically also includes a good number of fourth-year students, whose timetables made it necessary to defer enrollment in *Lit*.

9. Northrop Frye, *The Double Vision* (Toronto: University of Toronto Press, 1991), 38.

10. Northrop Frye, "The View from Here," *Myth and Metaphor: Selected Essays, 1974-1988*, ed., Robert D. Denham (Charlottesville and London: University Press of Virginia, 1990), 77-78.

11. Christa Wolf, "In Touch," trans., Jeanette Clausen, *German Feminism: Readings in Politics and Literature*, ed., Edith Hoshino Altbach et al. (Albany: State University of New York Press, 1984), 168.

12. Timothy Findley, "Turning Down the Volume," *Queen's Quarterly* 100 (1993): 815.

13. Christa Wolf, *Cassandra: A Novel and Four Essays*, trans., Jan van Heurck (New York: Farrar, Straus and Giroux, 1984), 20.

14. Jan Wong, "Margaret Visser's Taste for the Ordinary," Interview, *Globe and Mail* 13 Jan. 2001, R4.

15. Adrienne Rich, "When We Dead Awaken: Writing as Re-Vision," *On Lies, Secrets, and Silence: Selected Prose 1966-1978* (New York: Norton, 1979), 35.

16. Toni Morrison, *Beloved* (New York: Knopf and Random House, 1987), 252.

17. Bertolt Brecht, *Life of Galileo*, trans., John Willett (New York: Arcade, 1994), 98.

9   Technology and Society

Bob Hudspith

Editors' preface

With a few exceptions this course has been taught over the years by members of the Faculty of Engineering. For the first three years, it was taught by a member of the Department of Materials Science and Engineering (David Embury). Subsequently, it was taught, except for a few years when on leave, by the author of this chapter, who is currently the Director of the Engineering and Society Programme. Professor Embury's major objectives were to have students learn something of the way principles of technology, based on scientific knowledge, are used to solve technical problems, and to have them explore the effects of our technological environment (devices, systems, and other products of technology) on the way we live in society. Although these matters continue to be reflected in the course as taught by Professor Hudspith, it will be apparent from this chapter that other features of the relation of technology to society have taken centre stage.

The planners of the Arts and Science Programme believed that a full-year course on the place of technology in society was warranted by the growing importance of technology in our lives. They said of the aims of this course that it should provide "nonspecialists the opportunity to examine the ways of technology, the motivations behind technological development, and the impact of technology on the conditions and quality of life."[1]

In the early years of the Programme, a single, full-year course entitled "Technology and Society" was offered. Later, on my recommendation, this course was replaced by two half-year courses with the titles: "The Culture of Technology" and "The Social Control of Technology." This enabled students in the Arts and Science Programme to take the first course together with engineering students who are enrolled in McMaster's five-year degree programme, Engineering and Society. I thought this would be a desirable arrangement because the course objectives were entirely appropriate to the two groups, the differences in backgrounds of students in the two programs would enliven discussions, and combining the groups would make efficient use of limited teaching resources. My expectation of gains from the mix of students was fulfilled over the many years the course was conducted in this way.

In this chapter, I discuss the aims and content of these courses as well as my approach to teaching.[2] Because the content reflects my own perspective on the relationship between technology and society, I begin with a summary of that perspective. Although I have some strongly-held views on this matter, and presented them rather fully in these courses, it is important to say at the outset that I did not teach these views as truths to be passively received by the students. I designed the courses in a way that was intended to encourage students to react critically to my views, to consider alternative views, and to develop their own positions on the place of technology in our society.

Framework for the Courses on Technology and Society

I take a broad view of the place of technology in our culture, and that view strongly influenced the way I taught the courses. Our Western culture is technological, not just because of the abundance of technological devices and the infrastructure in our environment, but because our culture is imbued with a deep faith in the value of technical ways of doing things. Ellul's concept of "la technique" captures, in my view, the essence of that faith. By "technique" Ellul means "the totality of methods rationally arrived at and having absolute efficiency (for a given stage of development) in every field of human activity."[3] The development of technique proceeds by isolating a practice or task from its context in society or in one's life as a whole in order to find "the one best way" of performing it. The search for, and the application of, techniques affect every area of life. There are techniques to raise children, to plant gardens, to manage stress, to make friends, to teach, and to worship. Specific techniques come in many varieties, but the overarching commitment to the rational analysis of tasks in order to find the most efficient way to carry them out leads Ellul to speak of "la technique" as the defining characteristic of our age. Technique in this sense is found in all areas of life, including business, education, and religious belief. This is not to suggest that there have not always been techniques for accomplishing tasks, but in the past they were more closely connected to a local culture. "La technique" is a new phenomenon because of its purpose, which is to obtain the most efficient result by employing a decontextualized rationality. For example, Janice Gross Stein, in her book *The Cult of Efficiency*, argues that the quest for the "one best system" in public education has resulted in the adoption of a "factory model [where] the organization—if not the content—. . . was standardized , homogenized, and delivered as a mass market public good."[4] Other writers who also take a broad view of technology as pervasive include Ursula Franklin,[5] Kenneth Boulding,[6] and Arnold Pacey.[7]

The technological mind-set is pervasive in our culture, and the devices, systems, and products that it generates not only reflect that mind-set, but in subtle ways reinforce it. Consider, for example, the simple technology in classrooms with rows of fixed desks and a raised platform— perhaps a podium—for the instructor. The arrangement reflects a view of learning as transmission from the learned to the not so learned, but it also reinforces that concept and shapes the structure of the students' everyday experience with classroom learning.

According to Thomas Hughes, existing systems of technology also exhibit momentum.[8] They set the conditions for the success of future technological development. For example, the physical infrastructure that has developed to support the use of the automobile, together with a system of laws and regulations, constrains the alternatives for change to alternative fuels or means of travel. To consider another example, a large electrical power distribution network requires centralized management and authority to operate the system and to make decisions on the allocation and pricing of power. Once in place, that authority would have interests in the preservation of a centralized system for the production and distribution of power as against more decentralized alternatives.

There is now quite an extensive literature on the biasing effect of the technologies we have already created on the technologies of the future and on the political and social implications of technology.[9] I assigned readings in this literature because it deals with a central issue about the role of technology in society. It argues against the view that technologies are neutral and contribute to the public good or detract from it depending only on our choice as to how we use the devices, systems, and products that our technological culture makes available. It argues for the contrary view that technologies and technological ways of thinking play a powerful role in shaping how society is organized, influencing what we value, and even what we do with our lives. In other words, it argues that technologies have built-in characteristics that predispose us towards certain modes of operating. Exploring the biasing nature of technology in our society was one of the central objectives of both the first and second courses.

The deep and pervasive influence on our culture of material technology, and perhaps more important, of technologically shaped values and ways of thinking, raises a fundamental question: Can a technological culture steer the development of technology, and make it serve different sets of values? To answer no is to view technology as an autonomous determiner of cultural development rather than a facet of culture that can be controlled by other cultural values and agents. Although an examination of ways in which society seeks to steer technological development is the subject of the second course, "The Social Control of Technology," I presented for critical discussion one framework for thinking about the nature of technological determination in the first course, "The Culture of Technology."

To explore the question of the degree to which technology determines the development of culture one needs a model—a conception of culture. I relied heavily on the model of culture developed by Vanderburg in his book, *The Growth of Minds and Cultures*.[10] In this work, culture is defined as "the basis on which members of a society interpret their experience and structure their relationships with one another, their environment, their past, and their future (including tools, techniques, customs beliefs, institutions, laws, morals, religion, art, etc.) into a coherent way of life."[11] Vanderburg builds up his model by first considering how we as individuals grow and develop in a cultural context, how we learn to interpret our present experience based on past experience, and how we develop a "mental map" of reality. This understanding of culture as a mediation, or a lens through which we experience reality as individuals, is extended to explain how societies develop a coherent way of life in a culture. Cultural beliefs, described as a set of "myths," are the "truths" about life we believe to be totally self-evident and backed by experience. These assumptions about life include what we commonly call values, and they exist in a hierarchy, with some of them so fundamental that they become our "sacreds," without which life would be unthinkable. According to this understanding of culture, science, technology, economy, social structures, political and legal organizations, morality, religion, are not independent components but rather are related dimensions of our culture.[12] To say that technology affects our ways of thinking and our values, is to suggest that it has become one of our cultural sacreds and is no longer just a dimension of culture.

But can the myths and sacreds of our society be brought into the light, judged critically, and changed? To explore this question I present Ellul's seemingly contradictory view that although technology has an autonomous character we can work to oppose the consequences of this. To understand how Ellul can paint a deterministic picture of the technological system and yet hold out hope for social influence or control, requires an understanding of the use of dialectics in Ellul's thought. Ellul argues that we need to live in the dialectical tension between necessity (living as a cultural creature) and freedom (living with dignity and self-giving love). When applied to the role of technology in our lives, Ellul's view is that we should recognize that "technique" has become a sacred in our lives. In light of this we need to find ways to live that allow us to use fully and creatively our technical means without allowing them to remain as sacreds. I discussed other examples in which we are required to live in the tension of two seeming opposites: individuality and community, freedom and form, giving and receiving. Arnold Pacey's discussion of dialectics in the last four chapters of his book, *The Culture of Technology*,[13] adds to the picture by describing the positive impacts of technology. He discusses the need to be both iconoclastic and creative in our technology practices.

I presented to students for comparison with other views and for critical discussion my conclusion on the question of whether technology is an autonomous determiner of cultural development. I said that the answer is both yes and no. I take the position that if we recognize that our culture has become technicized, and if we think of technology as a means and not an end and de-throne technology as a sacred, then we can begin to develop a culture that is more holistic, where mystery is accepted and where place and context are important. But to the extent that we continue to approach life as a series of problems to be solved, where efficiency is a fundamental value, and where we seek "the one best way," we will not be able to control technology in any significant way.

In the second course, "The Social Control of Technology," the range of contemporary approaches to the steering and regulation of technological development are critically assessed.

From one perspective, it is clear that the market, the state, and the experts play a dominant role in the control of technology; it is also clear, however, that this control is heavily dependent on both the political structure and the nature of technology. Efforts to broaden the social responsibility of professionals and to open up decision making to public participation also indicate that the value-laden nature of technology is beginning to be recognized; there is now a concerted effort to shift the control of technology into the hands of the people whose lives are being affected by that technology.

While I think that it is vital to understand these mechanisms of control and to work toward reforming them so that one can develop technologies that are more responsive to the needs and values of people, I nevertheless raised the darker possibility that these reforms might be like rearranging the deck chairs on the Titanic. I wanted the students to grapple with the proposition that if, as I argued in these courses, a "technicized" mind-set has become deeply embedded in our culture, then the steering of technology to better serve human values will require fundamental cultural change. Arguably, the attempt to find the most efficient solutions for each narrowly considered objective or problem without regard for the way that solution affects the entire fabric of our social and natural environments may lie at the heart of our failure to achieve a sustainable, equitable, and satisfying way of life in society as a whole. Responses to those failures can be seen in the rise of such movements as "deep ecology," environmentalism, some expressions of feminism that stress holistic ways of knowing, and the growth of alternative communities. A study of what motivates these movements, how they work, and what they achieve, was an important part of this second course. Through a study of these movements much can be learned about the consequences of too great a reliance on the technological mind-set, and about possible avenues for cultural change.

Objectives

My overall objectives for both courses were to help students develop a deeper understanding of the nature of technology and of technological change in our society, and to further their skills in self-directed learning and inquiry. Although the courses engaged the students in some quite abstract philosophical issues, I encouraged them to reflect on their everyday experiences with the products of technology, technicized ways of doing things, and the beliefs and values associated with a culture of technology. I asked them to get started on what I hope will be an on-going interest in formulating their own position on the meaning of technology in our society and on the ways in which we as citizens can take part in making technology a better servant of our social goals. I emphasized self-directed learning and inquiry because I believe that such skills are essential ingredients for continual learning beyond the confines of courses and programmes.

In addition to common objectives, each course had its own focus. "The Culture of Technology" developed a broad conception of the place of technology in our culture and applied it to an analysis of how technicized ways of thinking, as well as the products of technology, affect our lives. "The Social Control of Technology" focused on existing and potential avenues for influencing the development and use of technologies by society, especially by the public.

Approach

I spent a lot of time thinking about and experimenting with ways of teaching these courses. The major tension has been to achieve a good balance between "teacher-directedness" and "student-directedness." I believe it is my responsibility to present a framework for thinking about the relationship of technology to society and culture, and to raise key questions about that relationship. But I also believe it important for students to develop and exercise the skills of critical thinking. I attempted to design an environment for learning that fosters self-directed learning and provides opportunities for students to learn from each other and to develop their skills in expressing their own ideas, both orally and in their written work. I used a combination of full-class meetings and seminars with groups of nine to twelve students in order to allow for a mix of teacher- and student-directed learning activities.

I presented my own framework, as well as introducing alternative frameworks, in meetings with the full class. Students prepared for these meetings through assigned readings. A typical class might be taken up with a short lecture, a small group discussion of issues that I had selected, and a full-class discussion. Because I wanted to engage students in the exploration of issues and to maintain a high level of interaction among all participants, I rarely lectured for a full hour. These sessions also afforded opportunities for guest speakers and group presentations. Seminar groups of nine to twelve students, that foster student-directed learning, were arranged in parallel with these full-class sessions. I say more later about the conduct of the seminars.

Contributing to the tension between teacher-directed and student-directed learning is the fact that students have very different preferences for the mix between teacher-structured activities and opportunities to follow their own interests in deciding what is worth learning and thinking about. Some students prefer the structure of assigned readings each week, while others find it frustrating to be required to spend time on matters of less interest while not being able to follow up on matters of greater interest. Although I always provided opportunities for students to choose among a set of issues that they wish to explore in more depth, I found that some prefer, and can use effectively, even greater freedom. Recently, I allowed the option of a learning portfolio in which they defined and pursued their own interests within the broad range of material that they encountered in lectures, discussions, and seminars.

The last comment I wish to make about my approach is that I experimented continually with new ways to meet my objectives. In addition to assessing their achievements, I tried to assess the ways in which students respond to the various parts of the course and I used this information to modify assignments and formats in an attempt to keep these courses challenging and stimulating. In what follows I discuss under several headings examples of the learning activities I have tried.

Full-Class Sessions

Full-class sessions were used primarily to introduce ideas and concepts, to discuss readings, and to provide a framework for seminars and group projects. To keep the learning active, I tried to include some small-group work in each session. In the first-term course, "The Culture of Technology," which included both Arts and Science and Engineering and Society students, small groups were formed with participants from each programme in order to take advantage of a diversity of backgrounds and outlooks.

I used various tactics to try to engage students actively in their learning. For example, in order to engage the students in a debate about the extent to which the ways we use technologies are set by (or dictated by) the built-in characteristics of the devices themselves, or on the other hand, are entirely a matter left to users who decide freely on how a device is to be employed, I gave a live demonstration of the outlandish, and messy, use of a chain saw to cut a pound of butter. The obvious point that the characteristics of a device set limits on how it will be used was, of course, just a starting point for examining in small groups the issue of neutrality versus bias. We certainly can freely choose to use a chain saw in this way, but it is built to make possible the rapid felling and cutting of trees, and people usually do with machines what they were built to make possible.

To take this one step further, and to engage the students in an examination of cultural practices embedded in technological devices, I have shown a video of a Canadian University Services Overseas (CUSO) water project in Togo and then asked them to prepare in small groups a debate on the resolution: "the Togo water project is an example of good development assistance." The video presents this project in development assistance as a highly successful one, but there are troubling aspects. It is clear that as the CUSO team guides the village in setting up an organization to utilize and maintain the pump, they are promoting changes in the village mores in the direction of such Western values as gender equality, democratic decision making, and efficiency. The debate and class discussion that ensued brought out the intimate connection between transferring technology and transferring cultural practices. It raised difficult issues about what constitutes good development assistance in the context of technology transfer, and showed the intimate connection between technological solutions and cultural values.

Reading Assignments and Reflections

The literature on technology and society is growing rapidly, and I made available to students a wide selection of shorter articles (rarely more than 20 pages) from this literature, collected in the form of a so-called courseware book, which they purchase from the bookstore. In the course, "The Culture of Technology," I included two short books as required texts.[14] Weekly readings were assigned paralleling the subjects of the lectures.

I asked students to respond, in writing, in various ways to their reading assignments. Sometimes I asked them to respond to a question which I posed, or to one which they posed. Sometimes I asked them to write a reflection on an article from the courseware book or on a topic we had discussed in class. I required that the written assignments be submitted before the relevant class meetings, and I found that this requirement led to more informed and more searching discussions in class.

Learning Portfolios

There always were students who found the assigned responses to readings and even the reflections to be restrictive, and who preferred a more open-ended way of responding to the ideas and issues in the courses. Some years ago I decided to allow students to make a choice between responding via weekly assignments and reflections or preparing what has been called a learning portfolio.

This option allowed for a wider choice in both content and format. The writing did not need to be confined to the readings; the students could comment on, or critique, what they were learning in the seminars or in the full-class sessions. There were a few minimum requirements: they were to include a critical analysis of two of the longer readings, a critical reflection of at least one other reading, and a final entry that was equivalent to the integrative assignment described below. The guideline on length was about 6000 words (equal to what the students who were writing assignments and reflections were doing), but few students kept to this limit.

Portfolios were collected and evaluated twice; the first submission was during the mid three weeks of the course and the final submission was at the end. Students submitted a blank cassette tape so that I could record my comments and suggestions. About one third of the class chose this option. Over 95% of the students indicated they would choose the same way if they had to do it again. For those who chose not to do portfolios, the desire for more constant feedback and the need for the discipline of weekly assignments were given as the chief reasons.

On the whole, the portfolios were very well done. Some prepared a diary or journal with regular entries. A couple designed a journal with articles, columns, and letters to the editor. A few even wrote a short story or a play as their integrative entry.

Seminars

Small group, student-led seminars always played an important part in each of these courses in encouraging students to learn from each other. I found that these very capable students enjoy the opportunity to teach their fellow students, to express their views, and to lead discussions. I adopted the practice of requiring the students to prepare and make available some written material to each of the other members of the seminar one day in advance of the seminar. This material must be read before the seminar meeting in which it is presented. During the seminar, presenters were asked to use half of their total time of approximately 45 minutes to present new material which extends the written material in some way. Some designed a game or a simulation or designed an exercise for the group to carry out. The remaining half of the allotted time was used by the presenter to pose questions for discussion, to answer questions, and to promote discussion. The last five minutes of the seminar were set aside for all the other members to complete an evaluation of the written material and the seminar session.

In the first course, "The Culture of Technology," each seminar group was assigned a technology (e.g., transportation, health care, communication, education, housework, parenting, etc.) for analysis. The first meeting of the seminar was devoted to identifying the issues and questions to be treated. In some cases the issues and questions addressed had as much to do with the nature of our technological culture as with the specific technology. At the end of this first session, each student had chosen a topic and the topics were put in a sequence, and a complete schedule for the seminars was established. Seminars concerned with general issues and questions about the nature of our technological culture were placed later in the schedule, when the students were better prepared for them. In the second course, The Social Control of Technology, the seminar topics were on specific modes of control, or attempted control, or more general issues about the avenues and obstacles to social control of the development and use of technologies. To help the students identify topics for their own seminars I provided a wide range of possibilities and suggested questions that might be raised about them. The schedule for seminar topics was created to parallel the progress of the lectures and other group presentations.

I experimented with the kinds of guidelines I gave students about the scope and purpose of their seminars. For years I asked them to develop and defend a provocative position on an issue related to their topic. Recently I changed the guidelines and asked them to prepare a proposal for an inquiry into their topic. This required them to formulate a central question, to try to anticipate alternative findings, and to make a beginning on carrying out research and analysis on at least one avenue of investigation relevant to their central question. Although all of the students in this course had a previous year-long experience with inquiry in the Arts and Science Programme, they needed to be reminded of the elements of inquiry and how an inquiry proposal differs from a position paper, or other attempts to present opinions or conclusions on an issue.[15] Despite some objections from students to the constraints imposed by the requirement to formulate an inquiry proposal, I believe that the emphasis on how to go about understanding an issue through research and analysis is at least as valuable as the opportunity to exercise their talents in expressing their views in a position paper.

Group Projects

Yet another way to foster active learning and to encourage students to learn from each other is to have small groups undertake projects that eventuate in their conducting a class in which they use their findings to teach their fellow students. I used this approach in the "Social Control of Technology" course. Groups of four or five students were formed based on student interests in the various topics which were suggested early in the term. The presentations were scheduled so that they parallelled the progress of the course. Although this meant that the first group to present had only two weeks to prepare, my experience shows that this is sufficient for these capable students, and that even when more time is available it is rare that more than two weeks is spent in preparation.

I asked the groups to prepare a two-page handout summarizing the main points and providing a list of references and further readings. The starting points for the group presentations were the issues being dealt with in lectures, class discussions, and seminars. Many students showed an interest in examining alternatives to our technologically shaped ways of doing things in such areas as education, health care, student housing, and agriculture. Because such projects required them to characterize the mainstream approach as well as to explore alternatives rooted in a different set of beliefs, they made for lively and controversial sessions. For example, the merits of such alternative medical practices as the home delivery of an infant using a midwife versus hospital delivery using a highly professionalized team raised broad issues about the tradeoffs between retaining a measure of individual control and independence, on the one hand, and the gains associated with the power of advanced technologies on the other.

These students required little encouragement to think creatively about how to lead their sessions. They adopted a variety of approaches, including role playing, dramatizations, participatory exercises, and case studies. One group undertook to plan and carry out a conference with public participation aimed at achieving a consensus on a proposal for public policy for waste disposal in the local community.[16]

Integrative Assignment

At the end of each of these courses I asked all students to carry out an assignment designed to lead them to a review and integration of what they had learned about the role of technology in our culture, or about the ways in which society seeks to control the development of technology. This assignment, which required writing a paper of about 1000 words, was a substitute for any other form of final exam. I experimented with various ways of defining the task for this paper. For example, I once asked them to write a letter to the editor in response to an article by Langdon

Winner on technological determinism.[17] At other times I asked for a paper articulating their own perspective on technology and its relationship to society and culture, with reference to the concepts and examples that had been explored in the course. I made it clear that they were expected to place their own views in the context of an assessment of alternative views.

What the Students Took Away From These Courses

In this concluding section I comment on what I believe students gleaned from the two courses. My comments are based on what students wrote on end-of-term course evaluations. While there were always criticisms and suggestions for improvements, it is clear that evaluations were on the whole positive and indicated that the full-year examination of technology and society had been meaningful in several ways.

The material in these courses caught most students by surprise. Those who were enamored by the latest high-tech devices expected an exploration of how technology might save the world. Those who were nervous about technology because they felt intimidated by its complexity thought that the course might be over their heads. Those who were convinced that technology was destroying the planet expected a recitation of a view of which they were already convinced. When they discovered something of the way technological values generate not only devices, products, and systems, but also ways of doing things in our culture, they began to think more deeply about the place of technology in our society and in their lives.

Many students talked about having their eyes opened; they felt able to ask new questions about the impacts of a technological culture on their lives. When a student commented that the course was constantly "shattering his belief in progress and Western culture" I took it as a compliment. My use of reflections and other assignments that asked students to consider theoretical claims in terms of their own experience, no doubt fostered their appreciation of the relevance of the issues and concepts in this course to their own lives.

One of the more important intellectual discoveries many students made as a result of this third-year course was the ability to see connections among the courses in the programme. For the first two years they tended to think of their courses as separate and unrelated undertakings. The cross-disciplinary (or, more accurately, non-disciplinary) nature of the technology and society courses, together with such other issue-based inquiry courses as the one on the media (p.109), or on the environment, led them to apply things they were learning in one course to other courses. This was most obviously true for the skills of critical thinking, formulating inquiry proposals, carrying out the many phases of research, making presentations, leading seminars, and, of course, writing. It was also true, however, at the more substantive level of concepts, and I believe that asking students for reflections, and for an integrative final paper, contributed to this development, which many students found exciting and enlightening.

Last, and perhaps most important, I observed that many students took away with them a realization that they could contribute to the shaping of the world around them. I think this has become increasingly the case as my experience in teaching these courses grew. In earlier editions of the course, some expressed bewilderment with the complexity of the technology-society relationship. But more recently I observed, in large part through their final integrative paper, that many students went through a three-stage process: first they saw that technology was more than machines; then they began to feel that technology was in total control of the future of society and there was little that they could do as individuals to change that; and then in the end they came to believe that there were things that could be done, even if the doing required some fundamental cultural changes. One student summed it up by saying that she felt now that she could be "an informed and active citizen," and was excited about that.

Notes

1. "Revised Outline: A New Baccalaureate Degree Programme in Arts and Science" (Report of the Planning Council chaired by H.M. Jenkins to the Senate, McMaster University, May 1980), 14.
2. Since I have limited my description of these courses to the period 1986-2001, I have used the past-tense when describing what was taught and how it was taught. The courses continue to evolve.
3. Jacques Ellul, *The Technological Society*, trans. John Wilkinson (New York: Vintage Press, 1964), xxv.
4. Janice Gross Stein, *The Cult of Efficiency* (Toronto: House of Anansi Press, 2000), 95.
5. Ursula Franklin , *The Real World of Technology* (Toronto: House of Anansi Press, 1990).
6. Kenneth E. Boulding, "Technology and the Changing Social Order" in David Popenoe, ed., *The Urban Industrial Frontier* (New Brunswick, N.J.: Rutgers University Press, 1969).
7. Arnold Pacey, *The Culture of Technology* (Cambridge, Mass.:The MIT Press, 1983).

8. Thomas P. Hughes, "The Evolution of Large Technological Systems", in E. Wiebe et. al., eds., *The Social Construction of Technological Systems* (Cambridge, Mass.:The MIT Press, 1987).

9. See for example, Albert Borgmann, *Technology and the Character of Contemporary Life: A Philosophical Inquiry* (Chicago: University of Chicago Press, 1984), Richard E. Sclove, *Democracy and Technology* (New York: The Guilford Press, 1995), and LangdonWinner, *The Whale and the Reactor* (Chicago: The University of Chicago Press, 1986).

10. Willem H. Vanderburg, *Growth of Minds and Cultures* (Toronto: University of Toronto Press, 1985). Vanderburg spent four years studying under Ellul in the mid 70s.

11. Ibid., xxiii.

12. Ibid., 270-278.

13. Pacey, *The Culture of Technology*, Chaps. 6-9.

14. Franklin, *The Real World of Technology*, and Jacques Ellul, *Perspectives on Our Age: Jacques Ellul speaks on His Life and Work*, ed., W. Vanderburg (Toronto: CBC Enterprises, 1981).

15. See Bob Hudspith and Herb Jenkins, *Teaching the Art of Inquiry* (Halifax, NS: Society for Teaching and Learning in Higher Education, 2001).

16. Robert Hudspith, "Using a consensus conference to learn about public participation in policymaking in areas of technical controversy," *PS, Political Science and Politics* (June, 2001): 313-317.

17. Langdon Winner, "Technological Determinism: Alive and Kicking," *Bulletin of Science, Technology, and Society*, vol. 17, no. 1 (1997): 1-2.

III

What Have We Done and Where Are We Going?

10   The Human Face of the Programme

Barbara Ferrier

Students

In-course students and very recent graduates were invited to offer brief comments about their experience in the Programme. These are inserted in this chapter and in Chapter 11. We pointed out to them that we were not asking for testimonials.

Student Progress

Many of the students admitted to the Programme have had star status in their high schools, and adjusting to being one of many equals has made the first few weeks difficult for some. Those who try to assert themselves as leaders are often unsuccessful, and others expect to be outshone and are unnecessarily retiring. For most, the assignment to them of a 'big sibling' eases the transition and they settle down by the end of the first term. Big siblings are upper-level student volunteers, and their selection and assignment to first year students are managed by the Society of Arts and Science Students (SASS).

> Interaction between the years is what makes Arts and Science special to me. I think this exchange fosters learning unique to such a small and special programme. (David Vanderburgh)

There are uneasy times when the first graded work is returned and some students receive grades of "B", "C", "D", or even "F", for the first time in their lives. However, with assurances that virtually all will have mastered the tasks by the end of the year and that grades will recover to be more like those they were used to, they settle down. At the outset, students are told that grades will not be adjusted to match some predetermined distribution and that the standards used in the rest of the University will be applied. If everyone were to earn an "A" by University standards, everyone would receive an "A". For cooperative learning in groups, which we emphasize, to reach its potential, trust in this grading principle is essential. Many students are skeptical at first about the benefits to them of learning in groups because in high school they often found themselves doing most of the work. They soon see, however, that with eager and able peers, groups can be productive and enhance the learning of all. They also come to recognize how much they gain from informal group learning through participation in classes.

> I remember, in my first day in Arts and Science, the magic of sitting
> in class and having a teacher ask a question and seeing those eager
> hands shoot up all around me. (Katherine Kitching)

As would be expected from their high admission averages, the grade distribution in Arts and Science courses is heavily skewed toward "A" grades when compared with the distribution in other undergraduate courses at McMaster. The question arises as to whether our intention to grade Arts and Science students within Arts and Science courses with the same overall standard used across the University has been carried out successfully. Annually since 1987 we have compared the number of "A" grades (A+, A, A-) students get in courses exclusively for Arts and Science students with the number they get in other courses offered by University Departments. The results show that our students do no better in courses designed exclusively for them than they do in the other courses. Apparently, Programme instructors are able to apply the same overall standards in Arts and Science courses as are exercised in the University as a whole.

Although all Arts and Science students had high school records of excellent performance in the arts, the sciences, and mathematics, consistent success is not maintained by all of them at university. From their results it appears that lower aptitude for subjects in the humanities and social sciences can be compensated for by hard work—rarely do grades in these areas fall below "B-", but the results in the required courses in calculus, physics, statistics, and biology, as well as in elective courses in the sciences and mathematics, appear to present a different challenge, since each year a small number of students struggle with these subjects. On anecdotal evidence, it appears that different high school teachers take very different approaches to teaching these subjects, and in extreme cases memorization is all that they require. Students with this background have been heard to comment on the injustice of being asked to tackle previously unseen problems in tests and examinations. It is apparent that high school grades do not always reflect the students' mastery of the material in these subjects.

A survey of one incoming class was done in 1997 to find out how closely the students' expectations of some aspects of university studies matched their subsequent experiences. This was done to provide information to incoming students and help with their transition from high school. Very soon after entry, the members of the surveyed class were asked to rate their expectations (using a Lickert-like scale) about the difficulty of their future studies, the amount of independence that would be required, and the amount of time that they would have to devote to them. Overall, they expected that more would be required of them in all three areas. The survey was repeated at the start of the second term, by which time they had finished their first set of exams and had completed substantial amounts of work in all their courses. Virtually all had found that the amount of time required was very much more than had been needed in high school, but that the difficulty of the work, and the independence expected, were not greater. It is probable that these results do not reflect the general undergraduate experience of first term at university. The students surveyed were, on average, stronger academically and with more extracurricular experience in high school than their peers. It is possible that the results would have been different with respect to the difficulty of the work if the survey had been done at the end of the second term rather than the first. Students often report that much of the work in the science and mathematics courses in the first term is a review of work done in high school. This is judged by instructors to be necessary to address an uneven level of preparation. The new work covered in the second term is much more challenging.

Some students have been very disconcerted by the amount of time they found they needed to devote to their studies and responded by abandoning all other interests, working long into the night, becoming sleep deprived and seriously stressed. For these students, academic achievement has been a very large part of their self-esteem and relationships. The Programme instructors, academic counselors and big siblings try to help by fostering time management skills as well as emphasizing the need for relaxation and fun in their lives. Students who managed the transition from high school well have acknowledged that good time-management has been an essential skill.

A large majority of Programme students adjust well, are happy with their studies and extracurricular activities, and get excellent grades. Those who complete honours degree programmes (Honours Arts and Science or Combined Honours Arts and Science and a specific discipline) almost all graduate with distinction. Attrition from the Programme is small. Very few students fail to maintain the Honours Standing needed to advance. A slightly larger number choose to leave in good standing. This is usually because they have found that they have a very marked preference for the arts or the sciences, in spite of their expectations that were based on excellent performance across the board in high school. It is expected that most students will develop preferences to some degree, and some who were aware of a preference on entry have been surprised to find that it had changed.

> A large component of my journey of discovery involved academics. Formerly my education was heavily centred on the sciences. Here, I embarked on a voyage through the arts and discovered my hidden love of and even talent for them. I came to appreciate the power of words, the beauty of silence, the need for speech, the open-ended questions answered by more questions. (Giselle Revah)

> I remember telling a fellow Biology graduate student that I had considered a specialization in East Asian Studies in my third year. She reacted with considerable incredulity when I told her that I had previously flirted with the idea of an Economics minor. I say with almost complete confidence that this speaks less to any personal intellectual breadth, but rather to the incredible flexibility that Arts and Science offers. (Manu Rangachari)

Although the Programme's planners designed a curriculum that led to an honours degree (B.ArtSc. Honours) after four years, they included the possibility of graduating after three years (B.ArtSc.). Students are encouraged to do the four-year degree to get the benefit of the complete curriculum and in particular of the senior thesis. However, up to a quarter of each class leave after three years, usually to attend a professional school.

The option of enrolling in one of the combined honours programmes (p.46) has been popular among Arts and Science students. About a third of the members of each class have made this choice. Fewer, however, graduate with a combined honours degree because some elect to graduate after three years, and some find that devoting all elective time to a single discipline becomes more constricting than they had expected. Over twenty different combined honours programmes have been offered. This number varies over the years because new programmes are introduced in response to student interest and others are eliminated when there has been no student enrolled for several years. The most popular subjects in combination with Arts and Science have been psychology, biology, biochemistry, English, political science, and economics. The appearance of psychology, biology and biochemistry on the list may reflect the attractiveness to many of a career in medicine, and they may have been chosen because they are seen as being helpful in preparing for that career, as offering an alternative, related career or simply as furthering an interest in human biology and behaviour. The popularity of political science and economics presumably reflects the students' interest in social concerns, both nationally and internationally.

Spending an academic year (almost always the third) abroad or at another Canadian university has been popular. This is managed through McMaster's various exchange programmes with other universities. Some Arts and Science students have not found what interested them among these programmes and have arranged their own "third year away" by negotiating directly with universities of their choice. It has also become fairly popular to take a year away from study. In this year students often travel extensively, often from a site where they had been volunteering or working in the summer with a development organization.

As would be expected from an academically gifted group, the students win many University prizes and awards. Often these are based on leadership and extracurricular activities as well as academic excellence. They have also been successful in external competitions; a Rhodes Scholarship, a Cambridge Scholarship, several Commonwealth and Fulbright Scholarships and other awards have allowed many to go for further studies to distinguished universities, including several in the United Kingdom and the United States.

Career Choices

Canadian Universities have for the most part been more like the British than the US model in that their undergraduate programmes have been specialized. Students often report that they had difficulty in persuading their parents to agree with their choice of the Arts and Science Programme. Parents kept asking, "But what will you do afterwards?" In fact, the

Programme's graduates go on to interesting careers of considerable variety, sometimes surprising themselves with their choices. When they are introduced to a wide range of disciplines and interdisciplinary studies in their undergraduate curriculum they discover previously unimagined possibilities. Some of their career paths are described in the section on graduates (p.199).

What is known about career choices is largely based on graduates' intentions when they leave the Programme. Work has just been completed to create a website which graduates will keep current themselves. Until that is done, conclusions must be tentative. One survey of graduates was done in 1997, and information from graduates and their peers is collected when they make return visits. Fortunately they have rich informal networks by which they keep in touch with one another. There are continuing requests for letters of reference, and many send letters or postcards. Information from all these sources supports the conclusion that the very large majority go on to further studies, some immediately after graduation and others after an interval of travel, work, and exploration of possibilities. The range of further studies is very broad.

It appears that the largest group go to graduate school. Common choices have been programmes with an interdisciplinary approach, e.g. environmental studies, development studies, communication, business, but many have involved research in single disciplines. Some of these disciplines are those in which the graduate had done a combined honours or a senior thesis. Some graduates have been allowed to bypass some graduate school requirements on the basis of the courses they have taken and the skills they have acquired.

Professional schools have been consistently popular, with medicine and teaching being attractive since the early years and law becoming more attractive over time. Some graduates see law as the most appropriate base for their intended work in social policy making. Medicine differs from other choices. Although it is by far the most common choice of entering students, a substantial number eventually make other choices as they become aware of other opportunities or find that science courses at the university level are not their métier.

The high academic ability of our students suggests that many would have chosen to go to graduate work from any undergraduate programme. However, the nature of what they choose to emphasize and the work they finally do suggest that they are influenced by the Arts and Science Programme's content and style. Some of the graduates' contributions to this book (p.202) support this. A sociologists' 1991 survey (pp.262-3) showed that 86% of the final year class acknowledged this influence, which for a number had been troubling, because it caused them to change direction and increased their self-doubts. Our graduates' careers show some recurrent themes. Whatever their postgraduate qualifications, many show interest in education (often in universities), the environment, and the developing world. Having been in a small programme in which there are close relationships with instructors who enjoy teaching, in which students are involved in its administration, and which for most provided an enjoyable experience, may have increased their pre-existing and idealized belief in the power of education. For many, concern for the health of the environment pre-dated their entry to the Programme and was enhanced by the many like-minded people and related activities they found at university. The Programme's first year Inquiry course on the problems of the developing world has led some to spend time there in the summers, often with Non Governmental Organizations. Together, these experiences appear to have fostered a long-term commitment to help. Overall, these young people show a keen interest, both before and after graduation, in the welfare of the earth and of all the species it supports.

Extracurricular Activities

It was the hope of the Programme's planners that its students would participate in many aspects of the life of the University and its larger community. This hope has been realized more fully than even the most optimistic could have imagined. On the first day of their formal orientation exercises the richness of the opportunities that surround them is pointed out to the students, and they are consistently encouraged to take advantage of them. Arts and Science students are generally represented in disproportionate numbers on University committees and task forces; they have taken many initiatives and can be relied on to be available whenever student volunteers are sought. Within the Programme they play important roles on all committees except Review and Awards; they are big siblings (p.195); they are ambassadors of the Programme at various information sessions and to their high schools. Their work as assessors of Supplementary Applications (p.51) is particularly important. They are always ready to be on the front line when the University holds open houses or participates in information fairs for high school students; they are responsible and articulate representatives in these settings. As would be expected of an idealistic and gifted group, they are always around when social problems are discussed and plans to address them are implemented. Over the years they have been involved in leading student anti-apartheid campaigns, organizing a Peace Camp to protest the 1990 Gulf War, setting up recycling programmes on campus, creating a McMaster chapter of Pugwash, working for the Ontario Public Interest Research Group and in a wide array of other actions.

Student Government has been attractive to them. Three have been President of the McMaster Students' Union and many others have been elected to other positions in this organization. They have also contributed substantially to writing, editing, and publishing the student newspaper and student magazines. Several were among the founders of one of the magazines which offered a place for debate on issues more weighty than were found in the student newspaper. They have been involved in all aspects of operating the student radio station.

Typical of bright and energetic young people, many are deeply involved in the creative arts, particularly music, literature, and drama, and they arrange several occasions each year at which their work can be presented.

The true essence of Arts and Science is manifested in the traditional event known as "The Coffeehouse." It is an evening to depart from our academic pursuits to celebrate the extraordinary and diverse talents of our peers. There is a strong, unmistakable feeling of unity as we all gather to witness the mesmerizing musical, satirical and intellectual performances. (Anjalee Gupta)

Considerable numbers are involved in sports and athletics. The University annually recognizes "Scholar Athletes," undergraduates who have achieved both academic and athletic distinction. There are usually more Arts and Science students among them than the Programme's size would predict.

The students' level of involvement, their academic success and their commitment to improve the lives of others have exceeded what the University could have hoped for when it took the step of introducing the Programme.

Graduates : Some Personal Histories

What is known about the career choices of the Programme's students is described in the previous section. About forty graduates of the Programme, who had left it at least two years previously, were selected to represent each of the years and as far as possible different areas of interest, and were invited to contribute to this book. They were told that what we wanted was "not a testimonial, but rather a personal history that might, but would not have to, include reflections on the Programme." We wrote to the most recent address we had; in some cases this was the address they had when they entered university. Six letters were returned as undeliverable. Of the thirty who agreed to contribute, twenty seven sent histories. These now follow. [Some explanations of local references are added by the editors].

Martin Smith ('85)
The Meeting or *Bibo ergo sum.*
(Castor and Pollux haven't seen each other for years. They meet as if by accident in a pub.)
Castor: Pollux!
Pollux: Castor! How do you, this many a year?
Castor: Ah, my life is over, biologically speaking.
Pollux: I don't understand you. "Biologically" is the only way you *can* speak: you must be living to speak at all, so that any speech is biological; and speaking of *life* you are per force speaking biologically. But since the evidence of my senses behooves me to insist that you are not dead, you need to tell me to which of these biologies you refer?
Castor: In fact to neither. As usual you have misconstrued me. I merely mean that I am biologically finished. Having created a posterity– man-child and woman-child created I them– I have had myself fixed.
Pollux: Indeed.
Castor: In deed and thought and word too.
Pollux: What remains then, in this post-biological life to which you find yourself relegated? Are you not yet happily married and so on?
Castor: Yes, emphatically so. It is a social and rewarding life nevertheless. There are plays to see, dinners to consume, wines to drink and songs to sing.
Pollux: How do you predominantly pass the days?
Castor: In going to school.
Pollux: To school? At your age?
Castor: Not where I am taught so much as where I teach.
Pollux: Good. I should have thought that even one as thick as you would eventually have had enough of schooling. How long *have* you been in school.
Castor: I started in kindergarten in the year of the Six Day War.

Pollux: That is how you remember it?

Castor: Yes. Conflict seems to punctuate existence. It drives novels. It lasts better in the collective memory than does love. I was born in the year of the Cuban missile crisis.

Pollux: This is an interesting view. What more have you?

Castor: I was married the year of the Air India Bombing, started my teaching career the year of the Gulf War. My son was born the year the World Trade Centre was first bombed.

Pollux: You are a morbid fellow if this is the way you remember your life.

Castor: Only if I were to let it get me down.

Pollux: How do you mean?

Castor: Well, if I tell you every cloud has a silver lining, then someone else might say that every silver lining has a cloud.

Pollux: I am going to let that invalid logical negation pass because I really have to get home, and I am waiting for the punch line.

Castor: Punch line? The joke is not yet half over, old horse, you haven't told me about yourself yet.

Pollux: Me? I have no story really.

Castor: That's a crock. You may not have been invited to reflect on your experiences, but that doesn't mean that you have nothing to tell. What have you been reading lately?

Pollux: You can't possibly care about that. Besides, how would that help you?

Castor: OK. You'll doubtless ridicule my disrespect for the language here, but if you can't tell me your life's story then at least give me the stories of your life.

Pollux: I'll try to take this seriously. I am actually embarked on a reading project.

Castor: That's good. Go on.

Pollux: Well. I have decided that I really ought to read some important books before I get too old. I saw a list someplace that contained a few things that I've already read at university, but which also had some others that I haven't read.

Castor: Such as?

Pollux: Ovid's *Metamorphoses*, Virgil's *Aeneid*, Sophocles' *Theban Plays*, Homer's *Iliad* and *Odyssey*, and the Bible. The list challenged anyone who claimed to be educated to read them. So I undertook to finish this project before I turned forty.

(Castor looks quizzically at Pollux)

	You are looking at me quizzically. I suppose you think that all this reading is likely to do is turn me into a white, Western, middle-aged male.
Castor:	No, I don't fear that transition.
Pollux:	No?
Castor:	It is foolish to fear that which has already come to pass.
Pollux:	Come on. How can you be so judgmental? A lot of Western literature takes its roots in the fertile soil husbanded by those classic authors. Besides, that's not all I do for amusement. There's cooking, programming, wine-making, writing satire, camping, playing chess on the internet.
Castor:	Whoa, friend. I am not *diminishing* your hobbies and interests. I only asked you to tell me about them. *Asking a question* is not the same as *questioning*, you know.
Pollux:	OK, sorry. I guess I got carried away. I have always had a hard time separating value judgments from ordinary statements.
Castor:	That is a disability.
Pollux:	I know it. But I have come to accept my limitations.
	(*There is an uncomfortable silence.*)
Castor:	Well, how is that for a punch line?
Pollux:	You mean the uncomfortable silence?
Castor:	Yes. It's a little like the music of John Cage.
Pollux:	He died the year I moved into my current house.
Castor:	Now you're doing it.
Pollux:	(*Rising from the bar stool*) Well. See you around some time.
Castor:	(*Rising also*) I wish you well. Take care.
Pollux:	Me too. You too.

(*Exeunt*)

Elham Afnan ('87)

My husband likes to tell new acquaintances how international our family is. He was born and raised in Norway, but has lived in both the Ukraine and Latvia. I was born in Iran, grew up in Canada, and spent several years in Israel, where my parents still live. Our son was born in Norway and our daughter in Russia. Of our three sisters-in-law, one is Russian, another Lithuanian, and the third an Iranian who grew up in Austria and New Zealand. I wonder (sometimes out loud) if people really want to hear about all this, because we know so many other people who are also of mixed backgrounds or who have lived in different parts of the world. But then I realize that it is still not so common to consider yourself a citizen of the world. And I begin to think that this is part of something more fundamental in my life.

My parents brought me up to look on all sides of a question. They taught me, by word and by example, that there is usually more that one point of view about any topic, and that differences of opinion don't have to lead to conflict but can often ignite a spark of understanding and shed new light on the matter. They encouraged me to learn new languages, to find beauty and interest in all cultures, and to discover something worth learning in everything I encountered.

Given this background, it was perhaps inevitable that when I found out about the Arts and Science Programme, I would think that it was just the thing for me. I was right. I loved studying Physics and English side by side and going from Calculus to Western Thought. When I later decided to do graduate work in English, it was with the intention of looking at literature, not in isolation, but in relation to science, to culture, to the world at large.

Writing my Ph.D. thesis was an enriching experience for me because it allowed me to look in theoretical terms at something that had been part of my world-view all along. I wanted to study utopian literature and found that the most rewarding approach to it was through a concept from physics: the concept of complementarity. Reality is a field of mutually interacting systems. In order to describe it, we need to use points of view that are different and may, at times, be mutually exclusive. We cannot fully understand the world unless we understand its seemingly contradictory manifestations.

In my life, learning and faith have gone hand in hand. I learned the language of complementarity in the academic world, but it is my faith that has taught how to apply it to life. Bahá'u'lláh, the founder of the Bahá'í Faith, wrote over a hundred years ago: "The well-being of mankind, its peace and security, are unattainable unless and until its unity is firmly established." Unity is not uniformity, but rather a dynamic process that is meaningless without diversity. Human society consists of a wide variety of individuals and cultures that are nevertheless interrelated in all spheres of life. Peace and prosperity, at the personal as well as the global level, are possible only through the recognition of the need for unity in diversity.

I see the applications in my daily life. Marriage, for example, is a perfect example of two separate and at times very different individuals coming together to form a whole that is greater than the sum of its parts. After we had children, I discovered that family life and a career are also complementary. At times, they appear to be mutually exclusive, but in the long run, combining them enriches one's life.

I have lived in five countries and visited more than a dozen others. Some days, when I am feeling lonely, I wonder if it is so great to have family and friends in three different continents. I would rather they all lived within babysitting distance. But then the feeling passes and I realize what a great privilege it is to live in different countries. It has taught me how to reconcile different customs, viewpoints, and ways of doing things, and allowed me to harmonize feelings that are sometimes at odds with one another: wonder, frustration, bafflement, admiration, and ultimately, a sense of how much we all have in common. I am glad I have had this chance to practice what I believe, to experience the reality of unity in diversity, not only in my education, but also in my life.

Rosanne Popp ('88)

There is no doubt in my mind that my decision to enter the Arts and Science Programme seventeen years ago was one of the best decisions I ever made. Like many high school students, I was at a loss as to what my next academic choice should be. I was at the time following a guiding principle which I continue to use when faced with difficult decisions: delay committing to anything for as long as possible. Therefore, when someone at the McMaster University Student Liaison Office told me I could apply to a Programme that did not force me to commit completely to either the Arts or the Sciences, I knew this was the choice (or lack thereof) for me.

I quickly realized that there were many other things that set Arts and Science apart from more traditional university programmes. The small class sizes helped the students develop a sense of identity and belonging. What other department was small enough to provide its students with periodic pizza parties, as the Arts and Science Programme could in these early years? Many a frazzled student was revived by the end-of-term "Pizza Plunge" get-togethers. Through informal activities such as these I developed some of the enduring friendships that are an important part of my life today.

As I slowly developed some sense of academic and career interest in the field of education, the Arts and Science Programme facilitated my growth in this direction. By doing a combined honours degree with Psychology, I was able to focus on the areas of learning and human development. Being given the freedom to choose a relevant thesis topic in my fourth year allowed me to do some research into the area of teaching reading skills. My second year Inquiry course in Peace and Conflict studies with visiting professor Dr. Anatol Rapoport [a distinguished social scientist from the University of Toronto] introduced me to the field of conflict resolution that has become an important focus in my career as a teacher. I have since taught conflict resolution skills to elementary students of all ages, set up peer mediation programmes at several schools, and completed a Master's degree in education with a thesis on the topic of conflict resolution. As an elementary school teacher, I am a generalist in that I teach everything from science and math to art and English. What better preparation for that could there be than an Arts and Science degree? I must admit that I'm still waiting to apply my knowledge of Special Relativity (that Dr. Goodings laboured so hard to help me comprehend) in my present position as a grade one teacher.

I've completed two other degrees at two different universities since my years in Arts and Science, but these other academic experiences have not had the same kind of impact as those first four years at Mac. Six years after I graduated from Arts and Science, when I was beginning to apply to graduate programs, I needed to contact the Arts and Science Office for some information. When I called "Commons 105", it was great to hear Joanne Miller's voice [long-serving secretary] again on the other end of the line. What was astounding to me, however, was that she actually greeted me by my name when I introduced myself simply as a graduate. Hearing her say, "Is that you, Rosanne?" after a six-year absence was a real sign that it was still a special programme and a special place.

Andrew Ide ('89)

My years covered the transition period from a Hooker fund-sponsored experiment to the entrenchment of the Arts and Science Programme at McMaster. I struggled with calculus and biology, which is somewhat ironic given that my other options for post-secondary education had both been in the sciences. Western Thought and the Inquiry courses were particularly important as they exposed me to ideas and concepts that I had never encountered before and would not likely have sought out myself. I remember burying my head in books and documents following strands of thought that went on forever. I remember Dr. Greenspan telling us one day to read The Republic for the next class; Dr. Kubursi exhorting us to consider the impact of economic growth and colonialism; and Professor Bowerbank urging us to find our inner voice. With its weird mix of courses and professors, the Programme was an eye-opener for this farm boy. I sometimes still wish that I had done more of the required readings.

The social side of Arts and Science was central to its success. Discussions with professors and students, parties, clubs, and all of the trial posturing we did made my years at Mac a lot of fun. Using the Programme's Reading Room, we kept in touch with students from other years, building friendships and exchanging thoughts. Late night study sessions there allowed me to get through from year to year. We talked, we listened, we grew. We developed research, writing, and speaking skills. We participated in the life of the university. We formed a community of bright-eyed scholars chasing ephemeral wisps of possibilities.

My wife thinks that some of us BS to a high degree. I don't know what she's talking about.

Since graduating after a very late night of thesis writing, I have come to realize that I have spent my life living or working in communities in progress. I worked with the mentally handicapped, travelled with Canadian Crossroads, did the graveyard shift in a variety store, volunteered in a Gandhian ashram in India, lived with Arts and Science vegetarians in British Columbia, helped a neighbour build an addition to his house, worked for Canada World Youth, took care of a troubled teen, taught in a James Bay Cree community (with a nod to my classmates and professors from the Native Issues Inquiry course), bought a language school, got married and had two kids. Now I teach in a federal prison, work on my French, nag my kids to pick up after themselves and burst with pride at everything they are learning to do.

Life continues to bring me interesting lessons. How I incorporate them into my life depends much upon the ideas and people I encountered in the Programme. The grads that I know have gone on to work, travel, study, dance, and raise families. We had wonderful opportunities to explore strange new worlds through the Programme and I think we are, in our own ways, continuing that experience.

Susan Frazer ('90)
I am an advocate. An advocate, according to Webster's, is one that pleads the cause of another or one that defends a cause or proposal. My profession is the practice of law. Fortunately, my profession allows me to be who I am and to earn a living. I try to take cases that I believe advance the public interest, primarily in the areas of mental health and policing. I am not sure how I became who I am. I suspect it comes from being raised in a family where I was taught to question the fundamental assumptions about the way the world works. I credit my high school (Thornlea Secondary School—a public but alternative high school now sadly

transformed into a traditional high school) for giving me the power and confidence to advance my own learning and my interests. Then came the Arts and Science Programme.

In my third year of the Programme, I ran for president of the McMaster Students Union and won. A woman had not held the position for ten years and, at the time of this writing, no woman has held it since. It was in that job that I learned that politics challenges advocates. Political expediency often leads to the abandonment of a cause or an idea. Good advocates will not be diverted unless the political end also serves the cause or client.

It is only now that I have had time to reflect (eleven years since my graduation). I understand that, although I didn't plan it, the Arts and Science Programme provided the perfect training for my profession. The Arts and Science Programme provided a pool of intelligent people interested in learning new ideas and operating in a climate of fear (of the future, the faculty, being found out and not fitting in). The curriculum provided advocacy tools: critical thinking, expository writing, and a smidgen of knowledge in every field to give its students the ability to go further. The best training for the advocate, however, is to encamp with others armed with ideas, facts, and a desire to trade. Only the practice of defending one's ideas amidst skilled advocates (and friends) allows the skilled advocate to emerge.

Anne Dahmer ('90)
People think I'm opinionated, that I ask a lot of questions, and that if something needs saying, I'll say it. These are not qualities I purposely nurtured or consciously pursued, they seem to be simply who I am. I have an uncle who claims that I developed these loud talents as some sort of survival skill as the much younger, only girl in a busy family. He figures if I hadn't learned to speak up for myself I might have been accidentally left at the mall as a toddler or been forced to wear cowboy-themed hand-me-downs until I moved out. My uncle's an engineer, not a psychologist, but I like his theory anyway.

My need to question everything and my reputation for speaking out have coloured my personal and professional relationships for as long as I can remember. I learned early on that not everyone appreciated my stunning wit. Not everyone was thrilled to see my hand go up in class. I spent my share of time standing in the corner or writing lines after school because I couldn't stop talking or argued just a little too often. However, there were moments of vindication. Once in grade 10 math my teacher unexpectedly presented me with a little certificate of achievement. He told everyone that it was because I was never afraid to ask a question when I didn't understand something. It happened again in grade 13 chemistry. My teacher, who made a habit of dressing up as an alchemist on Fridays and entertaining us with all kinds of explosions, once disappeared in a puff of smoke and reappeared in front of my desk, holding a gold painted test tube! With great flourish, he awarded me the "Golden Test Tube" because I always seemed to ask the questions that everyone else was thinking. Two weeks later, of course, I was unceremoniously removed (permanently) from my English class for wanting to discuss the origins of the Twelfth Night festival in Shakespeare's play when my teacher was definitely not in the mood. It turned out all right though, I opened the doors for an independent study program!

Apart from providing me with a rather colourful school experience, my drive to question and develop my own opinions gave me the push I needed to explore new challenges. I spent a year as a Canada World Youth participant in Manitoba and Colombia, and learned to question many assumptions about the world. I also enrolled in the Arts and Science Programme at McMaster University. I knew from the first day that this was the place for me. Arts and Science was the place to ask questions. We even had whole classes devoted to the art of making cogent arguments! I'm sure I drove some of my classmates a little crazy with the questions I asked, but others appreciated my persistence. One day in physics someone passed me a note, which read, "Please ask him to explain page 34. I don't understand it. Thanks." I also remember asking Dr. Jenkins a quick psychology question and being rewarded with a great discussion of Skinner boxes, B.F. Skinner himself, and the fine art of conditioning pigeons to peck at coloured lights, complete with hand-puppet pigeons! What a great environment for the curious mind!

I continued to make my noisy way toward adulthood. I traveled to the South Pacific and to Central America. After graduating with an Arts and Science degree, I completed studies for a Bachelor of Education degree and for a year taught elementary school in an isolated Native community where I learned a new approach to debate. These people were very quiet by nature, but a quick check from someone on the broomball court at fifty below zero could settle a disagreement swiftly and help raise body temperatures, too!

There is, naturally, some irony or cosmic retribution in my life story. After years of expressing my opinions and asking too many questions I have found great challenge and satisfaction in my present career. I teach Kindergarten. No creature on earth has more questions than a five year old!

Lisa Campbell ('90)
After I graduated from Arts and Science in 1990, I completed an MA in Environmental Studies and Geography at the University of Toronto, and a PhD in Geography at the University of Cambridge. In 1998, I became an Assistant Professor in the Geography Department at the University of Western Ontario. During the past four years, more so than at any time since 1990, I've found myself thinking about my undergraduate degree and experience. I make constant, often involuntary, comparisons between "now" and "then" and, while I graduated in 1990 and "then" isn't *that* long ago, "now" is almost unrecognizable. Frosh week, for example, is an entirely different beast, gender and alcohol aware and undoubtedly tamer. I have yet to see toilet paper strung on any tree branch, although Western seems to keep student residences on the outskirts of campus, so I may be missing it. While "then" we complained about food services, eating at UWO is like eating in a shopping mall, and when you've finished you can get your film developed, buy a new pair of glasses, or drop into the tanning salon, all available in the student community centre. While "then" I felt comfortable rolling out of bed and donning track pants to morning lectures, some of my students, male and female, apparently spend hours each morning grooming.

These differences are laughable, but there are others that are downright frustrating. Students interrupt my work regularly to request a stapler. A student phoned me from home once (and only once!) to ask if I would "pop down the hall" and check if the computer lab was open. Several students every term approach me with a paper or exam they've done poorly on and explain that, as they're an "A" student, I've obviously made a mistake. Maybe I just fail to command respect, but I visited professors for academic help only, and I never would have dreamed of asking Dr. Jenkins for a stapler. I write this not to complain (although these things are annoying), but to introduce what I see as the two most significant differences between "then" and "now". 1. Cost. Tuition at Western in 2001 is approximately $4,800, almost four times what it was when I started university in 1986. 2. Political climate. David Peterson's Liberals and Bob Rae's NDP [political leaders and parties in Ontario] were in power in Ontario during my undergraduate and MA years. Funding for post-secondary education was under pressure, but there was a sense that a post-secondary education, and I mean education in the broadest sense, was valuable. In contrast, the Harris Conservatives [Mike Harris, Premier of Ontario, 1995-2002] define post-secondary education (sorry, training) as a time-consuming and costly step on the road to contributing to a vibrant Ontario economy and earning a taxable income (had the Arts and Science Programme been proposed at any point after 1993, I doubt the proposal would have made it past the first level of university administration).

These two factors combine to create three defining characteristics of the contemporary undergraduates who pass through my office. Students are: frightened (they're not in engineering and are thus destined for unemployment); broke (one of my undergraduates, a twenty-four year-old single mother, graduated in 1999 with a $45,000 debt); and tired (many students hold down multiple part-time jobs). The end result? Student-consumers who see grades (I had written "education" and had to strike it) as something they've bought.

I'm making broad generalizations based on primarily anecdotal evidence (things a good Arts and Science education should preclude), and I teach some wonderful, intelligent, and energetic students. But my nostalgia for my days in Arts and Science, my gratitude for being encouraged and socially free to think for thought's sake, are more poignant after four years of working at the other side of the desk. I don't recall feeling anxious about what I would do professionally, at least not until the late stages of my undergraduate life. Part of this was certainly a function of being in Arts and Science, aware of its privileges, and surrounded by gifted peers. But I suspect it's more than that, that universities and Canadian society have changed. Now what was it that I learned about swing pendulums and cycles of history?

Merrilee Brown ('91)

I came to the Arts and Science Programme at McMaster much by accident. Visiting McMaster, intending to follow the Natural Sciences tour, I heard a description of the broad-based liberal arts mandate of the Programme and decided to change tours. After Dr. Jenkins impressed me with his vision for the Programme I knew I had found my niche. Where else but in the Programme's homebase could the works of the Marquis de Sade sit side by side on the shelf with "The City of God" by St. Augustine? I knew then that the Arts and Science Programme would be an interesting place to spend four years.

Orientation day merely confirmed my conviction that I had made the right choice. Dr. Jenkins delivered his legendary "world leader speech" where he addressed us as future titans of politics, commerce and academia.

He challenged us to take advantage of the unique opportunity we had been granted: a stimulating intellectual environment with students passionate about the joy of learning, access to some of the best professors at McMaster, and a curriculum that would stretch our intellectual and creative boundaries. Almost instantly, Commons 105 was transformed into a nexus of conversation and academic debate, nearly twenty-four hours a day.

What distinguished my experience in the Arts and Science Programme from that of my peers outside it was the totality of the experience. Arts and Science was not simply an academic curriculum but a community. It encompassed all aspects of my academic and extra-curricular experience at McMaster. We wondered at times whether the Programme was actually some "Skinner Box" of Dr. Jenkins' creation, to further his research in behavioural psychology. We bonded as we completed the Programme in a process that researchers called professional socialization. We put our hearts and souls down on paper for an Inquiry assignment, we lunched with Dr. Bob Hudspith after Technology and Society, we were "classically educated" in Western Thought, we experienced the "Brute Logic" of our first year course, and we had our creative writing dissected critically. These experiences were all part of the trials that bound us together. Many of us lived, breathed, and ate Arts and Science twenty-four hours a day. Many students lived together in houses that became legendary: Napier Street, Women on Main, the House at Pooh Corner. They were not just places to live; they were places to think, philosophize, debate, and dream with like-minded other Arts and Science types.

The extra-curricular activities stand out for me as important in our forming a cohesive group. We protested the Gulf War at Peace Camp, we objected to McMaster's financial investment in the Apartheid regime in South Africa at the time, and we collected three thousand signatures on a petition to eliminate a Student Council by-law we felt was unjust. We wrote murder mysteries and cooked Moroccan food for our formal dinner dances, we met every Tuesday night for vegetarian potluck dinners, and we performed our various talents at our regular "Coffee Houses." We attended movies at the local repertory theatre, we sang and danced and celebrated like all university students. But all along, our involvement in the Arts and Science Programme nurtured our idealism and our sense of social justice in and out of the classroom.

How has my experience in the Arts and Science Programme influenced me? I am not a world leader nor a philosopher king. I read with pride about my peers from Arts and Science in the media, and how they are creating opportunities for the child victims of war or fighting for the rights of the Innu people in Labrador. However, my life is a little more conventional. I qualified as a Family Physician several years ago, married, and we just welcomed our first child. I work as a small-town rural general practitioner delivering babies, attending to emergencies, taking care of the seriously ill, attending the dying, and teaching medical students and residents the art and science of medicine. I know that my experience in the Arts and Science Programme has nurtured my compassion for those who are suffering, my sense of social justice, my focus on the social determinants of health, my commitment to my community, and my role as a citizen of this country and the world. And who knows what the future may bring—I may yet become a philosopher king!

Robert Kapanen ('91)
The Arts and Science Programme truly inspired me to be myself in my educational and career choices. I now live in Berkeley, California, with my wife, Deirdre, and our two year-old daughter, Chloe. I work in Silicon Valley at the world's third largest software company, where I manage partnerships with consulting firms and hardware companies. I do not believe I would have even entertained this outcome had I not been in the Arts and Science Programme to establish crucial groundwork.

Prior to the Programme I knew I wanted to learn a lot quickly and be exposed to a broad base of ideas from history, to literature, to science. I was thirsty, and the Programme delivered more than I had expected; instilling a passion and confidence in learning and expressing ideas and an openness to new ideas.

The first thing that struck me about the Programme was that the professors really seemed to care. I mean really care—the way a parent would carefully ask what a child wants to be when he or she grows up. It was nurturing and competitive, but mostly nurturing. The professors instilled a respect for full participation and a spectrum of ideas, so that we were not competing—we were collaboratively building insights using analytical skills and creativity.

I combined the Programme with an Economics Honours, and considered continuing in that stream. I would later learn that the real attractions for me were diplomacy and business with an international scope. So then I considered working at the UN, after one of my role models, an Arts and Science professor who occasionally had to cancel class because he was "stuck at the UN" or "couldn't get out of Lebanon." There were more than enough role models to choose from within the Programme. So, I went into law and pursued international law. I then worked at a boutique international law firm doing commercial litigation and corporate law. I liked it, but Internet activity was heating up, I was increasingly interested in business, and I liked to dream of what technology might enable. And so, like any Arts and Science student, I returned to school yet again, this time to do my MBA at the Richard Ivey School of Business, at the University of Western Ontario. I was homing in on my ultimate career.

I also traveled extensively. During legal studies and work, I traveled for one year in Central America and a few months in Europe. The Programme's students and graduates as a body have probably covered the entire globe. So, during the MBA, it felt right to join a student-operated initiative to teach business in emerging Eastern European countries for the summer.

So now all the flavors of the Arts and Science Programme have commingled for me: international experience, travel, new concepts and technologies, and a great appreciation of those who inspired me during those very special four years in it.

Mary-Beth Raddon ('91)

I am practising to be an embodiment of three-faced Maitreya.

"My right face is black, and my left, white. My main face is yellow, saffron-like in colour."

Has Maitreya ever known such a warm day in late October? I am seated draped in sunshine, on a log on a yellow-leafy river bank, watching the sparkle and depths of the water.

"Each face has three eyes: each is peaceful and smiles."

I have retreated to this log in the woods to recite the Sadhana. I retreated from Toronto to the Dharma Centre in Kinmount to reflect on my life. According to Buddhism (and the river in front of me), the nature of life is flux. Breathing in and out, I know it. Only three weeks ago I took my oral defense and submitted my thesis to complete my PhD in sociology. Very recently my marriage ended. In a time of major world events and minor life transitions, a retreat on the theme of World Peace seemed the right time for my first exploration of the Dharma Centre. So, here I am in the woods.

"Heavenly silks cover the upper half of my body, and I wear a rainbow-coloured skirt."

How strange that I, raised a Baptist (a church that eschews religious images and goes light on liturgy) and turned Quaker (a religious society that avoids ritual and has no official doctrine or clergy), now find myself along with so many of my WASPish co-retreatants, practising a Tibetan form of visualization meditation on deities such as Maitreya.

Rinpoche had instructed us to physically turn our heads, to practise looking left, right, and centre through the three eyes of Maitreya's three faces. I do it. Maitreya breaks out laughing! A Baptist-Quaker-Buddhist! Now the strange is familiar, Maitryea is everywhere and throughout my life.

Maitreya was present in my Arts and Science years, supporting me not to specialize too narrowly; present with Bob Hudspith the day he lectured on "living in the tension," and with the teachers and directors who loosened disciplinary boundaries for all of us. Later, my PhD thesis became Maitreya's vehicle as I wrote about local money experiments as gift economies, where payment is not at odds with the sense of reciprocity between friends and neighbours. Maitreya sustains my intellectual work in the university, my attempts to understand and teach about the processes through which social institutions–family, state, economy–become gendered, racialized, and unequal. Maitreya, I fancy, gives the nod to my political involvements, too, my wish to champion the many small movements for more sustainable, local economies in the face of the dominant, centralizing thrust of corporate globalism. Quietly and surely, behind the scenes Maitreya directs my moments of play, as on the day my sister and I sculpted two large sheets of cardboard to make Ruby, the Parallel Universe Horse which we then rode down Bloor and Yonge [Toronto streets].

"The Wisdom Beings merge and become non-dual with me."

Three-faced Maitreya befriends contradictions and bathes them in the glow of the sunshine face. Dark/light, soft/hard, matter/spirit, good/evil, feminine/masculine are not resolved out of existence, but embodied in one being, whose main qualities are compassion and loving-kindness. Maitreya refuses to split, but actually amplifies opposites, allows ambiguity, sees through all eyes at once. Maitreya brings all my parallel universes into view and lets me live in them with others.

And what about World Peace? That is the theme of this retreat and my biggest concern, after all. I look for "peace" in the text and do not see it. Wait, it could be this: "Maitreya is seated on a Lion Throne, legs pendant in bhadrasana."

Maitreya enthroned; the definition of peace.

"OM MAITREYA SVAHA!"

"May all sentient beings come to possess happiness and its causes."

Jim Dunn ('91)

The Accidental Arts and Scientist: A Personal Confession

Those of you who carefully selected the Arts and Science Programme from a number of other competing programmes, who scraped and scratched for every grade point in high school, and who carefully and diligently prepared exquisite letters describing why you were intrinsically well-suited to study Arts and Science (supplementary applications were introduced the year after I was admitted), all to get into the Programme, may be a little disturbed by this confession: my admission to Arts and Science was largely accidental, and when I applied to Arts and Science, I really had no idea what I was getting myself into.

In my initial application to McMaster, I had applied for Natural Sciences, not really out of any enthusiasm for natural sciences, but for lack of a better option. But then my parents went to a soirée where they heard about the Arts and Science Programme from the daughter of one of their friends. They conveyed this information to me, and after reading some materials in the guidance office at my high school about AandS, I concluded that it sounded "a hell of a lot more interesting than Natural Sciences" and proceeded to amend my application. I received an offer of admission a few months later (I have wondered what I would have said on a supplementary application and what my chances would have been). I was happy to be admitted, but since my grand plan was to go to Mac for just three years and then skip off to law school, in some ways it didn't really matter what I studied, so long as it was tolerable.

An auspicious beginning, to be sure, but it gets worse. On a sunny afternoon in early September 1987, I remember sitting with my incoming class being welcomed by Dr. Jenkins to the Arts and Science Programme. I don't remember much of what was said, except for one thing. I remember Dr. Jenkins, almost as an afterthought it seemed, asking how many of us, by a show of hands, intended to go to medical school. I remember the thought "what a strange question" flashing across my mind in the nanosecond before some two or three dozen or more arms shot up into the air. As quickly as the previous thought had flashed across my mind, so the next thought shot: "Yikes, what have I gotten myself into?"

I spent the first year trying to figure out what the Programme was about, patiently tolerating all the course assignments that were difficult or seemed tangential to my ambition to make a clean getaway to law school. My efforts to crack the code of Arts and Science were confounded by the myriad of strange and apparently unrelated things we were studying:

debt crises in the Third World, calculating the rate of decomposition of a corpse after a murder, OMSITOG [An acronym for a step-by-step process for evaluating arguments developed by David Hitchcock, first instructor of Informal Logic], and the Jerusalem Bible. Not only did these things seem unrelated to each other (and remarkably dull in many cases), they seemed acutely unrelated to my ambition to go to law school and my classmates' ambitions to go to medical school. We were studying everything from soup to nuts, and increasingly it seemed like the Programme was more nuts than soup! What *had* I gotten myself into?

The upper year students had told me that it would get better after first year, and they were right. Increasingly I began to see some method to the madness, the materials became more interesting (with the exception of biology, for which my lack of interest was partly driven by ineptitude), and I think I may have even begun to grasp why the med-school enthusiasts had gravitated to the Programme. The way I came to articulate (much later on) my own attraction was drawn from a letter explaining "what Arts and Science is" (always a challenging question, as we all know). Dr. Jenkins had kindly furnished this clever letter to help students seeking jobs and admission to further education. My own reading of the letter centred on the notion of inquiry, which he called "the art and science of inquiry into problems of public concern." In retrospect, this has become a mantra for me in making sense of what exactly I had done with those four years of my life. In my third year, I can see now, I began to catch the inquiry bug in nearly all my classes. This manifested even, to my own surprise, in a sudden reversal of my desire to bolt to law school.

What caused this change of heart, this new embracing of Arts and Science? The negative answer is that around this time I began a part-time job in a law firm, where I learned that dictating letters for days on end is the staple of some of the more boring but lucrative legal specialties. (As a footnote, I should say that the people I know from Arts and Science who *did* go to law school are doing really remarkable things that I never would have dreamed possible with a law degree—labour law and constitutional law in particular.) But more affirmatively, although unarticulated at the time, I think I began to relish the idea of spending my time in deep and thoughtful "inquiry into problems of public concern." I guess I had been successfully acculturated into Arts and Science. The first objects of my newfound interest in inquiry were environmental issues, and I also had a brief dalliance with peace issues during the Gulf War. But in the final term of my programme (luckily) I took a course in "health geography" where the issue of the large and persistent inequalities in health which exist between social classes in industrialized societies caught my imagination, and has held it ever since. Eleven years later this is what I now do on a day to day basis, and it can be at least partially attributed to the appeal of inquiry. Ultimately, I guess, what makes inquiry endure for me is that it presupposes, I would argue, that society is a human construction, not simply something that occurs like the weather, and that the way things are is not necessarily the way they must be—that social change is possible.

Of course, all of this could simply be a *post hoc* explanation of how I arrived at the time and place where I currently sit [Assistant Professor, Department of Community Health Sciences, University of Calgary], an explanation that I've repeated to myself so many times that it now passes for the truth. Maybe so, but it seems to work, and I'd be shocked if it didn't resonate with more than a few other graduates of the Programme. As for me, in spite the serendipitous chain of events that had me enter it, I expect that "the art and science of inquiry into problems of public concern" will be a mantra for me to live by for a long time to come.

Larry Innes ('92)
Telling something about our lives will always reveal something of who we believe ourselves to be. I've always fancied myself as a traveler, and I've been an eager seeker of new horizons to explore. The Arts and Science Programme was the point of departure for many of my own journeys.

As Barry Lopez observes, what one experiences while traveling is a result of at least three things: what one knows, what one imagines, and how one is disposed. If knowledge, imagination, and desire mediate our experience of the world, as students in the Arts and Science Programme, we learned to travel well.

Although I must still confess a complete ignorance of calculus, what I've found invaluable about an Arts and Science education is knowing something about how my society orders its understandings of the world. It's like being able to read a map: to be able to situate particular facts within a general body or region of knowledge, and to quickly relate one region to another in ways that emphasize connections.

Imagination and desire lead us to take the risks and seek the rewards of new experience. These qualities were nurtured within the Programme, ostensibly through Inquiry seminars and in other courses, but I found that they came about at least in equal measure in kitchens, coffee shops, and late-night study sessions with fellow students.

My life has taken a number of interesting turns since graduating from the Programme. Climbing and kayaking trips on the West Coast led to volunteer work in West Africa, and then to graduate work in environmental studies back in Canada. I now live in Labrador, where I work with the Innu Nation on land and resource issues, in the context of their ongoing land claim negotiations with Canada and Newfoundland. I've also started a family here, and I'm now busy helping my daughter, Manish, begin to explore her world.

The Innu are great travelers, having spent millennia as nomadic hunters. But they are also indigenous to this place, and they have a deep knowledge, appreciation, and respect for the land. As a newcomer in Innu territory, I've learned just how inadequate my own knowledge of a place can be. But I've also come to appreciate that a traveler's perspective can reveal new possibilities. This is especially apparent in negotiations. There is still a long way to go in that process, as the Innu are trying to leave behind the trauma, dislocation, and other colonial legacies of the past. I've come to understand that while Canadians believe Canada to be a liberal and progressive society, the Innu and many other Aboriginal peoples continue to experience domination, dispossession, and assimilation at our hands. From the vantage of someone who has learned to live and work in "two worlds", I've come to regard my role as a sort of "cultural interpreter" helping both Innu and government participants in the negotiations get past some of the barriers that situated perspectives can create.

As travel accounts reveal so clearly, our interpretations are often inadequate to the richness of what is there. Explorers in the nineteenth century were certain of their own privileged perspective on the world. But I've come to believe that we all have a responsibility to be open to different ways of being in the world, and to the possibilities for positive change that can result when we choose to learn to live with different and imperfect understandings, instead of trying to impose our own interpretations on a place.

I'm fortunate to share this perspective with some of my fellow travelers from the Programme, and all the more so because many of our paths still cross.

Kathryn Denning (entered '88, transferred '89)
If someone had told me in October 1988 that in October 2001 I would be e-mailing a writing assignment to Barbara Ferrier and Herb Jenkins from my desk on the McMaster campus...I would have asked, "What's e-mail?"

Once past that conceptual hurdle, I would surely have raised an eyebrow or two and wondered if I was really going to be thirteen years late with my first Inquiry paper, and still living in Brandon Hall.

It would certainly not have occurred to me that I would leave Arts and Science, complete a BA and MA in Anthropology at McMaster, travel overseas to do a PhD in Archaeology at the University of Sheffield, teach university in British Columbia and Ontario, return to McMaster in the Department of Anthropology in 2001 as a postdoctoral fellow, and then, out of the blue, receive a lovely invitation to contribute some thoughts about life after the Arts and Science Programme to an upcoming book.

No indeed. In October 1988, the most inconceivable of all those eventual realities would have been the first—that I would leave Arts and Science. It was, after all, my dream programme, and I was enjoying it thoroughly. Sure, some aspects of that first year were somewhat alarming— I remember clearly my wonder at Professor Bowerbank's meticulous dissection of my first essay, and my dismay over my first calculus test— but I was nonetheless excited by the challenges, and happy to be part of a scene so energetic and intense. But my fledgling fascination with archaeology and anthropology soon developed a ferocious appetite and a will of its own. By the end of first year, I was convinced that I couldn't survive without oodles of anthropology courses. I simply had to have *all anthropology, all the time*! I was hooked. I transferred that summer.

I also had extraordinary teachers in Anthropology and am still smitten with the field—obviously!—but I have somehow managed to take Arts and Science with me on this journey through life and academia. Precious friendships with fellow Arts and Science students (you know who you are) lasted throughout my undergraduate years and beyond, and continue to inspire me. My research endeavours have been relentlessly interdisciplinary in true Arts and Science style. And principles I learned from Arts and Science professors in that crucial first year continue to guide me: Ask. Search. Look outwards. Listen harder. Find the edges of the problem and work into it, beside it, around it, through it, and don't be surprised when the edges move or dissolve. Read the book again. Think again. Revise again. Cooperate. Start something new. Make something better. Remember differential equations…?

Yes, I'm surprised to report that, although I'm currently studying the representation of archaeological knowledge, I still use calculus regularly. I only hope that Professor Stewart won't be disappointed that what I draw upon is not the math, but the experience of being humbled and awed by something I had thought I understood.

In October 1988, I would never have expected that thirteen years

later, I'd be as grateful for that unimpressive midterm mark as for all the other mind-expanding moments of my year in Arts and Science. But I am.
     And in truth, I *am* still working on that Inquiry paper.

Robert Sinding ('92)
I have great memories of my undergrad experience—life was so new and had so much potential and promise. Compared to those formative years in Arts and Science, my subsequent university education lacked the same level of close friendships, encouragement, and inspiration.
     I came out of high school wanting to improve society and hence I fit into Arts and Science very well. I was the Arts and Science student president in '91-'92. I then worked for a year in two NDP MPP [New Democratic Party, Member of Provincial Parliament] Constituency Offices, where my suspicions were confirmed that, unfortunately, very little time in politics is spent attempting to solve social problems with informed policy considerations. The experience helped me develop my opinion that much more can be done to change the existing policy landscape if one learns to pick one's battles and to specialize, to influence a narrow policy field rather than every possible area. I observed that decision-makers are only too glad to give tremendous deference to the work of experts in order to get a file off their desks.
     Then I attended Ottawa Law School, and returned to a third MPP's office for a summer after the first year. I did a combined LL.B. and M.A. degree, the latter at Carleton University's Norman Paterson School of International Affairs (NSPIA). I was in good company at NPSIA and in Ottawa generally, with many other ArtScis.
     My M.A. thesis related to the effect of globalization on workers and labour standards generally. It eventually was developed into a book co-authored with my two supervisors, *Toward a Fair Global Labour Market*, published by Routledge. Thus when I moved to Toronto after four years in Ottawa, to article at a labour law firm, I was able to maintain my interest in labour issues.
     After articling and doing the Bar Admission Exams, I accepted a job in Kenora, Ontario, a 24-hour drive from Toronto and 3-hour-drive from Winnipeg, doing criminal and aboriginal law. I experienced a completely different world working with native people and living in a truly rural, isolated and beautiful environment by Lake of the Woods. Another great aspect of the job was being a sole practitioner in association with two other lawyers, and hence being my own boss. I highly recommend

this for anyone caught up in the rat race. It is nice to know you can always fall back on self-employment as an alternative to working in a career you are no longer happy with. I found it much easier to become self-employed than I had imagined.

Kenora was beautiful, I canoed and mountain-biked a lot, I gave up my vegetarianism (try explaining this diet to a native Chief) and I made frequent flights in small aircraft to remote native communities to assist in the administration of northern justice, complete with sentencing circles and other cutting-edge attempts at restorative justice. Canada's First Nations are, without a doubt, the most disadvantaged of Canadians, and it would be hard to find legal work that is more important and meaningful. However, I left Kenora after two years because I was involved in a long-distance relationship with a girl from my high school with whom I had become reacquainted.

I was planning on setting up my own practice in Peterborough, but I decided to apply for a few jobs and have been a Crown Counsel for the Ministry of Labour since May 2001. My main responsibility is enforcing provincial labour statutes, primarily through prosecuting corporations violating the *Occupational Health and Safety Act,* so my criminal law experience ended up being extremely helpful. It is hard to predict how your various experiences will influence your future. It is interesting to note that several people advised me that if I was truly interested in practicing labour law I should stay in Toronto because a move to Kenora would amount to career suicide. Instead, I did what I thought was best for me at the time, and I am certain that my unconventional career choices, such as working for the NDP and working up North, helped me get the job. I was doing serious trials, mostly in criminal law, on my own in my first year of practice while other first year associates, I hear, were keeping the photocopier warm. Also, the Ministry of Labour assigned me to the "Northern team", presumably due to my familiarity with northern life.

I am starting a Master of Law degree (LL.M.) in the fall at the University of Toronto, so I may end up as a professor of law, but for now I am pretty happy with my career, and I am attempting to find some synergies between my work and my academic research.

Dwayne Hodgson ('92)

And you may find yourself living in a shotgun shack
And you may find yourself in another part of the world
And you may find yourself behind the wheel of a large automobile

> And you may find yourself in a beautiful house with a
> beautiful wife
> And you ask yourself – Well. How did I get here?
>   – from *Once in a Lifetime* by David Byrne and Chris Frantz

I'm asking myself that same question these days as I'm taking refuge from the November heat under a merciful ceiling fan as the ants crawl over the coffee table and onto my legs and the sweat drips down my neck and back and I'm simultaneously enthralled by the life here and homesick for the CBC [Canadian Broadcasting Company], my bike, and snow. My father said that I should become a banker. But no! Here I am sweating away in Tanzania working for a Canadian church-based NGO. Well, how did I get here?

I suppose, however, that when I look back and trace the lines of Providence, serendipity, and/or just sheer dumb luck, I can see the waves that converged and cast me upon the shores of Dar-es-Salaam.

One is faith, I am a Christian—although I'm not so fussy about wearing the brand name of any one denomination. Does that make me a saint? Hell, no! Just someone who is trying to live out what they have experienced of God. And I think that among other things, God calls us to live and work for justice for the poor and to steward the Creation. And for now, that work has brought me here.

The second wave is a car accident that I survived in 1988, just as I was half-way through my first year at McMaster. Two friends died and others sustained serious, life-altering injuries. For myself, the numbers speak for themselves: one broken nose, two broken legs, eight lost teeth, four months in hospital, seven operations, eleven months of physiotherapy and years of struggling about what this all means on an existential level. No, I didn't lose my faith, but I still have lots of questions. And I still cry at sappy homecoming scenes in movies and I find it hard to see people suffering. So yeah, here I am trying to do something about it, although I still have a lot to learn about how to help.

The third wave is the remarkable five years I had in the Arts and Science Programme. Remarkable not only for the great learning environment and the sheer range of subjects that we could sample, but also for the community of free-thinkers, hippies, activists, artists, scholars, med-keeners, politico-wannabes, and bohemians that moved through the Programme's territory.

To be honest—and this is where the dumb luck comes in—I entered the Programme largely because I couldn't decide what type of degree to pursue—Arts? Science? Arts? Science? I left equally unfocussed, but with an integrated perspective on development and environment issues, and some wonderful experiences of campus activism that might as well have been considered as core requirements for many Arts and Science students at the time (along with a compulsory year off, of course). It was definitely the best academic experience I've had—loads better than the MA I subsequently did. But more importantly, I still count it as one of my richest experiences of community, one that tested my faith, shaped my thinking and blew wide-open my world view.

To this day, I find that what I learned there has shaped my ways of thinking about development, (and ensured that I can hold my own at cocktail parties anywhere). I also find that I can connect with many Arts and Science grads instantly—not that we necessarily agree on everything, but that we have shared a common experience and an understanding of how to question things. In fact, one of these grads is my wife, Tricia Wind (Arts and Science '94). And while we certainly don't agree on everything, we tend to see things form a similar eccentric perspective. And together we have come as far as Tanzania.

So yeah, looking back, I can see the path that brought me here. But looking ahead? Hmmm, that's a different thing altogether. If my hindsight is 20/20, I'm pretty near-sighted when it comes to the future. Who knows what's next? I'll have to see which way the currents take me.

Letting the days go by/ let the water hold me down
Letting the days go by/ water flowing underground
Into the blue again/ after the money's gone
Once in a lifetime/ water flowing underground.
            – from *Once in a Lifetime* by David Byrne and Chris Frantz

Malcolm Pellettier ('93)
I was delighted to be given this opportunity to reminisce; my capacity for rose-tinted nostalgia exceeds that of most war veterans and aging pop stars. I suppose my desert island, all-time, top six most memorable Arts and Science moments would have to include the following:
1. Spending more time on that first calculus essay than on my undergraduate thesis.
2. Locking myself in Mckay Hall's bowels for four days in late November, to complete my first Inquiry paper.
3. Living with seven other students in the "unofficial" Arts and Science house on South Oval, surely breaking several provisions in Hamilton's fire code.

4. Writing Arts and Entertainment articles for the *Silhouette* [McMaster student newspaper], and getting to meet several of my rock and roll heroes with a paltry *Silhouette* press pass.
5. Performing a grunged-up version of "Like a Virgin" and "Madonna's Got a Crush On Us" for one of the Coffee Houses, only to have an especially convivial first-year student write an excoriating review of our performance for a student newspaper. He described our sound as a "dissonant dirge with an atonal singer," and then lamented that we couldn't sound more like Bob Dylan; the irony obviously escaped him.
6. Spending the summer of '91 working in London, England, where I became a shameless Anglophile and an inveterate popular music collector. The trip included a pilgrimage to Manchester and the fabled Hacienda at the crest of the Madchester craze, perhaps the most important youth cultural movement of the past fifteen years. I wrote a short story about the excursion, modelled somewhat after James Joyce's "An Encounter," which later won the Agora's [Arts and Science student magazine] short story contest. I can remember my thesis supervisor, Dr. Ferns, asking, quite rightly, why a Mancunian street urchin kept slipping into a Scottish brogue; my command of the Northern dialect obviously left something to be desired.

Looking back, I realize now that the times were remarkably tumultuous, while I was caught up in the sort of quotidian, work-a-day obliviousness of pursuing my undergraduate degree: there was Free Trade, the Recession, Soviet dissolution, Anita Hill, Meech Lake, Charlottetown, Oka, the L.A. riots, Waco, Bosnia, Bob Rae, Preston Manning, Lucien Bouchard, and Bill Clinton. The most divisive issue on campus, however, was unquestionably "Operation Desert Storm." Vietnam, in part because it was the first televised war, managed to stratify a nation, but it also galvanized social and intellectual movements of lasting and profound influence. The Gulf War, on the other hand, merely satiated our technology fetish, with the Pentagon's carefully sanitized pyrotechnic display. CNN swamped us with continual twenty four-hour coverage until there was nothing left but a sense of banality about the entire enterprise. I think what I recall most is the overwhelming sense of impotence that I felt in the face of our bellicose neighbours.

When I moved on to pursue a masters degree, I realized how much the Arts and Science Programme had spoiled us. It was basically four years of graduate studies before graduate school: small classes, bright students, and lots of research. I suspect that some of us may have received a rude awakening in grad school. Some of us, like myself, may have even been under the misguided impression that all universities were progressive, left-leaning affairs; but then, I had the misfortune of pursuing doctoral studies at another university, where I encountered nothing but supercilious conservatism. Even McMaster, at the time, was itself a curious mixture of pedagogical progressiveness and pockets of old-school haughtiness. Fortunately, we were situated squarely in the former category.

Today, the importance of a liberal education cannot be overstated, especially in the face of neo-conservatism's scourge, though after six years, I'm becoming inured to Mephistopheles', I mean Mike Harris's [Ontario premier, 1995-2002] tyranny. The ongoing contraction of the humanities and the calls of an erstwhile Education Minister (who incomprehensibly lacked a post-secondary education!) for funding based on job placements demand vociferous apologists for a catholic education. At the risk of whingeing, critical appraisal skills are intensely political tools that enable students to resist rhetorical persuasiveness and to recognize the ideological heritage behind legislative policies. In fact, I wouldn't mind seeing the introduction of Critical Theory, or Continental philosophy, the Parisian rather than the Frankfurt variety, and minority discourses (dreadful term), feminism, queer theory, and postcoloniality into the curriculum, but then, I may be succumbing to my own disciplinary biases.

In the end, I'd like to thank the entire Arts and Science faculty for their vision and dedication, basically reinvigorating an old idea in the face of increasing specialization, for providing invaluable intellectual life skills, and for providing me with some wonderful memories.

Jennie Barron ('93) and **Erik Leslie** ('95)
I hardly ever read anymore. Not unless you count bedtime stories or e-mail. I start books; I even buy them occasionally. But I don't read them. Maybe it's that things—work, errands, laundry, buying a house, moving (we've moved five times in the last three years), toddler playgroup, yardwork, attempts at exercise, keeping up a correspondence with friends and family, just putting food on the table—these and other things get in the way. So maybe reading is the dessert I never get to. Or maybe, after many years at university, I still associate reading somehow with work. But I have a third idea. It is possible that the reason I never read is just that I am living out the pendulum's swing from the abstract to the concrete. Or in Wendell Berry's words, the word and the flesh. Maybe this is just the way things are meant to be right now.

In university, I thought a lot about how life ought to be lived. In Tech [Technology and Society course] we studied planning for sustainability; we looked at architecture and design, and how the identification of patterns that work could transform our homes, cities, and rural areas. In Work, Media, Nuclear, and Environmental Inquiries, we busted myths and assumptions, engaged new paradigms of thinking, and conducted theoretical evaluations of the Great Whale Hydroelectric project and the Gulf War. We dealt mainly in this abstract world of ideas. And so, as rich and challenging and liberating as those years in Arts and Science were, I always had the feeling that my "real" life was still in the planning stages.

By the end of university I craved "real life." It seemed that I had only read about it and that the life I'd been living had been of another sort altogether. (Indeed, people told me it was.) It wasn't that I didn't do my own laundry, or hold a job, or rub shoulders with people on the street; I was not that cloistered in an ivory tower. It's more a question of where my head was. Graduation hit like a proverbial ton of bricks. In spite of all the planning (vague and dreamy as opposed to practical), I wasn't ready for my real life to begin. I didn't know even where to start.

I knew that I wanted life to be more visceral, less theoretical. I wanted to feel myself living. I wanted to work with my hands, put my mind to practical problems. Leave the city. I—now we—jumped at the chance to house-sit a working sheep farm—with 120 ewes, two rams, and 250 rolling acres in Grey County—for a year. Along with two of our close friends, we raised 200 lambs, shovelled tons of manure, planted vegetables, canned fruit, drove tractors, cut wood, repaired rusty cars, and made maple syrup. In the quiet evenings before falling asleep at around 9 p.m., we also read novels and rural history—anything but critical social theory. When the role-playing was over, we got jobs at a commercial apiary down the road. Beekeeping—now that's visceral! We got stung half a dozen times a day in that job. Beekeeping is also very gruelling, physical work. We had never worked so hard or produced so much— ninety thousand pounds annually is a lot of honey.

All this was visceral, but it still wasn't very real. It wasn't a lasting life choice, and we continued to search for a life that suited us. We thought seriously about buying forest with friends, and developing a sustainable, working demonstration forest. (We still hope to do this eventually.) By this point, it had become clear that the pursuit of an idealized lifestyle needed to be reconciled with the mechanics of making a living

Today we live in a little post-war bungalow in a small town in the British Columbia interior. Erik works full-time as an eco-forestry consultant and forest planner. Jennie does some contract work and a bit of writing, but mostly she stays home with our two-year-old son Quinn. (It might sound mundane to some, but it's as real as any life, grounded by blood, bread, earth, tears.) We're not living out the romance we thought we might: the hard-knuckled "pure" existence of living in a cabin in the woods, or at least in a self-reliant community. But it's not for lack of conviction. It's more that everything changes when the world of free, abstract ideas gives way to the act of living them out.

It's not that ideas—and ideals—have suddenly become expendable. In fact, if it weren't for all the philosophical brooding and intellectual sparring that we had time for in those Arts and Science years, we surely would not have made the life choices we have. It's just that testing and trying to manifest those ideals takes a long time. And the ideas evolve.

Most of our ideas now come directly from our own lives. There are fewer of them, but they are more grounded, less global. No longer do the authors we read or the essays we write determine how we see ourselves. Now we sculpt our identities from the real-life decisions we make—those with price-tags and actual consequences; decisions like where we live and school our children, how we derive a livelihood and spend money. The idea of sustainability is now manifest in our day-to-day choices, and our visions of family life. The idea of community is manifest in little things we do, like volunteering for Co-op Radio, and sharing regular weekly meals with neighbours. We've finally settled in enough to dust off our youthful ideals and see to what extent we can make them real. And we're learning more that what distinguishes practice from theory is that practice takes a great deal more patience, and some compromise.

Meanwhile the tasks of daily living take priority. Erik is gone ten hours a day for work; Jennie is busy making Quinn a monkey costume for Halloween; we're organizing with our neighbours, building furniture, cleaning leaves from the eavestroughs. We're doing many things we didn't have to do, or even think about doing when we were in university. And having the time to do them is a privilege we want to indulge right now.

Which all comes back to saying that we hardly read anymore. In this bookless interlude of our lives, our vocabularies may not be increasing. But as the pendulum swings back toward the word, as it is sure to do, the flesh—that substrate upon which our understanding of all we will yet read is built—is getting richer. So when we finally get back to William Cronon, dian marino, Thomas King and the others who sit patiently, unread, on our bedside tables, we will appreciate and engage their words that much more, for we will have something to add to the dialogue.

Brenda Matthews ('94)

It has been a long road for me through academia, one which I am still happy to travel. While in high school, I had already become strongly interested in science but remained passionate about the arts. I remember well taking a second English OAC [Ontario Academic Credit course] in my final high school year. The goal of the course was improvement of writing skills, and the teacher, after announcing that this course was really for those who intended to pursue English or related subjects, asked each of us to state why we were taking the class. When my turn came, I stated rather blatantly that I intended to pursue science but that I felt communication was vital to good science, and that hence I had every reason for being in his class.

I guess it was this philosophy that led me into Arts and Science, and despite a brief period of angst at the end of my first year about the difficulty of specialization, I have never regretted my decision. I combined with Physics, which stretched my degree from the typical four, to five years. The road was sometimes stressful, to which my various roommates over my undergraduate years would no doubt attest. Fortunately, between my Arts and Science courses and physics courses, I found time to take all the astronomy courses McMaster offered. For my undergraduate thesis in my final year, I knew I wanted to try an astronomy project. I spent a year, and then a summer, working with Dr. Christine Wilson on the history of star formation in two regions of our galaxy, and I was hooked.

The choice to continue on to graduate school was easily made. The University of Calgary beckoned, and off I set for the West. I spent two years working on my Master's with Dr. Russ Taylor in the shadow of the Rockies. My project resulted in the identification of the oldest known remnant of a supernova explosion, the death of a very massive star. The presentation of this work garnered me an award at the 1996 annual meeting of the Canadian Astronomical Society.

Later in 1996, following a lifelong dream trip, an African safari, I returned to begin a Ph.D. with Christine Wilson. Doctoral programmes are so different from Master's; they're longer and ideally much more in the control of the student. I spent the better part of the next five years investigating the prevalence and geometry of magnetic fields inside molecular clouds, the birthplace of all stars, using a new instrument on the James Clerk Maxwell Telescope in Hawaii. Travel to Hawaii is just one of the perks of doing original research in astronomy. During my doctoral studies, I was also fortunate enough to travel to California, Holland and Spain.

The transition from graduate to postdoctoral work is one of the largest filtering processes in academia. This is also the point at which many Canadians must leave the country in order to continue their work; since postdocs are considerably more costly than graduate students, they simply cannot be supported on the grants of the average Canadian faculty member. I accepted a position at the University of California, Berkeley. My choice was made for the chance to work and make contacts outside the Canadian community. With luck, and a faculty position, I hope to return to Canada eventually.

Liz Darling ('94)
I started the programme in 1989. Like a number of my classmates, I had been directed towards math and science in high school but wasn't ready to commit. I had a vague notion that I wanted a "classic education," and no idea what I wanted to be when I grew up! First year did provide the foundation for which I had been hoping. Even more excitingly, I found myself a class full of students who were interested, thoughtful, and eager to share their perspectives. Of all my courses that year, Inquiry probably had the biggest impact. It taught me how to transform inquisitiveness into scholarly inquiry, and fostered not just critical thinking but also social criticism. On the other hand, my large, lecture-based Chemistry class completely turned me off science courses.

As a new student, I felt welcomed into a community by faculty and students in the years ahead of me. Formally, SASS [Society of Arts and Science Students] events like Milk & Cookies nights and coffee houses helped build that sense of community. Informally, the Monday night club, communal living and the participation of so many students in a plethora of extra-curricular activities made the community vibrant. Much of the learning and debate that I cherish from my Arts and Science years took place outside the classroom. My memories of second year, shaped primarily by the Gulf War, are almost entirely extra-curricular in nature! One of the influences of my fellow students was their propensity to "take a year off." By the end of second year I was feeling directionless. I decided that a year away from school would offer new learning opportunities, and hopefully a little inspiration. I spent the summer volunteering in West Africa, in Togo. The remainder of the year, I worked and travelled in B.C. with various Arts and Science friends. When I returned to McMaster in the fall of 1992, I had a new focus. Somewhere in my travels I realized midwifery would allow me to bring together the arts and the sciences in a way that was right for me. In my final years, I appreciated the freedom to take electives from a range of disciplines to explore this interest. In the core Arts and Science courses, I continued to relish the unparalleled passion and involvement of both faculty and fellow students. A highlight for me was the Literature course taught by Jean Wilson.

After graduating, I studied midwifery at McMaster and have been working as a midwife since 1997. I have found a profession with a philosophy that fits perfectly with my personal values, offers rewarding work that is never dull or predictable, and challenges me in new ways every day—although it does not always leave enough time for all those extra-curricular activities that I would like to do! The Arts and Science Programme continues to have a lasting impact on me, particularly through the people I met. Perhaps the programme's greatest achievement has been to attract and nurture people who are creative, reflective, adventurous, principled, and involved. In the many different ways they are living their lives, my friends from Arts and Science continue to inspire me.

Karen Bakker ('95)

I arrived at McMaster in 1990 and, quickly becoming immersed in the campus environmentalist culture shared by some other ArtScis, bought a bike, learned to love lentils, recycled dutifully, and thought of creative ways to reuse the hundreds of plastic Astro yoghurt containers piling up in the kitchen cupboards of our communal household, that I didn't have the heart to throw out. Shrugging off the "Arts & Crafts" label, we carved out a bounded life of environmentally friendly rituals. Each squeaky styrofoam cup, each car belching fumes, was a moral as well as an environmental assault. Lobbying the city council for cycle paths, devout vegetarianism, writing on both sides of your notepaper, communal kitchens in communal houses, and wearing reusable plastic mugs strapped like badges of honour to our knapsacks were the answers. Political statements, I believed, were best made through personal, local action, through living lightly on the earth, even in the city.

Arts and Science was a good place to be working through these ideas: a quirky mix of people—from vaguely left-leaning to libertarian; politically active, politically correct and politically quiescent; from outdoorsy types on mountain bikes to urbanites with BMWs; some earnestly engaged in the search for "right livelihood," others intent on entry to the right professional school. Mostly middle class, and not very ethnically diverse, many of us had our horizons stretched by our teachers— our professors, and sometimes one another—intent on asking critical questions, and interested in individual students' answers. We were privileged in being in a programme with more time and resources per student than most, able to foster an environment that would encourage students' appetite for ideas, and designed to teach us the skills we needed to engage in debate—logic, writing, research, numeracy, scientific and philosophical literacy. This is the sort of experience most university students have at the graduate level, rarely as undergraduates.

In 1995 I won a Rhodes Scholarship, moved to Oxford, and began graduate work in geography. The contrast with Arts and Science was stark. My education here as been as much about the acquisition of cultural capital as it has been about intellectual training. As a colonial arriving in England, in a weird echo of the imperial civilising mission, I've become adept with cutlery (although eating green peas properly with a fork still defeats me), and learned to adopt, clumsily, the artifice and veiled ritual codified as "manners" in some segments of English society. If at McMaster I learned to cultivate my bioregionalism and my roots, people here cultivate their mobility and their antennae: students here are usually well travelled and multilingual, but with no idea (nor interest) in where the water in their taps comes from. Oxford is not only a university with highly competitive admissions, but also a training ground for the elite from around the world, and particularly of Britain and its former colonies, producing fine scholars but also attracting people who, as Gary Snyder puts it: "make unimaginably large sums of money, people impeccably groomed, excellently educated at the best universities—male and female alike—eating fine foods and reading classy literature, while orchestrating the investment and legislation that ruin the world." Perhaps it should come as no surprise that the spirit of critical inquiry does not thrive here—professors, as well as students, are often incurious about the rest of the world, not to mention other academic subjects. In my first few months here I was often reminded of Jean Wilson's discussions about the margins—geographical, intellectual, social—being a greater place of freedom than the core.

The traditions of academia, at least as I've lived them at Oxford, often work against curiosity and a relentless spirit of critique—qualities I was taught (by some fellow students as well as profs in Arts and Science) to believe are essential to being a political intellectual. Academics here specialise in specialising, and are suspicious of innovation; "new" subjects like the environment, and "interdisciplinary" work are regarded with scepticism. One dominant trend in contemporary academia is the division of knowledge into distinct terrains—creating mutually unintelligible languages about common problems. I now understand why academics belong to "disciplines"—because becoming an academic requires restraint and discipline, as you are taught not to "think outside the box," but to reinforce it. And so, several years after leaving McMaster, I now realise how lucky I was to be in Arts and Science, which was more radical than we perhaps realised: in dispensing with disciplines; emphasising problem-definition rather than problem-solution; in providing us with the tools we needed to think critically; and in trying not only to teach us how to answer questions, but also how to ask them. As I move into an academic career (I'll be an Assistant Professor of Environmental Geography at UBC starting in 2002), I'm appreciating all the more that this is a precious and by no means easy task.

Patrick Feng ('95)
When I entered the Arts and Science Programme back in 1991 (a whopping ten years ago—where has the time gone?!), I didn't know where it would take me. Little did I know it would take me halfway around the world. Now, as I type these thoughts from Beijing, where I am a visiting scholar, I think back to fond memories from my artsci days.

I remember hearing about the Programme while in high school and thinking to myself: "this would be a good place for me." While I was interested in math and science, I didn't want to give up the more "artsy" subjects either, and so I found choosing a major difficult. Luckily, with Arts and Science, I could make a classic "non-decision" and postpone choosing what to specialize in. My parents, needless to say, were suitably aghast, urging me instead to choose a more practical, concrete programme of study (preferably pre-med). Sometimes I think they're still in disbelief.

Strange but true: my first admissions letter from McMaster said I had *not* been accepted into Arts and Science. (I think I actually cried when I read that.) But the letter was accompanied by a cryptic phone message, left on our answering machine, asking that I contact the registrar's office ASAP. Turns out they'd sent the wrong letter—I had been accepted after all! Talk about a jittery start. Arts and Science has had a big influence on my professional life. In fact, my going to graduate school was a direct result of an artsci course. In my third year, I (along with my classmates) took *Technology and Society* with Bob Hudspith. For many of us, this was the first time we'd been challenged to think critically about technology, and take stock of its pervasive influence (both good and bad) on modern life. As students in Bob's class, we asked ourselves: "Why do we have the technology we have? Is this the only way tech could have developed? How could things be different?" My experiences from that class would later lead me to pursue a Ph.D. in *Science and Technology Studies,* focusing in particular on the political and social implications of new technologies. So, in a very real sense, Arts and Science led me to my current career. Just as importantly, Arts and Science has enriched my personal life as well. For one thing, I think that having met so many gifted and caring people has made me a better person. My interest in international development was fostered by my time in Arts and Science: beginning with first-year inquiry—of which I still have fond memories, despite (or perhaps because of?) the all-nighters involved—my desire to gain a global perspective on things has continually grown. As with numerous other alums, I did a volunteer stint with *Canadian Crossroads* after I graduated, and still consider that to be one of the highlights of my life. This spirit of volunteerism and thinking globally I learned from my artsci friends. Finally, aside from providing professional guidance and personal enrichment, Arts and Science was simply fun! Here are a few of my best memories from university life at MAC: talent shows; artsci parties, formals, and semi-formals; milk and cookies night (yes, that's really what we called it); late night editing sessions of *The Agora* [Arts and Science student magazine]; midnight walks through Cootes [natural forest area adjoining the campus]; Creative Arts course trips to the theatre; impromptu music performances at Prof. Stewart's house; going to class in my pyjamas.

Now, as the Arts and Science Programme turns towards its next twenty years of teaching and learning, may I wish my fellow artsci grads all the very best for the future!

Cheryl Lousley ('96)
Dark and quiet in Toronto, but for the rain.

When I left my apartment at 5 a.m., the night was cold and dry, the city still asleep. Now the rain has started and the wet seeps into my cycling shoes. We are searched by the police when we arrive at City Hall—the rain pounding down by this point, a few cars starting to swish through the streets, but I am calm as the faces and badges appear out of the darkness of an October morning. It is still so early that we don't have the energy to protest, but blankly hand over our bags, swallowing the words of non-consent with the coffee we are forced to drink down or dump before venturing further. I am required to leave my dangerous weapons—an apple and a water bottle—behind on my bike, and I join my friends to huddle under a cement canopy. Drums beat steadily on the other side of the square where more bodies mass and crush together out of the rain. Tension, fear rises with the rhythms and we look at each other steadily, not smiling, touching fingers as we move to join the other demonstrators with the Ontario Common Front.

Neo-conservatism came to power in Ontario just as I was finishing my Arts and Science degree, and in the five years since graduation I've walked picket lines, waved placards, written countless useless letters to assistants of assistants of politicians. I have stood again and again on the grass at Queen's Park [Toronto] staring at the impassive legislative building looming behind whichever speaker of the week. I have knocked on doors canvassing for elections, ridden joyfully through the streets of Toronto with hundreds of other cyclists in critical mass, debated political strategy for hours in living rooms, pubs, streetcars, and beds, receiving derogatory, threatening e-mails in response to organizing a women's group at a university. I have been tear-gassed in Quebec City.

"Get a job!" some guy yells from his car, stopped by the demonstration from getting through Bay Street. And it's true, politics is almost like a full-time job when you take it seriously. When you believe in creating the world in which you live. And I believe I help to create this world in which I live and love and dream and despair and wonder at its beauty, oh so beautiful these people around me and this singing I hear and these hands I hold in mine and the speed wind glide of my bike flying like the butterflies which danced over my roof in September migration, so beautiful this world, this life.

There are people in my life who suggest that I will grow out of this "political phase," as if politics is adolescent and apathy is more adult.

We set out into the streets once the darkness eases into grey morning, streaming between the cars stalled on University Avenue, placing flowers on windshields, and smiling at the coming day.

Jenny Macdonald ('96)

Looking back on my first degree, five years after it ended, it seems impossible to imagine who I might have become with it. If the Master's I just finished taught me about a subject, Arts and Science taught me about life. I remember very clearly my first day. All the new students had gathered to meet with Dr. Ferrier and some of the professors. Dr. Ferrier encouraged us above all to cultivate balance in our lives. At that time I breathed the same sigh of relief that I had when I first found out about the Programme. It had been such a thrill to discover a university programme that embraced complexity rather than simplifying life through compartmentalization. When I arrived and saw that notion in action it was exhilarating. The meeting of like minds was electric; the excitement of being constantly surrounded by students and professors who were intelligent, critical, aware, questioning, and engaged. Most of my closest friends remain those that I met in art/sci. They are people who want to challenge their minds, widen, not narrow their thinking, and try to live with integrity in a complicated world.

The struggle for balance, or for "living in the tension" as we used to say in Tech. class, has not been a simple one. I emerged from art/sci with at least a vision of who I was and how I wanted to live, and I have been working with the ways to make it reality ever since. The lessons in undergraduate experience were sometimes overwhelming. I was confronting what my personal success actually meant or might do for anyone else in the world. I was overwhelmed by the inequalities of race, gender, and class, and becoming concerned and active in refugee and world development organizations. The inquiry courses and the Human Rights Theme School [a McMaster programme, equivalent to a minor] gave me a chance to intellectually confront those issues. But it was the third year with Tech. and Environment [Inquiry course] that was an intellectual and personal watershed. I felt that year that I was returning to things I had always known without ever realizing I knew them. Technological progress, and in many ways everything we had been taught to try to achieve in our lives, were suddenly on the chopping block. It was amazing and terrifying. It is funny to realize how many of the paradigms for living that were a revolution to me then are commonplace in my community now. Of course, an inevitable frustration resulted then from feeling so strongly that we were living in unhealthy ways, while simultaneously overextending ourselves with coursework and extracurricular commitments. The idea of balance sounded good—the idea that there needed to be time in life to cook, to have conversations with friends and to visit people in hospital—but it would be another two years before I felt I could do it myself.

When I graduated I moved to Scotland, purely on a gut random instinct of the kind that I now realize speaks rarely, or at least can rarely be heard, and so should be listened to above all other voices in life. I think I felt at that time that my life was a high speed train and if I didn't jump off painfully and dramatically, I would realize at seventy that I had lived only from opportunity to opportunity, with no time for reflection or integration.

The mission was to broaden my understanding of the world as fast and furiously as I could. I also wanted to make some personal peace with my social justice ideals; to "walk the walk" a little more. To live more simply, to listen more and talk less, and to be aware of the lessons that had always been close at hand, those from friends and family. I wanted to get my hands dirty and to do hands-on work. I was tired of books. During my time as a carer at a nursing home, I loved the exact and obvious necessity of our work. If someone cannot bathe herself, bathe her, if someone is lonely, talk to her. But very quickly I missed intellectual practice and my community. And I found that when I began working for the Edinburgh Fringe Festival I felt so at home in an artistic community. I had a similar feeling about the academic world when I did some research work in Dublin for a history professor in Canada.

Seeing a European lifestyle where people walked everywhere, shared accommodation, spent less on things and more on living, I returned to Toronto and tried to live similarly. At that time I almost felt that life was more important than work, or rather that I wanted to do work that would facilitate the lifestyle I wanted to have. It is amazing to me how rarely the idea that lifestyle can be a series of choices comes into consideration for people for whom work is very definitely a series of choices. When we are young we are encouraged to think only what we want to do, not where we want to do it, how we want to live, and indeed who we want to live with. Bob Henderson [instructor of Environment inquiry course] introduced me to such considerations. So many people, especially of the high-achieving art/sci variety, I think place unfortunate judgements upon themselves when they realize that they care about other things as much as their career. I lived in a communal house, rode a bike, shopped at a food co-op and ate organic, worked part time for a small theatre company (The Tarragon), and began to freelance write, both for mainstream publications which could afford to pay me and for alternative press which could not. I learned that all work gives opportunities to cultivate activism, and that art, for the way it flies in the face of all capitalist reason and cultivates the worship and appreciation of life, is a perpetual protest against so much of how we live. My friends in Toronto were similarly living and working by the values we had all discussed so much in the art/sci days.

All along there had been academic itchings. I found myself always living near university campuses and going to hear lectures after work. I realized that all the lifestyle choices I had made were possible in a context of study, perhaps even more possible there than in others. After an introduction to just about everything in Arts and Science, I decided that this time I wanted to study only my greatest love as a discipline, English lit. My favorite writers were Irish, and during the research in Dublin I had fallen in love with a city and a country. I chose the Master's at Trinity College, Dublin because there was a creative writing Master's in the same building. Since leaving McMaster, I have worked more and more on creative writing, but never put it on the front burner. I still felt that having not taken as many English courses as I wanted to as an undergrad, I wanted to do a critical Master's, but it was a great advantage to have the creative writers in the same building. There were constant readings, two writers in residence, and the chance to do workshops with them. Education access became the focus of my activism, and there were still bicycles and organic food and protest. It was a magical year in a magical city and in a culture where many of the things we struggled to create in Arts and Science, like respect for balance and creativity, are inherent and taken for granted. Still feeling motivated by the year, I decided to stay on to do writing workshops and an administrative job on campus at night. I don't feel ready to leave Dublin yet, and another lesson I have picked up along this crazy life is not to leave places before you are ready.

In art/sci I was trying to figure out how to live, and that in retrospect took the greater part of my days. Now at last I have in place some rhythms and systems for navigating in a world that can seem to fall on a scale from confusing to insane. I have perhaps gained just a little wisdom on the way. Of course there is still so much to learn. If art/sci taught me one thing above all, it is that we always have more to learn than what we already know. I guess my ultimate lesson is that there are choices, constantly choices. This is exhausting, but allows us to continuously affirm who we are and what we believe. We only have one life, and the pressure to live it wisely for both ourselves and others can again become paralyzing. Sometimes we do have to take one road and not another for a time, and sometimes despite our best efforts to research and control things, there is no particular reason why, but that is all ok. Sometimes even us critically conscious art/sci types just need to defer to the mystery.

Azim Essaji ('97)
This has been a difficult piece to write. I have struggled hard to produce something interesting. Unfortunately, regardless of the spin I have tried to put on my life, I have been unable to dress up the facts into something exciting. What follows, then, is my mundane (but true) personal history.

I was born in Nairobi, Kenya. As a fourth generation Kenyan Asian, I considered Kenya my home and never dreamed that I would live elsewhere. During the 1980s, however, growing anti-Asian discrimination convinced my parents that we had to leave. We thus emigrated to Canada in 1988.

While I understand my parents' reasons for moving, I must confess that my first years in Canada were not happy ones... being thirteen is difficult; being thirteen in a place with radically different norms, without friends, is horrible. In high school I fell in with a crowd that did not mind my odd accent or my nerdiness. I encountered some dedicated and inspiring teachers who encouraged my academic interests and pushed me to do better. My school also provided extra-curricular opportunities, such as anti-racism work and the school newspaper, which helped me integrate into the school and the community at large.

Having enjoyed a variety of courses in high school, I was naturally attracted to Arts and Science's multi-disciplinary curriculum. However, the decision to come to Arts and Science, once I was admitted, was not easy. Being cash-strapped, I was tempted by the stay-at-home University of Toronto option, or the co-op programme at the University of Waterloo, which actually promised to let me make money. Ultimately, I chose Arts and Science because of the enthusiastic endorsement of somebody I knew in the Programme, and a gut feeling that McMaster was the school that best suited my temperament.

Whatever the reasons, I am glad that I chose Arts and Science. The Programme helped me forge my closest friendships. I am not sure whether we came together out of genuine affinity, or whether, like recruits at boot camp, we bonded because we needed a support network to get through first year. I suspect that it was a bit of both. The Programme also expanded my intellectual horizons. It not only passed on substantive knowledge, such as how to measure forces acting on a pendulum hurtling through space, but taught me to think and write critically. I learned that to understand an issue, one had to look at the many sides of the problem: when reading a text, one had not only to pay attention to what was said, but what was left unsaid. Through all of this, I was amazed by the professors' dedication to their students. I cannot count the hours I spent with professors, outside class, discussing assignments, projects and future plans.

I only began to think seriously about life after Arts and Science at the end of my second year. Law school soon became the leading candidate. I had been interested in social justice issues since high school. and law seemed a powerful tool for effecting change. I therefore decided to apply to law school at the beginning of my third year. When I sent in my forms, though, I did not have an LSAT [Law School Admissions Test] score, so

I had no idea whether I would be accepted; I figured that if they did not take me in this year, I would apply again in my fourth year. Surprisingly, I got in. After some wavering, I decided it was too good an opportunity to forego, so I left Arts and Science.

The doubts that emerged about applying to law school lingered and were amplified when I actually started law school and was a bit overwhelmed. Unhappy, I looked for an out. While in Arts and Science, I had taken some economics courses; armed with them, I managed to convince McMaster to allow me to do a Master's in Economics. This worked out well. The year away from law allowed me to gain perspective on my life, while the MA programme itself gave me some useful knowledge and a powerful set of analytical tools.

I returned to law school and enjoyed my second year much more than my first. It was during this year, though, that I realized that I did not want to practise any of the conventional types of law.

Ever since my first year in Arts and Science I had a strong interest in international development issues, an interest reinforced during my work for my Master's. Realizing that the combination of legal and economics training could be useful in the development field, I decided to switch into the combined LLB/PhD (Economics) programme at the University of Toronto.

The work in the combined programme has been challenging and fulfilling. In many ways, though, I still face the Arts and Science dilemma. While I have narrowed my sights, I still do not know where I should aim to fulfill my interests: an international organization, a university, an NGO? What has changed from Arts and Science, though, is that this future uncertainty does not bother me (as much). I have learned that where you begin has little to do with where you end up. As a child in Kenya, I never thought that I would live in Canada. In high school, I could not have imagined a programme like Arts and Science. If you had told me four years ago that I would do a PhD in Economics, I would have thought you were crazy. Life can take some interesting turns; to use a hackneyed expression, the pleasure lies more in the ride than in the destination.

Cindy McCulligh ('98)
Life can change in an instant, and no one knows what the next moment will bring. So, I wonder about my personal life history. Amongst the millions of people who have come and gone from this earth, how important are the intricacies, the material successes and failures of one life? Perhaps my life history would be but a living obituary: Born September 9, 1974 in

Oakville, Ontario. No children. Short, bereft of detail, perfunctory, a name in bold on newsprint.

For I am full and without appetite, as stuffed as after a holiday feast and with no hunger whatsoever for the hyperbole and pride, for the victories and sorrows each life is bound to accrue; accrue like degrees, framed on the walls of the ego, shining with ostentation in blank smiles. Sported when necessary, in all of those conversations that begin with, "So, what do you do?" Badges of honour, fortifying the walls of self, well-insulating the world of "I am," from devastating questions with no apparent answer.

But I am happy to stay with the question. Not to assert that I am Cindy McCulligh: an environmentalist, social activist, wannabe writer— or whatever other signifier or title I might be tempted to add. I will leave the question open, still trying to know why a heart beats and life breath flows in my body. I always appreciated, thinking of my time in the Arts and Science Programme, that Sylvia Bowerbank [supervisor of Cindy's senior thesis] always asked questions. She would return drafts of my thesis full of questions and, when we spoke, always answer my questions with more questions—never answers.

Several years have past since then.

And now, it is knowing that I don't know the answer to those open questions of the self, that gives me hope.

Matt Wohlgemut ('98)
Among other things, these days I am making pots. When I first learned to make pots, I hoped, as do most beginning potters, that my pots would rise off the wheel, their clay walls giving shape to the spirit and firing the imagination. What I was not prepared for, like most beginning potters, was the fact that throwing any form on the wheel is a tenuous process, a fragile and dynamic tension between hand and moving earth. Most crucial to the eventual possibility of form are the initial processes of preparation: after the clay has been cleared of air pockets, and before any move towards the vertical can be made, the clay must be centred on the wheelhead. I spent hours that felt like weeks learning to gather the clay and, gently and firmly, bring its axis in line with that of the rotating wheel.

What brings me to this topic, in this place, is not to cast a narrative of myself as unformed clay, now a lovely pot, nor is it to wonder at the master's hand whose mark I bear. It is to consider the process of preparation, the process of making possible.

I remember that there was a certain feeling in the air whenever someone invoked the Arts and Science Programme as "preparation" for medical school or for any other future programme. It caused the elders of the community to wrinkle their noses and lift their chins. I absorbed the significance of this reaction even before I understood or shared some sense of resentment towards stripping off the inherent ends of education, leaving only naked means. As my Arts and Science years went by, this process became a particular under a more general cultural/philosophical suspicion that I was developing: any instrumental rationality that served to reduce an experience to the constituent conditions necessary for and separated from a distant master value made me edgy.

Wandering back over things done and times past, my experience of Arts and Science as preparation never traveled the route of being reduced to linear gain in-the-service-of. Preparation, as it now looks to me, is not the assembly of constitutive parts for a preconceived end, but a gathering together that makes space for new possibilities. The Arts and Science Programme was a preparation for me in the sense that it gathered the ground and made a clearing where new possibilities became imaginable. These possibilities might have been categorically available as plans back then, even as now I might plan on making "a bowl" or "a vase" before I attempt to make one. There is, however, a specificity of the form arising from the prepared ground that is utterly new and unimaginable before it is present. The form is given—realized as present—from out of the potentiality. It is almost always surprising, but never quite in the way that I thought it would be. Preparation projects a horizon of possibility into entirely new worlds. These are the worlds that I now inhabit.

I have come to terms with making pots. Sometimes the clay just seems to do its own thing: handles crack, mud flies, and walls falter and slump. The clay must be gathered again, patiently, and centred on the spinning wheel. This is a process to be repeated again and again: to gather, to create, to make possible. To prepare well is to clear a space for vital and meaningful possibilities to emerge. I am pleasantly haunted by my preparations past: I dwell in the landscapes of possibility that are present because of those preparations.

Instructors

Selection

The method by which payment is made for the release of McMaster faculty members from their home departments to teach in the Arts and Science Programme is described on p.49. The release of the faculty members is negotiated by the Director of the Programme with the Chair and Dean of the relevant Department and Faculty. Instructors are invited to teach in the Programme on the basis of their academic expertise and a record of interest and success in undergraduate teaching. They are usually pleased to be asked, because the reputation of the students as able and eager learners has made teaching in the Programme a prized and sometimes actively sought after opportunity. Appointments were originally for three years; this was modified to "three teaching years" to account for any intervening research leave that would otherwise result in the extravagance of an instructor preparing a course only to offer it twice. Appointments, subject to satisfactory performance, may be renewed as long as there is a reasonable turnover of the overall teaching body. This turnover is seen as essential to ensure the introduction of fresh ideas, to promote ongoing informal review of the Programme curriculum and administration, and to widen the group of faculty at McMaster who care deeply about the Programme.

Participation

The Director and all other instructors constitute a Council of Instructors, on which students also serve. The Council operates as a Curriculum Committee. The Council reviews the curriculum and may recommend changes. Instructors also serve on the various committees required of a free-standing programme (committees of a kind that exist in the Departments and Faculties to manage undergraduate matters), and they are often asked to represent the Programme at the variety of events at which information about the University is offered to the public. A substantial amount of volunteer instructor time is devoted to assessing Supplementary Applications for admission to the Programme (p.51).

Members of an External Review Team[1] commented individually and collectively on the characteristics of the Programme's instructors, noting that they "find their involvement to be a substantial learning and development experience" and that "their commitment and dedication to the ideals and to the realities of the Programme is impressive. Their profound respect for the students with whom they work is palpable. This respect is, in turn, reciprocated by the students." The Team's Report noted that "The Programme's instructors contribute their talents with academic rigor and with great enthusiasm," and that "It is not uncommon for the Arts and Science Programme instructors to make personal sacrifices (e.g. overload teaching, extended office hours) to be involved."

The nature of the Programme requires instructors with many different interests and from a range of University Departments. This range is shown in the pattern of recruitment from the University Faculties. Most have been from the three large undergraduate Faculties of Humanities (17), Science (19) and Social Sciences (21). In addition there have been contributions from Engineering (2) and Health Sciences (4). Short term replacements for instructors on research leave have usually been visiting professors or contracted part-time instructors (20).

Although the principal attraction of the Programme for instructors is its students, there are others. The opportunity to work with colleagues from different disciplines who would otherwise remain remote is enriching. These colleagues bring not just their disciplinary expertise, but also their different approaches to teaching and learning. The synergy that is possible in discussing teaching with peers within one's discipline becomes greater when representatives of other disciplines participate. Inter-instructor relationships are almost always respectful and harmonious. An important reason for this harmony probably lies in the fact that little of the management of their careers is done in the Arts and Science Programme. The Programme Director is expected to contribute assessments of the instructors' effectiveness when career decisions (tenure, promotion) are made, and occasionally to participate in discussions of contentious situations involving individual faculty members, but the Chair of each instructor's Department retains responsibility for his/her career progress. As a result, ongoing disagreements, jealousies and politics that are endemic in the departmental environment can be left behind, and suggestions and criticisms can be given, debate can occur and initiatives can be taken without consequences for the instructors' career or professional relationships. The pleasure of academic interactions can be fully enjoyed.

Instructors have high expectations of the quality of their students' work, but their relations are for the most part relaxed and students are aware of the pleasure that the instructors get from the teaching they do in the Programme. Many instructors attend and participate in student-arranged extracurricular events such as debates, plays and coffeehouses at which anyone may play, sing, read or otherwise entertain. They gladly take part as judges of short story contests and poetry workshops. Most feel that they are part of a community.

Evaluation

Course evaluation by students is mandatory at McMaster and includes an assessment of the instructors' effectiveness and the learning achieved. In addition to the standard questions, the Arts and Science Programme asks for suggestions for improvement and allows instructors to add questions to help them plan their courses for subsequent years. This information is collected at the end of the course. In the case of full-year courses, an informal course and instructor mid-year evaluation is done at the end of the first term. This is seen as being particularly important for first-year courses to encourage students' sense of responsibility for their learning.

Since excellence in teaching is a criterion for instructor selection, it is not surprising that their evaluation by students is generally very favourable. These are not students who mince their words. Several Arts and Science instructors have won University, Provincial and National awards for teaching, partly on the strength of their endorsement by these students.

Instructors' Personal Experiences

Some of the course descriptions in Part II give a clear picture of what the instructors give to and get from their teaching. In addition, past and present instructors were invited to submit any personal reflections they had about teaching in the Arts and Science Programme. Their submissions follow.

Roy W. Hornosty
Department of Sociology and instructor of the upper level Inquiry course on Work

An Experiment in Non-directive Teaching

When I was a graduate student/teaching assistant in the Department of Sociology at the State University of New York at Buffalo in the mid-1960s, part of the buzz in the department centred around the philosophy of education and non-directive teaching methods of Nathaniel Cantor. I was favourably impressed with this approach to teaching and learning, but when I came to McMaster in 1967, I found myself teaching basic, required courses with predetermined content, at a time of burgeoning enrolments and large classes. The conditions were not right for experimenting with non-directive teaching methods. The opportunity to do so presented itself in 1983 when I was invited to teach an Inquiry seminar on Work in the Arts and Science Programme, and I jumped at the opportunity. It was one of the most rewarding experiences of my twenty-eight-year teaching career at McMaster.

Non-directive teaching is based on the assumption that each student is unique and will learn what he/she wants to know in his/her own way. I also adopted as a working premise the view, "No man can reveal to you aught but that which already lies half asleep in the dawning of your knowledge" (Gibran), and I encouraged students to free themselves from institutional and disciplinary constraints and follow their mind wherever it led them. I regarded my role as that of a facilitator and fellow traveller, and I was delighted to follow their intellectual journeys as they developed their individual course papers. One student started out studying retirement in Canadian society, then decided he should look at the phenomenon from a cross-cultural perspective, and then discovered that he wanted to know more about the origins of our cultural biases. He ended up studying the philosophical roots of modernity.

It was quickly evident that Arts and Science students were brimming with creativity and imagination, so after my second year of teaching in the programme I invited the students to initiate and carry out group projects, either with the class as a whole or with smaller groups, for 25% of the grade. At first the groups cleared their projects with me before beginning, but with each succeeding class the groups chose to involve me less and less. On two occasions, I had no idea what the groups were doing until presentation time, when I was told to go to a particular room at a particular time and plan to stay for three hours. One group produced a TV programme, based on TV Ontario's documentary series on the Future of Work, complete with interviews and visual and audio effects. I still enjoy viewing the video tape. Another group set up an assortment of booths and displays in the Arts and Science lounge one weekend and performed little skits illustrating the various topics they were studying in the course. Another group presented me with an abstract painting done by the group on a 3' x 5' canvas intended to depict the themes discussed in the seminars. This hung on a wall in my office until I retired and moved to Victoria.

To this day I have many good feelings about my six years in the Programme, and when I meet students from those classes, I often thank them for the personal pleasure I derived from this experiment.

Bill Harris

Department of Physics and Astronomy and instructor of the Physics course, 1995-2001

There are lots of memories, but one of them seems to say it all. Over the six years that I taught the Level II physics course—which adds up all told to something like 400 to 450 lecture sessions—I walked over to almost every one of them with a spring in my step.

Walking back to my office after class, I was often flying even higher: I could hardly wait to get on with the next meeting, already planning in my head how to involve the class in the next bit of material, or how to adjust what I had just done so that it would run better next year.

On a daily basis I often didn't care all that much about the broader context of the Programme; I was just having too much fun. Sometimes I wondered (though usually not for long) whether I really ought to be feeling guilty that I was apparently getting more out of the course than the students were.

What a pleasure to know I could generate a good discussion in class about virtually anything that came up. Part of the reason, of course, was the students' dependable liveliness and intelligence (well documented and commented on elsewhere). But part of it was precisely that they were not classic "physics students" already committed to the subject and just buckling down to learn all the techniques and details without questions. Instead, they could take an outside, fresh viewpoint. Almost every month, I could depend on someone raising a question that was astonishingly and wonderfully new to me. Bravo for interdisciplinary minds!

Throughout the whole experience I had a terrific sense of freedom. I could design a curriculum very different from my Department's normal offerings, and change it substantially from year to year or even month to month. I could delve into the history and people in my own subject and not just spend all the time on its nuts and bolts. I could experiment with topics, styles, and links that would have belly-flopped elsewhere.

Aside from rediscovering over and over again—to my endless delight, frustration, and fascination —that the most effective way to learn your subject is to try to teach it to someone else, what else did I learn about the Programme as a whole?

I learned that good teaching is not, repeat not, a one way street. It's a matchup between the instructor and the class, as a shared enterprise. The best individual ingredients just don't always produce a decent stew.

I learned that it's actually incredibly hard to "teach" anything in a deep way even to the best imaginable audience of undergrads. The gods themselves cannot prevent the absolute determination of junior undergrads to put off even large amounts of work till the last minute. But after all, deep learning comes only with far more experience than we can give them in a few weeks. At first I thought this problem might be a feature of just my subject—after all, physics thinking is a relatively recent invention in human history, and it really does not come naturally to most people, no matter what anyone might claim—but now I don't think so. As some clever scholar once remarked, the nasty rumor that high culture is hard brainwork is, in fact, true. It doesn't matter what field you're in.

A corollary to the above: most of what students learn in university happens outside of class, and even outside of their courses. University is a total social environment, and works best if it is a community of manageable size.

I learned that the nicest way to do something of quality is to get in among a lot of good people, and better yet, ones from a wide variety of disciplines.

As far as the students are concerned, did I change anyone's life? I'm not really sure. Maybe a few. Time will tell, and maybe neither I nor they will fully know.

The widespread view of the Programme is that it is supposed to be giving bright and broad-minded students the closest thing to a classical liberal education that a modern campus can manage. For some students, I think that's indeed what it does. For many others, it doesn't entirely do that, because so many of them come in already strongly pointed to a particular career channel (medicine, law, or other things) and are just using the Programme as a good route to their own goals. Those people stay so focussed on their own intended careers that they miss out on a lot. Ultimately I don't know if there is anything that can be done about that. To everyone's credit, however, I believe the Programme maintains a vibrant, supportive, and challenging working atmosphere year in and year out, and that is really all that can be asked.

Here's the bottom line for me. For six fascinating years, I felt that I was taking part in a small university-within-a-university: but a university functioning the way it was intended to be.

The environment created by the Programme for its members, not its curriculum, is the keystone. As a learning community, everything in it builds from the fact that it is large enough to be diverse and challenging and yet small enough to be personal. Long may it thrive.

Michael Ross

Department of English and instructor of the first Literature course

My opening question to my first Arts and Science Literature class, a dozen bold pioneers, was routine enough: "So how do you feel about this book?" The response was anything but routine: all hands promptly shot up. My prior years of classroom exposure had prepared me for nothing like this; a "Someone else break the ice" reaction was what I'd grumpily come to expect.

Those who have taught Arts and Science courses tend, I believe, to think of their involvement as even more a learning than a teaching experience. One of the first things I learned was that the standard "trickle-down" model of educational economics, whereby gleaming drops of knowledge rain from the instructor's lips and saturate the brains of the listeners, couldn't be applied to Arts and Science students, who consistently balked at being cast as passive "absorbers." One's role as a teacher tended to be less that of oracle than that of facilitator, and occasionally referee. I realize, of course, that my specific subject, literature, may have lent itself more readily to such a model than other, more technical Programme courses. Moreover, the model worked all the better because of the broad spectrum of interests the students brought with them. Literature is a field open to inquiry from a variety of standpoints, so that a class primed to think in interdisciplinary terms was likely to approach any given text from multiple angles. But even more important was the prevailing intellectual climate in the Programme. With notable exceptions, undergraduates pursuing more conventional degrees often seem to buy into a peer-group code of disengagement. According to this code, showing keen interest in your subject, participating conspicuously in class discussion, and igniting controversy are branded as "uncool." Among the majority in Arts and Science the opposite holds true: what's uncool here is yawning indifference, zipped-lip diffidence and the evasion of risky issues. In this milieu "peer pressure" acts in reverse fashion: it paradoxically encourages engagement and the vigorous voicing of individual or even "eccentric" views. It follows that discussions often take unpredictable twists and turns; after an especially dizzying session, the instructor may be chagrined to discover that his or her long-pondered class-plan has zipped gleefully down the tubes.

I consequently found that a peculiarity of teaching in the Programme was the giddy changing of gears that had to happen between a conventional English course and a typical Arts and Science session. The sort of question that had provoked a contentious uproar in the latter might provoke no more than a jittery silence when put to, say, a class in Modern British Literature. One danger of such comparisons (and perhaps of teaching Arts and Science generally) is that they can foster distinctions of the "sheep and goats" type—distinctions essentially unfair to students in more traditional programmes. Those admitted to Arts and Science tend, as everyone knows, to be intellectual high achievers; it's therefore no surprise that they are often vivid (sometimes even irrepressible) performers in the classroom. One wonders, however, how much of the vibrant culture of the Programme is determined by the Programme's very nature and structure. If one is to have *esprit de corps*, it obviously helps to feel one belongs to a *corps*—a feeling harder to come by for students in larger, less personal, more routinized programmes. As with most so-called "gifted" courses of study, the difficult question arises: what influence does being labelled "gifted" have on the mind-set and self-image of the individual so labelled? The impact of the occasional Arts and Science students who cropped up in my regular English courses may suggest at least an oblique answer. By demonstrating their own willingness to engage with the subject and with controversial issues, they offered models to other, normally more reticent students, encouraging them to breach their own local codes of non-involvement.

At a university like McMaster, small class sizes don't guarantee participation by individual students; a group of thirty-five or forty may be likelier to contain the minimum "critical mass" of willing participants needed to detonate a lively discussion. Typically, though, an Arts and Science student constitutes a critical mass of one; that's why, in my first small cluster of pioneers, my "opener" surprised me by producing a prompt and general response. I must confess that by my final year of teaching the course to a group of forty-five odd, I found the situation hard to manage; forty-five Arts and Science students aren't a critical mass, they're a critical avalanche. If there was ever a case calling for small class size, the Arts and Science Programme is it. Since our famous "fiscal restraints" apparently rule out this ideal for many courses, I can only trust that the task of managing a stampeding herd of resolutely individual minds is a challenge for which current instructors are finding creative solutions, more effective than my own uncertain expedients.

Elizabeth Inman
School of Arts, Drama and Music and instructor of the Drama section of the Creative Arts
course, in which she was assisted by David Inman.

How was I going first to design and then teach a course on Drama to the undoubtedly intelligent and sophisticated senior Arts and Science students? I was terrified that I might talk down to them. On the other hand, I did not want to lead them into the labyrinths of academic dramatic theories. My own experience in Drama was in the practical arts of directing, acting, and staging. This was where my passion lay; this was what I taught. Here I received criticism, almost verging on horror, from some of my colleagues in Fine Arts and Music. "Surely you are not going to let them perform?" they exclaimed. "They are totally without training, It would be a desecration of the discipline." etc, etc.! But that is exactly what I did.

This course was unlike any other I have ever taught. To work, it needed students with a high level of intelligence and commitment. The course took huge risks in that, basically, it was designed to be student driven. That the students rose to the challenge every time, was what made it one of the most exciting and unforgettable courses I have ever been lucky enough to teach.

In the first class, I gave an introductory lecture, one of very few, on the process of bringing a text—the book—to the final production. I identified the following main areas of production; direction, acting and design of set, lights, sound and costume. The students were all given the text of the same play, and asked to choose which of the production areas interested them the most. Miraculously, this almost always divided them into six groups of roughly the same size. Each group then worked outside of class time to come up with its idea of how to act, direct, and design the play, concentrating only on the group's chosen area. These ideas were then later presented to the class as a whole, the only instruction being, "Be creative in your presentation as well as in your ideas. In other words, make your presentations performances." Wow! I could write a book on all the clever things we saw: a puppet show, each character exquisitely and appropriately dressed; beautiful models of theatre sets; musical scores on tape; scenes acted in deliberately contrasting ways to emphasize choices; lighting choices illustrating the psychological significance of different colours—yes, a lot of research as well as imagination went into these presentations.

This imaginative work became even more significant, because the chosen play was always one being presented by one of the professional theatres in the area. We would all board our trusty school bus and go to the theatre, to see what the professionals did with the same material. A written evaluation of the production was to be handed in at the beginning of the next class. "What, in just one week?" was the anguished outcry, but it had to be so, because the rest of that class was taken up with an animated—sometimes very animated—discussion of the production.

These class-room discussions were great, but one of my favourite memories is of an out-of-classroom discussion. It was after a performance of Strindberg's *The Father* at the Tarragon Theatre. Members of the audience were invited to stay behind and ask questions of the stage manager and some of the actors. Well, we had spent a lot of time identifying Strindberg as one of the fathers of twentieth-century realism. The Tarragon production was, however, deliberately outrageous. Our students grilled the members of the production, asking them to justify their choices in a way they certainly did not expect. It was all extremely good-tempered and it was clear that everyone on both sides of the footlights was having a whale of a good time, but we were not letting them off lightly. When question time was finally brought to an end and we were leaving the stage area, the stage manager caught up with me on the stairs and said with wonderment in his voice, "Who *are* you ?", meaning us collectively of course. When I told him we were a class of university students who had been studying and discussing production options for this very play for the last few weeks, he looked visibly relieved. He said it had all been great fun, but he was glad he didn't have our like in every "question and answer" session.

This was the pattern of the class for the first half of the course. Finding appropriate plays was one of the greatest challenges. Once, our text was a novel. For the second half of the term we gave the students their head and let them put on their own productions. Each year we selected a Shakespeare play and asked the students to use the play to find a theme on which they would base a collective presentation lasting no more than twenty minutes. The class was divided into four groups. David and I were each assigned to two groups, for whom we acted only as resource people. The students did everything—found their theme, wrote their scripts, (parts, of some of them, in perfect iambic pentameter!), played the parts, found their costumes, did the lights, made their sound tapes, and kept everything secret from the other three groups till the last class—the performance.

Some of my best remembered of these are an outdoor production of scenes from *A Midsummer Night's Dream* in a courtyard with hundreds of fairy lights, and Puck high in a tree; *Hamlet* as seen through the eyes of Ophelia, as her ghost watched and commented on the scenes from the play; another *Hamlet* inspired production—HPD (Hamlet Prince of Denmark), a great take-off on the movie JFK. Of course, the standards of the scenes varied greatly, but each group had to face and surmount the problems encountered in putting on a production, and they had only four weeks. It was a lot of work and also a lot of fun.

"Fun"; that was probably the word that came up most frequently in the course evaluations. "It was such fun!", the students wrote. I know this worried some of the faculty in the Arts and Science Programme. Perhaps it should have worried me, but it didn't. Several years after I retired I met a former student at an alternative theatre in Toronto. We reminisced; we laughed. "Oh", she said, "it was all such fun." I shared with her how that word had almost come to haunt me. "Oh it mustn't" she said. She then went on to tell me that it was because of this course that she found and pursued her love of theatre and was now in a theatre related job. "Yes", I said to myself, " I knew it was OK to let them perform and to have fun."

Lorraine York
Department of English, member of a team that formally reviewed the Programme and instructor of the Literature course

Teaching Experience (Brief)

In the autumn of 1990, my partner Michael Ross, who taught the Arts and Science Literature course, had to undergo minor surgery at the beginning of term, and the question of what would be done to cover his Arts and Science course naturally came up. I started to speculate that I could probably take over his classes for a couple of weeks while he recuperated. When Dr. Barbara Ferrier, Programme Director at the time, called to consult me on this question, I tentatively floated my suggestion. She seemed, frankly, relieved and she accepted my offer. There was only one (small) complication: I was eight months pregnant and on maternity leave. Was this the best time to dust off my copy of Homer's *Odyssey* and embark on a journey of my own?

I sailed (galleon-like in girth) into the Literature class the first day, announced (perhaps unnecessarily) that I was not Dr. Michael Ross, and proceeded to experience the most stimulating discussion of the question: what is a literary text? Of what does its "literariness" consist? Each day I returned to the class, several students would revert to this initial discussion and take it up, test it, anew. In my experience, students rarely recalled what was said on the first day of class meetings: they came, they saw, they picked up a course description. But Arts and Science students rarely forget what you tell them, and I think that this may be both the boon and the bane of their instructors' existence. My teaching experience with Arts and Science students was brief, but this was one thing I did learn. Arts and Science students put into action the advice that the esteemed American novelist Henry James offered in "The Art of Fiction": "Try to be one of the people on whom nothing is lost." Arts and Science students do not even have to try.

Experience Evaluating the Programme

In 1996-97, I was fortunate to be a member of the team that carried out the first comprehensive, formal review of the Arts and Science Programme.[1] I say "fortunate" because this project allowed me to work with two especially thoughtful colleagues, Adam Hitchcock, from McMaster's Chemistry Department, and Norman Gibbins, from the University of Guelph's Microbiology Department. Norman, the head of the review team, had extensive experience administering Guelph's Akademia programme, an academic unit with objectives similar to those of the McMaster Arts and Science Programme, and that experience, along with his collegiality and scholarly generosity of spirit, was invaluable to the task at hand. As the only humanist among us, I felt that my role was to represent and support the vital role of the humanities—the "Arts" in Arts and Science—that was eloquently forged by humanists on the original Planning Council and later supported and strengthened by humanists who taught in the Programme and served on its Advisory Council, especially Alwyn Berland, former Dean of the Faculty of Humanities, and upheld by all of the directors to date. Accordingly, one section of our report, on the "balance between the arts and sciences," reminds Arts and Science administrators to "ensure that one of the programme's primary *raisons d'etre*, namely its interdisciplinarity, be maintained and enhanced." In this endeavour I had the full and enthusiastic support of my scientist colleagues on the review team.

Another concern for the team was the administration's interest in possibly opening up the Arts and Science Programme to larger enrollments. The programme had garnered praise from various quarters, and attracted top-of-the-line students who otherwise might have been tempted to attend so-called "prestige" institutions with which we are in competition. In our report, we came out unequivocally in favour of retaining smaller class sizes. I believe, in fact, that this is the central theme of our report. We bluntly stated that "In particular, budgetary pressures should not be used as a rationale for the reduction of financial resources, or an increase in class sizes. Increasing the class size will jeopardise the success of the programme." As a team, we recognized, to quote our report once more, that "The concept and structure of the Arts and Science Programme were established by visionaries," and we determined that, on this question, at least, the visionaries should carry the day.

Notes

1.   "Review of the McMaster Arts and Science Programme" External Review chaired by N.Gibbins, (McMaster University, 1997).

11   What Have We Achieved?

Barbara Ferrier

In-course students and very recent graduates were invited to offer brief comments about their experience in the Programme. These are inserted in this chapter and in Chapter 10. We pointed out in the invitation that we were not asking for testimonials.

The Climate

Most outsiders who have experience with the Programme and with its students are struck by the energy, creativity, and enthusiasm of the participants. One has noted that "Within the rich and mutualistic environment of the Programme, the quest for individuality and the intellectual independence of each student participant is largely successful."[1] These characteristics have resulted from and have reinforced the particular culture that has been created, both by intent and good fortune.

> I can only shake my head when I try to think about what my life would have been if I hadn't been an "artsci".The formula doesn't look that complicated: a broad core curriculum; a warm, personal atmosphere; a strong emphasis on student participation and the pleasure of learning. But it was enough to change my life—both my love of philosophy and my desire to be engaged in the world grew out of the environment provided by the Arts and Science Programme, and as a result I can't even begin to imagine the debt I owe it. (Eric Tam)

I have learned how to critically engage with the world around me,
It is here that I found my own, authentic voice and people who
were willing to listen to it, sometimes challenge it and most of all,
encourage it. (Karen Murdoch)

Most of the students, instructors, and administrators feel themselves
to be part of a distinct community in which scholarship is respected,
individual interests are supported and collegiality is a reality.

I feel that I am part of a community that extends to all levels of
Arts and Science, including the professors. The Programme fosters
a sense of belonging that encourages students to take ownership
and initiate change. (Sarah Dobson)

The factors that may have contributed to this result are the small
size of the Programme, the layout and location of its assigned space that
provide an intellectual and social centre removed from classrooms, and
characteristics of the students themselves—high academic potential,
acceptance of a spirit of cooperation and idealism.

What is Arts and Science? The most eclectic collection of interests,
thoughts, and dreams I have ever seen; a truly mind-opening
experience; a lesson in diversity, inquisitiveness and eccentricity;
the realization that those who are most unlike you are often, on a
more fundamental level, the most similar to you. (Sachin
Pendharkar)

Some pressure has been exerted to increase the size of the
Programme, and it did increase in small increments for a few years to its
present limit of sixty. Pressure to increase beyond this number in recent
years has been successfully resisted (p.270) based on the argument that
some important positive characteristics of the Programme would almost
certainly be diminished and that its continued success might be jeopardized.

A space set aside for the Programme has contributed to the positive
climate. This space consists of a reception area, offices for the Director
and the two staff members, a reading room, and a seminar room. It is
located in a building in which there is no other undergraduate teaching
department or classrooms and which is usually thought of as being devoted
to the system of student residences. As a result, students and instructors
have a sense of a space apart. Students attend classes elsewhere on campus
but return to their home base to meet others, to complete administrative

business, to study, and to plan their academic and social activities. It is used heavily in the evenings, when students have access with the use of a sign-out key. It is their study centre and an intellectual centre, and there is often serious debate on whatever issues have engaged the students' interests. Instructors have felt that they are back in graduate school when they hear the seriousness—and sometimes self-indulgence—of the discussions. Indeed, the community resembles a graduate school in other ways. Student independence, skills, and motivation are akin to what is expected at the graduate level.

> I have been ambivalent about my enrollment in Arts and Science throughout the course of my time at Mac. Sometimes I worry about lack of focus and rigour. However, there has been a very beneficial aspect of our education here, in the sense of being empowered to bring my own interests and values to the work I do. Being encouraged to develop my own opinions and pursue my personal areas of interest contributes to the feeling that I matter as an individual, as a whole person, and not just a machine to crank out essays and assignments. (Eleanor Alexander)

The students enter the Programme with a record of success in academic and extracurricular activities, and as a result most are self-confident, motivated, and engaged with the idea of study and of involvement. Most leave the Programme with these qualities enhanced. It is possible that they simply continued on the path on which they were already set, and the Programme's role was permissive rather than formative. Even avoiding harm would be something of an achievement, but most students and observers believe that its role was indeed formative.

Some students and other faculty members of the University have expressed concern that the Programme fosters elitism of a favoured subgroup. Students in the Programme have sometimes shared this concern, and report being heckled in residence by peers in other programmes. There is no doubt that there is something special about them. Although individual Arts and Science students are not certain to be the most intelligent of McMaster's students—all of its undergraduate Faculties have some excellent students—the average intellectual ability of the group is higher, and instructors find that they do not have to spend so much time on the less able as they do in most other University courses. Perhaps more important, their involvement in extracurricular activities and their commitment to each other's education are clearly greater than average.

The students see themselves as different in their motivation and involvement. They recognize an Arts and Science "type," and also recognize that there is potential danger of excluding those who cannot be described this way. The characteristics of the type do allow for individuality; indeed, the differences are appreciated. It had not been the intention of the planners that Arts and Science students would create or find themselves in an isolated community. They took steps to encourage interactions with students from the rest of the University by requiring substantial elective work from University course offerings and by assuring that assignment of rooms in residence would not put Programme students together. The wide involvement of students in extracurricular activities has also helped to prevent their isolation. A survey carried out in 1991 by a group of McMaster sociologists as part of a research study of Arts and Science students included questions about the nature of their associations with other students.[2] It showed that 46% mixed with both Arts and Science and non-Arts and Science students, 33% mainly with Arts & Science students, and 21% mainly with non-Arts and Science students.

On several occasions, small groups of students have raised the possibility that the Programme might move to a pass/fail system for student evaluation. They believe that this would promote more genuine learning and remove residual competition. There has been some sympathy for this position from instructors, even though those who have worked in such a system know that it greatly increases the work of assessment. Two matters have so far kept us from moving to institute a pass/fail system: the difficulty of dealing with two disparate systems of grading—pass/fail for Arts and Science courses and the conventional system for all other courses—and the reality of the students' need to compete for admission to graduate and professional schools and for grants and scholarships.

In the 1990-1991 academic year the sociologists' study explored the students' experience at McMaster and especially how they had adapted to the Arts and Science Programme's demands. They interviewed students, graduates, instructors, and staff members; they attended a range of extracurricular activities from the academic to the purely social; they held focus groups; they fielded a survey of all in-course students; and they spent a considerable amount of time just "hanging out" with students. Their reports are extensive, and some results have been presented and published.[3] Little of what they found came as a surprise to those in the Programme, and no common beliefs about it were dispelled. It was very useful, however, to have impressions validated by impartial observers. Although this research was completed ten years ago, there is no reason to believe that major changes have occurred.

One very interesting aspect of the results of the study and of the investigators' interpretation of them that had not been recognized or explained before related to the Arts and Science students' very obvious idealism. The researchers' review of the literature, and some of their earlier work, suggests that idealism of students usually fades as they proceed through university. This attrition is particularly marked in professional schools but has also been noted in general undergraduate programmes. Yet the idealism of the Arts & Science students increased. This is apparently paradoxical, because the students clearly identify their increased realism. One explanation of the decrease of idealism usually detected is students' confrontation with the constraints of reality. It is suggested that increased knowledge, critical ability, and experience made the Arts and Science students rethink their idealism. They "feel that their idealism is better grounded and that they can address issues in a more informed way. They feel that they have a better sense of what is possible and can act in a more pragmatic manner. They feel that they are better positioned to know where their actions might make a strategic difference." Many have taken steps to change their lifestyles and have identified and implemented feasible projects to benefit others. Some have altered their career choices or have recognized a route to take within their original choice that would allow them to meet their goals as idealists.

The researchers suggest that those students who are idealistic on entry to the Programme retain their idealism in modified form under the influence of their peers and of their experience in the Programme, which, through its scholarly concern with social issues, supports their idealsim without preaching about it. A similar result was found by one member of the research team in studies of students and graduates of a particular School of Pharmacy with well articulated social goals with which the curriculum and teaching approaches were congruent.[4]

Assessment of the Programme's Effectiveness and Impact

There are several sources of information for evaluating the Programme. There are the usual course evaluations, input from students and instructors on an on-going basis, a survey of graduates, research by a group of sociologists, and two formal reviews with membership determined by the Provost (Vice-President, Academic). Overall these indicate successful achievement of the objectives, although criticism and suggestions for change have not been lacking.

Course and instructor evaluation is carried out systematically. As would be expected from the selection of experienced and skilled members of McMaster's faculty as instructors, they are usually very favourably evaluated. Their average score on the required questions is consistently high (over 8 on a scale of 1=very low to 10=excellent). The Arts and Science students have high expectations of their teachers; sometimes their evaluation of substitute instructors (who are usually hired to replace regular faculty members on research leave) can be very harsh.

The graduate survey was carried out in 1992.[5] The response rate was only 54%, possibly because one of the Programme's weaknesses has been its failure to put in place a good system for tracking its graduates. The survey was sent to the last known address, which was usually the address of their family home when they first entered the Programme. An attempt to remedy this weakness has been the recent creation of "grad-web", a web site which each graduate will be expected to keep up to date. The graduates were asked to assess the Programme in the context of their present situation. Questions about features of the Programme were deliberately open-ended to avoid any steering effects. The response rate differed by year of graduation, with the first class, the pioneers, responding at the highest rate. It is not uncommon that the courage needed to attend an untested programme brings future commitment to it.

The graduates were asked whether they would enter Arts and Science if they were starting university studies now. A large majority (92%) said yes, one person gave a conditional yes, the conditions being related to specific course changes, 4% were unsure, and 3% said no. Most of those who were unsure or would not enter the Programme believe that a more focused curriculum would have prepared them better for their careers.

Those who would have chosen the Programme again were asked to identify what had been its particular strengths for them. Since the question was open-ended, the responses were grouped in categories. By far the most frequently identified strength was the multidisciplinary design (94% of respondents). Approximately a third of respondents identified the skills acquired, the learning style, and the Programme's size as strengths. While the peer group was explicitly identified by only 20%, it was indirectly referred to by many in responses put into other categories. It continues to be a very important feature.

> Through the Programme I have felt empowered. I knew that when it comes to rough times, I could count on my peers to support me and have the courage to stand for what we believe. (Meghan Burke)

The answers of all survey respondents to a question about the changes they would like to see made were similarly categorized. The largest category (41% of respondents) included suggestions for changes to specific courses. There were no discernible patterns in the suggestions made. The next most frequent response category was that of the student selection process. Concern was expressed about the very high grade point average that had become necessary for admission.

Finally, graduates were asked to identify which features of the Programme should be protected. The Progamme's size was most frequently identified (79% of respondents), then came inquiry courses (41%) and the range of required courses (31%).

While the sociologists' study of Arts and Science students was not intentionally evaluative, inevitably some evaluation did occur. In a survey (see note 2) they asked in-course students whether the Programme had influenced their career choices. A large majority (86%) of the final year students said that it had by increasing their sense of responsibility and their interest in the third world and by opening up new academic disciplines and options to them. For some, however, it had increased their self-doubt in relation to their chosen career. They were also asked if they would recommend the Programme to others. Twenty three percent said yes, 75% said yes with reservations, 2% were unsure and none said no. The reservations were almost all related to the necessary match between the student and the Programme.

One indirect, but possibly valid, indicator of student satisfaction is the substantial number of applications for admission from younger siblings of enrolled students and graduates.

The Report of the External Review done in 1997 (see note 1) identified the Programme's strengths as the quality of its students, the commitment to and support for the students, the emphasis on inquiry and small group learning, the high quality of the physical environment, and the students' appropriate workload. The Review Team also identified some weaknesses; a small number of students thought that there was a left-leaning political bias among some faculty members. But the team members qualified this concern by noting the openness and emphasis on the quality rather than the conclusion of arguments. Too much competition was identified by some students as a weakness, but the team found that this was compensated for by the high level of student cooperation. Finally, they found a lack of clarity in some of the committees' mandates and interrelationships.

The overall assessment of the Review Team included the

statements, "Judged by any measure applicable to an undergraduate experience, the Arts and Science Programme is an outstanding success," and "The participating students are all overwhelmingly enthusiastic about their experience," and "[It] is an academic jewel within a fine and highly respected university."

The Team's Chair, Dr. Norman Gibbins, in a cover letter wrote, "The increasing complexity and diversity of the modern world requires, in its leaders, an extraordinary capacity for broadly based intellectual synthesis, and the application of the results of that synthesis and creativity to the real world. McMaster University has found a truly effective way of moving substantially toward this educational goal."

Here are more comments from students.

> It has given me a changed outlook on academics, on my way of interacting with people from different societies, and a renewed faith that a university degree can give you something more than a piece of paper—a real, tough and enlightening experience. (Alpna Munshi)

> So much energy and innovation come together in one place and that, I believe, is the Programme's main strength. (Katherine Kitching)

> The last four years have been full of moments of discovery, questioning, excitement, sorrow, and love. I've been challenged to move beyond limits I never understood before. I've been involved in a wonderful atmosphere, met some of my greatest friends, and was able to pursue my crazy dreams wherever they led me (astray or otherwise). (Cynthia Soullière)

> The Arts and Science Programme is about ideas. It's about questioning our perception of the world in an informed manner, and encouraging others to do so well beyond the classroom. (Matt Lannan)

> I came to Arts and Science with a slew of unfair expectations. Some part of me thought that I might finally find the elusive guidebook to making sense of the universe: at the least, I hoped to be provided with a clear analysis of the ailments of Western society. I soon realized that we are provided with no answers, only questions. (Lisa Mu)

> Arts and Science captures the true essence of education, learning for its own sake. Whether one is talking to the professors, participating in a class discussion, or simply socializing with fellow artsis, there is always something by which to be challenged or

some way for one to be stretched. (Christine Shalaby)

The people are amazing! I feel that I've learned as much outside of class talking to both professors and students as I have doing the coursework. (Dave Dawe)

The value of a university education is quickly degrading as more and more in-coming students regard it merely as a stepping stone to a lucrative future career. This is a notion that the Arts and Science Programme has been rebelling against since its inception, insisting instead, albeit quietly, that learning is an endeavour with its own rewards. What is Arts and Science to me, you ask—my profs, my study-buddies, my friends, my big sib, my great big sib, my little sib. thinking, talking, laughing, playing, gossiping, crying, sleeping, eating, dancing, studying, trying, caring, loving, and yes, the classes, but more, so much more. (Britt Braaten)

Arts and Science is a coming together of marbles. The marbles roll together and form a luminous shape, a unique pattern of colour. This small world is achingly brief; time quickly scatters the marbles. This world, this shape, may be mortal. but the shine each marble gets from the collision of the spheres endures. (Laurence Scott)

Transformation.
A web of support and guidance in the forefront of Science and
Art: the never-ending kaleidoscope of symmetrical loops
Promoting freedom to be and to do
Learning the difference you can make
Granted permission to explore
And see life through freshly opened eyes. (Debbie Sin Yan Too)

Notes

1. "Review of the McMaster Arts and Science Programme," External Review Chaired by L. Norman Gibbins, (McMaster University, 1997.)
2. Roy W. Hornosty, Dorothy Pawluck, R. Jack Richardson, and William Shaffir, "Summary of responses to a questionnaire to gather information about students' experiences in the Arts and Science Programme," (McMaster University, 1991).
3. Dorothy Pawluck, Roy W. Hornosty, R. Jack Richardson and William Shaffir, "Learning the Ropes: The Experience of Gifted Students in University," (Paper delivered at the Qualitative Analysis Conference, Carleton University, Ottawa, 17-20 May 1991); "Student Responses to a Liberal University Programme," (Paper delivered at the Annual Meetings of the Canadian Sociology and Anthropology Association, Learned Societies Conference, Queen's University, Kingston, Ontario, 1-4 June, 1991); "Fostering Relations: Student

Subculture in an Innovative University Program," in *Doing Everyday Life: Ethnography as Human Lived Experience*, ed. M. Lorenz Dietz et al., (Toronto: Copp, Clark and Longman Ltd., 1994), 340-353; "The Construction of an Idealistic Self: Idealism among Select Undergraduates," (McMaster University, 1991).

4. Roy W. Hornosty, "The Development of Idealism in Pharmacy School," *Symbolic Interaction* 12 (1989):121-137; Roy W. Hornosty, L.J. Muzzin, and G.P. Brown, "Faith in the Ideal of Clinical Pharmacy among Practising Pharmacists Seven Years after Graduation from Pharmacy School," *Journal of Social and Administrative Pharmacy* 9(2) (1992):87-96.

5. "Summarized Results of a Survey of Graduates of the Arts and Science Programme" (McMaster University, 1992).

12   Future Directions

Gary Warner[1]

Graduates of the Arts and Science Programme continue to demonstrate the unique strengths of the Programme. How many programmes can graduate students who, as a recent graduate indicated to me by way of expressing the difficulty of the choices facing her, receive simultaneous admission offers to Law School, Medical School, and Graduate School? Many of our students continue their leadership roles after their graduation from the Programme and bring to a variety of fields the benefits of the skills in critical thinking and the interdisciplinary perspective that they have acquired. The range of fields to which graduates of the Arts and Science Programme have gravitated is most impressive, including the medical and legal professions, business administration, architecture, journalism, and a wide variety of fields in the life sciences, physical sciences, environmental sciences, social sciences, and humanities. Many students have contacted former professors to express gratitude for the profound influence particular courses have had on their lives. One recent correspondent pointed out, for example, how the Environmental Inquiry course had led a group of four students to varied careers, one to naturopathic medicine, another to Arts education and street theatre in Europe, another to organic farming, and the fourth to architecture.

The experience of the past two decades demonstrates conclusively that the creation of this programme was a successful experiment. The challenge facing us, then, is how best not only to preserve but even strengthen this programme in the years ahead.

A key contributor to the quality of the Programme has been its small size. That has made possible student-student and student-faculty interactions which have resulted in a vibrant community of sharing and learning. But over the years, the senior administration of the University has suggested more than once that the number of students admitted to the Programme be increased substantially. Recently, this was suggested again as the University prepared for the double cohort of university-bound students resulting from the phasing out of the fifth year of secondary schooling in Ontario, the province of origin for the majority of students who register in the Arts and Science Programme. Despite the pressures, we have successfully made the case that the suggested increase would jeopardize one of the Programme's sources of strength—its exceptional quality as a community of learners—and with it, the varied contributions, both academic and extra-curricular, which the Programme's student body makes to the University as a whole.

The launch in the 2003-2004 academic year of a new optional Experiential Learning component for academic credit in the upper two levels of the Programme represents a new curricular development. We envisage Experiential Education as defined by the Association for Experiential Education, namely "a process through which a learner constructs knowledge, skill and value from direct experience." This initiative builds on a strong culture of both voluntary and paid community service, as well as local and international travel that is characteristic of Arts and Science students. It is noteworthy that students played a major role in the development of this initiative. The new Experiential Learning courses will have a strong academic component. Students who choose these courses will register in 3 units in Level III and 6 units in Level IV. Such students will be required to complete experiences in three areas, broadly defined as work/service, travel, and creative/active pursuits. For each experience students will present to the course committee an academic proposal including areas of investigation, goals, the nature of the inquiry, and an evaluation plan. Students will work with a faculty advisor to develop their proposal. The advisor will ensure that the experience and assignment proposed are suitable for academic credit. Common class time will be scheduled for seminar presentations and student reports. There will be a final defense for each course at which students will make a presentation to the course committee. These courses are not intended to replace the activities which these students have been embarking upon on their own initiative for many years. Neither were they framed to provide the students with a work experience relevant to their future careers. Rather, the goal of the Experiential Learning courses is to add to the Programme a new opportunity for learning. Their purpose is to enhance the achievement of the core objectives of the Arts and Science Programme, to allow the students to integrate several disciplines, to inspire them to undertake imaginative learning experiences off campus, and to provide opportunities for developing their leadership and organizational skills. The students' learning from these experiences would be reflected upon and evaluated by University standards. Our challenge is to implement this option in such a way that it constitutes an effective component of student learning and of the academic quality of the Programme.

The Arts and Science Programme was designed with a four-year curriculum leading to the B.ArtsSc. (Honours) degree. It was recognized that some students might prefer to finish in three years, and the option of a modified curriculum leading to the B.ArtsSc. degree was offered. Most who take up this option do so to attend medical or law school. The number of students graduating after three years has ranged in recent years from five to fifteen. These students miss the benefits of the final year courses, among which are the Thesis and Independent Study that allow them to draw on their previously acquired knowledge and skills, while pursuing in some depth an area of study that holds particular interest to them. The aims of these students can also influence the experience of other students. Because they are working to meet the requirements of medical or law school, they are sometimes more restricted in their course selection and in the time that they can devote to other activities. This is certainly by no means true in every case, and there are indeed notable exceptions to this observation. The view that completing the four-year curriculum benefits all students is reinforced in conversations with students at the end of their fourth year, and by the experience of a number of students who deliberately deferred their admission to medical school at the end of their third year so as to derive the maximum benefit from the totality of the Programme. The elimination of the fifth year of high school in Ontario made it timely to re-examine this issue, and preliminary agreement has been expressed within the Arts and Science Council about giving serious thought to eliminating the three-year Bachelor's option and thus discouraging applications from students who are not committed from the outset to experiencing to the fullest the liberal education that the Programme was designed to offer.

The Programme has achieved remarkable success in recruiting outstanding students over the years. Colleagues in other departments constantly express their pleasure in having Arts and Science students in their classes. Academic supervisors, particularly those who have not previously supervised Arts and Science Theses or Individual Study projects, often remark at the end of the year on the calibre of the work done by the students. This does not mean that improvements in the pool of students are not possible. The ethno-cultural diversity of the students enrolled in the Programme is adequate in terms of students from Asia, but not in terms of students of African or Aboriginal heritage. Expanding this diversity is limited to a large extent by the composition of the pool of applicants. We have initiated efforts to recruit a small number of qualified Aboriginal students, but so far without success. Many of our students are children of professional parents or come from families who do not appear to experience financial hardship. The recruitment of students from a wider range of socio-economic backgrounds is probably beyond our control because of the financial factors involved; for example, the limited availability of suitably substantial scholarships or other financial assistance. Fine-tuning our admission system is one area in which we can make some modest change. We plan to experiment with offering a small number of admissions to otherwise eligible candidates who receive outstanding Supplementary Application results but who would not be offered admission on the basis of the normal calculations. This mechanism, which is intended to catch special cases, will, of course, have to be closely monitored.

The structure of the Programme reflects a balance which allows students to share a common core of Arts and Science courses, selected to provide them with a liberal education while allowing them to pursue more specialized study to the degree that they wish in the field of their choice. The two courses that have sparked queries in recent years are the required Level I Biology course and the Eastern Studies requirement, the only required courses for which enrolment is not limited to Arts and Science students. In the case of the former, students have often asked to have a Biology course specially designed for the Programme. (The first of the Technology and Society courses admits Engineering and Society Programme students as well as Arts and Science students.) It is, of course, healthy to have our students take one of their Level I courses outside of the Arts and Science Programme and come into contact with other students in the context of another Faculty, rather than spend their entire Level I in classroom contact exclusively with other Arts and Science students. However, in the case of Biology, students have repeatedly noted that the content and teaching methodology of the regular Level I Biology courses, necessary as they are as a base for Science students intending to take more advanced courses in this field, are inconsistent with the more participatory learning style and broader interdisciplinary objectives fostered by the Arts and Science Programme. Preliminary work was begun on creating a broadly-based Arts and Science Biology course that would be offered as an alternative to the regular Level I Biology courses for students not needing to complete the regular Level I Biology course as a prerequisite for further courses in Biology, but the preparation of this course has been put on hold, largely because of problems related to staffing it.

The Eastern Studies requirement was introduced in recognition of the perception that the exclusive focus on Western Civilization was a weakness in a programme that sought to provide a liberal education in the context of a modern multicultural university. The introduction of two half-year Eastern Studies courses, supplemented by a limited menu of courses with an Eastern Studies content taught by other units, has been the Programme's response to the call by students for greater inclusivity in this area of the curriculum. The choice of Eastern Studies reflected both student interest and the depth of scholarship available at McMaster in this field. A small number of students have expressed their preference for a single dedicated year-long Arts and Science Eastern Studies required course. However, the current arrangement has the advantage of offering students the flexibility of meeting this requirement from different disciplinary perspectives, and no change is presently being contemplated.

The success of the Programme depends as well on having instructors whose scholarship is solid, who have demonstrated pedagogical skills, and who share the values and objectives of the Programme. The practice of recruiting from the University's faculty members, as discussed earlier (see p.244) can be onerous for the Director. It is possible that the problem could be alleviated if a small number of key joint appointments to Arts and Science could be negotiated. Care to retain flexibility and renewal of the teaching staff would have to be taken.

The Arts and Science Programme owes its existence to the winning combination of the vision of the key planners of the Programme and the commitment and decisiveness of the top academic leaders of the university at the time of its creation, who backed the programme with the resources it needed to succeed. Inquiry-style courses are now commonplace in almost every Faculty at McMaster University. A few other Canadian universities have either instituted one-year liberal arts programmes, for example, the Foundation Year Programme at the University of King's College, Halifax, Nova Scotia, or have launched degree programmes spanning the arts and the sciences, for example, the Renaissance College undergraduate degree programme at the University of New Brunswick, launched in September, 2000, or the Bachelor of Arts and Science Programme launched at the University of Guelph in the fall of 2001. A key distinguishing characteristic of McMaster's Programme is the substantial number of core required courses which were designed as an integrated programme specifically and exclusively for its students; these core courses, which are neither cross-listed nor assimilated courses from another academic unit, constitute approximately 60% of the courses taken by a student completing a four-year Honours Arts and Science degree. This structure requires a significant commitment of resources. There are no signs that the commitment of the academic leaders of the University is waning, which augurs well for the future of the Programme. The vision of a liberal education and the twin goals of intellectual development and social engagement that inspired the Programme are even more relevant in these early years of the twenty-first century, confronted as we are with pressing challenges such as threats to the sustainability of our biosphere, growing global and local income disparities, and destructive violence and conflicts that threaten peace and security in many parts of the world. Graduates endowed with a keen intelligence, who are equipped with strong skills of inquiry, critical thinking, and communication, as well as an interdisciplinary perspective, are a valuable social asset and are well prepared to make important societal contributions to addressing the multidimensional problems of our age.

Notes

1.   Gary Warner was appointed Director of the Arts and Science Programme in the year 2000.

13   Reflections

Herb Jenkins, Barbara Ferrier,
Louis Greenspan, and Michael Ross

The premise for these reflections on the Arts and Science Programme is that it has been successful. It attracts excellent students who make good progress toward a liberal education in their university years. Moreover, many go forth eager to make a difference in the lives of others, and with a belief in the relevance of scholarship for achieving that end. The premise of success does not mean that we see no problems or areas in which the Programme falls short of ideal. The purpose of this chapter is not only to reflect on the things that have made the Programme a success over more than twenty years, but also to discuss some of the ongoing tensions and problems that call for continued attention.

We have been helped in the preparation of this chapter by a series of small meetings with some of the key people associated with the Programme. They included teachers, an administrator, and an educator with a university-wide concern for the quality of teaching and learning. The discussions were wide-ranging and free-flowing, and much of what we say here was said in those meetings. But the usual caveat about the views expressed applies to what has gone into this chapter—its authors take responsibility.

We choose to organize the discussion around four critical elements of the Programme: its students, faculty, pedagogy, and structure.

Students

Unquestionably the Programme attracts unusually capable, high-achieving students who are serious about learning, willing to work, and able to resist the security offered by early specialization for the less tangible values of acquiring wider knowledge and a broader set of intellectual skills. These students are active in university-wide student groups, are disproportionately represented at public lectures, and often take the initiative for campus-wide meetings and actions on contemporary political and social issues. As one of our meeting participants put it, they come to us with concerns as well as interests.

That there exists a substantial number of high school students with these characteristics is one of the more important truths to which the experience of the Arts and Science Programme at McMaster testifies. We of course hoped that would be the case at the outset, but we did not know. Moreover, it may well be that our students were not fully aware that there were many other students who shared their interests, concerns, and intellectual potential until they met and came to know their fellow students. Students with a serious interest in their education and a willingness to work hard at learning may find themselves outsiders in the peer culture of many of today's high schools, and even universities. But in the Arts and Science Programme, these attributes are respected by their peers. The discovery by the students of this "counterculture", with its supporting as well as challenging aspects, is, we believe, a strong justification for our Programme's deliberate effort to attract the best students out of high schools. While these students would be expected to do well in any programme, here they form a community within which they are stimulated to perform at a very high level and to contribute to the education of their peers.

Is the community of Arts and Science students all that it might be? One of our concerns is about diversity. Although the community is ethnically diverse, and students are protective of the traditions of their own cultures, they may in certain other, more subtle ways be too much alike. Most are from southern and central Ontario. While we are not free to make a study of their backgrounds we have the impression that many are from upper-middle and middle-class homes with university educated parents, a substantial proportion of whom are professionals. In short, they tend to be a privileged group.

Another characteristic of the admitted students is a cause of concern. When they start in the Programme, a high proportion, certainly more than half, express an interest in going to medical school. We are concerned about this because it suggests a lack of diversity in outlook and aspirations amongst our students. Furthermore, we sense that some, although certainly not all, of the aspirants for medical school are so focused on grades that they make less of a contribution to the learning community of Arts and Science students than they might otherwise do.

We could seek remedies for these problems along two avenues. One is to increase our effort to recruit students whose backgrounds differ in significant ways from the typical Arts and Science pattern. It is easy to see how we might do that with respect to geographical origins, but much more difficult to see how that might be done with respect to other characteristics. A second avenue is to introduce specific biases in the criteria for admission. Our present admission procedure involves assigning points for high school grade average, and points based on a supplementary application which asks for background information about the interests and achievements of applicants outside of their academic performance (p.51). It seems apparent to some faculty involved in the Programme that this way of doing things has not produced as diverse a community as they would like, but there is a reluctance to attempt any more explicit biasing rules on admission scores because they would exacerbate the perplexing issue of the proper balance between fairness to individual applicants and community interests in diversity. It is an issue that continues to be debated among faculty and students, but there can be little doubt that a greater effort to make the Programme known to students of varying backgrounds, possibly by publicizing the Programme in media of interest to minority groups, should go forward.

There is an even broader question about the student body. The direct consequence of having far more applicants than places (taken together with the conviction that merit in academic performance should carry a heavy weight) is that the admission average for successful applicants is very high (p.50). Some of us have argued a case for diversity on the dimension of academic achievement level as well as on other characteristics. Part of that case is that students with good, but not outstanding, performance in high school could, provided they are eager to learn on a broad front, profit as much from this Programme as do the more exceptional students to whom admission is now restricted. Although this point is generally accepted, one would need a very strong argument on the community value of diversity in entrance performance levels to defend a decision of this kind which could be seen to jeopardize fairness to individual applicants.

As the long-standing controversy in the United States over the constitutionality of affirmative action in university admissions shows, we are not alone in facing these complex issues of admission procedures for sought-after programmes. One of the factors which discourage us from attempting more proactive measures to increase diversity in the community of students is the widespread appreciation of the positive qualities of the community of students we now admit, as is so evident from accounts instructors give in these pages of their experience in teaching Arts and Science students. We will continue to debate these matters while moving only cautiously toward new procedures.

Faculty

Not a few skeptics thought that the Arts and Science Programme would founder on the unwillingness of faculty to teach in it. The grounds for skepticism will be familiar to anyone who understands the ethos of research-intensive multiversities. The work of these institutions is organized by departments whose identity rests on being professional practitioners of a discipline. Their *raison d'être* is developing new knowledge within the discipline, teaching the established knowledge of the discipline to students, and guiding graduate students in research. Departments have the dominant role in the recruitment, retention, and advancement of faculty, and in these matters the ability to advance knowledge through research, scholarship, and publication will play a major part. The ability to teach effectively within the department's programme will be given some weight, perhaps more in recent years than a decade ago, but rarely one that equals or exceeds the weight given to productivity in research. In any case, it is fair to say that to obtain comparable recognition for teaching in the university outside of one's departmental programmes, is an uphill battle.

Despite ample reason for apprehension about the prospects, our experience shows that there is a group of faculty willing to give a great deal of time and thought to teaching undergraduates in a programme that is not administered by departments. So much is evident, we trust, from the contributions to this book by instructors talking about the courses which they designed and taught to serve the purposes of the Programme. Some reflections on why, despite countervailing pressures, they are willing to do so are in order.

First, some are attracted by the opportunity to develop and teach a course that takes a larger view of what is significant about their field of knowledge than is typical in the more narrowly focused, building-block courses of departmental degree programmes. One of our instructors, whose own discipline is Religious Studies, said that he had always wanted to teach a course in which students read in the Bible, Darwin's *Descent of Man*, and Freud's *Interpretation of Dreams*. Others are attracted by the opportunity to help students acquire a level of academic skills beyond that usually achieved by undergraduates. Our experience strongly suggests that in order to reap the benefits of this kind of excitement, one must give a great deal of responsibility to instructors in defining the aims, methods, and content of their courses.

Second, they look forward to teaching students who really want to learn, will do assignments, are forthcoming in discussion, argument, and debate, and can function as part of a community in which everyone is learning from everyone else. The quality and motivation of the students are no doubt the major inducement for faculty to devote so much thought, time, and energy to teaching outside of their home departments.

Third, they take pleasure in meeting and working with other faculty members in the context of a shared concern with the total educational experience of undergraduates. They enjoy the chance to know more about the interests, viewpoints, and insights of faculty in other disciplines. The atmosphere in the community profits from the relative absence of competitive pressures that might exist within departments. Moreover, the Programme's reputation for excellence makes it an honour to be asked to contribute. It is our belief that McMaster is not unique in having a pool of willing and able faculty members to mount a liberal arts and science programme. The same inducements to involvement could be present, we expect, in any good university.

On the other hand, it would be a mistake to minimize the countervailing pressures on faculty. We recruit instructors in consultation with Department Chairs and Faculty Deans (see p.244). Excellent teachers are always a scarce resource, and the reluctance of Chairs and Deans to lose some of their services from existing Departmental programmes is understandable. Our success in recruiting to date rests in part on university administrators who are persuaded of the gains for the University as a whole, including of course Departmental programmes, from the establishment of the Arts and Science Programme. Our continued ability to recruit excellent teachers depends on the maintenance of that conviction through both good and hard times for university finances.

Aside from their strong interest and high ability in teaching, the faculty members who become instructors in the Arts and Science Programme are a diverse sample of the faculty as a whole. Some have very strong achievements in research, some do not. Some are junior faculty, some are senior or even emeritus faculty. The diversity in career paths, stages, and appointment status among instructors reflects the fact that excellence in teaching is not restricted to any one set of these variables.

Pedagogy

We agree with Christopher Lucas when he writes: "Undergraduates no less than graduate students [we would add, instructors] must be taught to appreciate the very profound truth that a college education is not something done 'to' or 'for' them as passive recipients. Nor can education be directed 'at' them with much hope for success either. Quite the contrary it must be conducted with them as active collaborators in a shared enterprise."[1] The Programme's success is, in our view, closely tied to success in making this philosophy an everyday fact about intellectual life within it. Our students have developed skills as collaborators, have taken their responsibilities conscientiously, and learned much from one another. The emphasis on collaborative projects has also helped to create a community in which thought and debate about things that matter go on outside course boundaries as well.

In courses named Inquiry, but by no means confined to them, the philosophy of teaching and learning as a shared enterprise is most salient. These courses are explicitly aimed at engaging inquiring minds in formulating critical questions about important, almost always complex, issues and developing the skill of using research to better understand them. Instructors vary in the degree to which they assume responsibility for presenting background information, current views on issues in the domain of the inquiry, and in designing specific reading or other assignments. In all cases, however, students are responsible at some stage for formulating their own questions and carrying out all the phases of research to which those questions lead. There would be broad agreement among Inquiry instructors with the characterization of inquiry by Knight and Maguire as a hybrid process involving self-directed as well as instructor-guided activities (p.109). Approaches have also differed in the weight given to projects undertaken within groups or by individuals acting alone, but in every case collaborative teaching and learning play a significant role in inquiry courses, as they do in other core courses designed specifically for the Programme.

Virtually the entire spectrum of skills expected of a liberally educated person has a role in the process of inquiry and in the effective communication of the fruits of inquiry. But the role of inquiry in the

Programme reaches beyond the development of skills to encompass the conviction that multidisciplinary scholarship has an important place in addressing issues in society. The first year Inquiry on Third-world issues has supported our students' high level of social concern and has been influential in the career choices of more than a few of them over the years. Samantha Nutt ('91) provides a case in point. She is a physician-humanitarian, cofounder and Executive Director of War Child Canada. She wrote to say: "When people ask about defining moments in my life, I tell them Arts and Science, because more than anything else, the Programme taught me to think critically and creatively, and to be a voice for change. It was my first real exposure to international issues, as well as to the spirit of activism."

We welcomed the publication of the Boyer Commission Report[2] and its espousal of inquiry-based learning. In one important respect, however, our use of inquiry-based learning is not in accord with the view expressed in that report. In keeping with their central aim of creating through undergraduate education participants in a future research faculty, the report recommends the engagement of undergraduates in projects arising from the faculty members' frontier research. Undergraduates are to be inducted as apprentices in a faculty-led team of researchers which would include graduate students. Our aim in undergraduate education is broader than the creation of professional researchers, and accordingly we have taken a different view of the role of faculty members when leading Inquiry courses.

Few Inquiry projects in our courses reflect the specialized research interests of the faculty member teaching the Inquiry. The range and breadth of questions raised go well beyond those encountered in an instructor's professional research. We believe that teachers who are experienced and accomplished in research and reflective scholarship can help students understand and practice principles of good inquiry even when (perhaps, especially when) the topic for inquiry is not one with which the instructor has had first-hand involvement as a researcher. Our goal is to help students learn how to use inquiry to make progress on broad questions that arise from their own concerns and perceptions about how we live. We share the skepticism expressed by Pocklington and Tupper[3] in their recent critique of undergraduate education in Canadian universities about the feasibility of what might be called the apprenticeship model of a research-centered undergraduate programme, especially in the context of a programme such as ours which is committed to fostering breadth of understanding in the arts and sciences. There is, however, a place for apprenticeship in the Arts and Science Programme. In their fourth year students take an independent study or thesis course under the guidance of one faculty member. The students take the initiative and make agreements with a willing faculty member from any Department of the university. Especially in thesis courses, the topic typically lies within the professional research interests of the faculty member and so conforms more closely than do our Inquiry courses to the apprenticeship model of the Boyer Commission Report.

Inquiry-based learning has become a part of many Arts and Science courses other than those named Inquiry. In Technology and Society students write short seminar papers consisting of an inquiry proposal accompanied by some initial, illustrative research findings. Students are urged to develop and pursue critical questions in other courses as well. The commitment to inquiry in the Arts and Science Programme, and our years of experience teaching it, have contributed to a concerted effort at McMaster to introduce inquiry-based learning in the Faculties of Science, Social Sciences, and Humanities. Moreover, inquiry courses are central to the curriculum of the Engineering and Society Programme offered by the Faculty of Engineering.

Despite the pervasive role of inquiry in our Programme, some expectations of its planners for the place of inquiry have not come to pass. It was hoped that these courses might be a major help in integrating knowledge acquired in other courses. Although they do bring together skills in logic, argument, writing, speaking, interpreting data, and reading literature closely, their role in integrating more substantive knowledge is limited. In retrospect, the reason seems apparent. Although Inquiry courses explore a broad topic area, the formulation of questions for individual inquiry typically has a specific focus and requires specific kinds of information. For example, an inquiry on the question of why Haiti has become the poorest nation in the Western hemisphere would involve examining its history and culture. But even a student who has had courses in history and cultural anthropology is unlikely to have considered Haiti. For the most part, individual Inquiries focus on questions that are too specific to be illuminated by the subject matters of other courses the student has taken. Inquiry seems better suited to the development of new knowledge than to the integration of knowledge acquired from other courses. Another consequence of the narrow focus of many inquiry questions is that students may become so engaged in the pursuit of their own question that they pay too little attention to learning about the broader inquiry topic that the course is devoted to understanding. Thus the teaching of inquiry is a hybrid process—one in which attention must be paid to the broad domain of the inquiry–the big picture–while each student is investigating just one of many questions that need to be understood.

In the early stages of planning some thought that the study of modes of inquiry, or ways of knowing, in the various arts and science disciplines should be emphasized as a theme within core courses. However, as these courses took shape in the hands of the faculty members ultimately responsible for teaching them, the theme modes of inquiry, although frequently addressed, did not become pervasive. From our present perspective, we think that is a wise development. Examining epistemological underpinnings of disciplines is a highly abstract undertaking. It is hard to imagine, for example, a fruitful study of historiography in the absence of familiarity with some body of historical writings, and it is doubtful that the effort would be very meaningful to students in their early years of university. Moreover, had the planners insisted on an overall theme of this kind, it might have taken too much from the responsibility of instructors to follow their own lights in the design of core courses.

In summary, our approach to pedagogy rests on the broad conviction that teaching and learning in the university should be a shared enterprise among students and between students and teachers. This philosophy is clearly manifest in Inquiry courses, where the most important role of the instructor is not in presenting expert knowledge, but in helping students acquire their own new knowledge through the arts of inquiry. Effective collaboration is one of those arts—one which we have fostered with enthusiasm, not only in Inquiry courses, but throughout.

Structure

We have spoken of the need to give instructors freedom to design their courses while respecting only very general guidelines about aims and content. The potentially negative side of freedom is incoherence and needless repetition in the curriculum. Has the Programme managed a good balance on this matter? In general, our students think so. As they proceed in the Programmne, and notably by their third year, many say that things are coming together and they see connections across arts and science courses. We believe this happens because some of the same fundamental concepts and deep questions are being addressed from different perspectives in several courses. Such questions as, What is knowable?, What are the limits of science and logic as sources of truth about the human condition?, Can one believe both in free will and in the possibility of a science of behaviour?, What are the springs of ethical conduct?, are engaged in many courses including Writing and Informal Logic, Technology and Society, Literature, Western Civilization courses, Calculus, and in Inquiry courses, to cite just some of the more evident examples.

Among members of the Instructional Council opinions differ on the question of whether a more deliberate effort should be made to draw attention to connections across the curriculum. One way to foster that would be have meetings in which instructors address each other on the principal issues that are treated in their courses. (In the early years when courses were being brought forward for the first time instructors met to discuss a proposed course outline, but the practice has not been sustained as later generations of instructors come into the Programme.) Although to some this appears to be a missed opportunity, others feel that making connections is a creative act that has to take place, and is taking place, in the students' minds, rather than being put forward explicitly by instructors. Given the choice between spending more time in meetings with other instructors, or more time on the teaching of their own course, some prefer the latter. The question of what is worth doing to enhance the integration and connectedness of knowledge and approaches across the disciplines will continue to be debated.

We have written often in these pages of the intellectual-social community of students and faculty in the Arts and Science Programme. The character of this community, centered on teaching and learning, is, we believe, an indispensable feature of the Programme's success as a vehicle for fostering liberal education. That we have established a programme, and not merely a collection of new courses, has provided an essential context for community.

Students enter the Programme as a group, on equal footing, and have a common experience with the core curriculum. As they become senior students they maintain their engagement with the community by becoming mentors, helping junior students, or by becoming teaching assistants within the Programme's courses. They graduate together, receive the same Arts and Science degree, and many stay in touch through a network of the Programme's alumni. The twentieth reunion on campus was attended by the largest number of alumni from any programme in McMaster's experience.

As noted previously, the Programme has its own space which has contributed to its cohesiveness. The Director's office, to which students have always had easy access, is immediately off the small, informal meeting area. The Directors, of whom there have been three to date, have been deeply committed to the Programme's success. Among their formal duties are the appointment (in consultation with administrators) of instructors, the chairing of the Programme's Advisory and Instructional Councils, the recruitment and admission of students, and the academic counseling of in-course students. In addition, each of the directors has taught in one or more of the core courses. Perhaps their most important role is in maintaining good communication among all the participants, a vigorous intellectual climate, and an open and friendly social climate for students and teachers alike.

Over the years the Programme has been well served indeed by a dedicated staff who understand and believe in the Programme and who are often the first contact for prospective students. They counsel in-course students generously and wisely, and are seen by them as concerned and supportive. This tradition owes much to the first, long-serving administrator, Kathy Ryan.

Could the benefits of community be realized for a group much larger than the sixty or so students we admit each year, or is there something in small size that is basic to the formation of community? It is our view that having numbers small enough in relation to instructors to allow for genuinely interactive teaching is essential. Indeed, we feel that we are often on the edge of what is possible with the present numbers. One could imagine creating parallel cohorts of students and increasing the faculty complement accordingly so that interactive teaching and learning remain feasible. But even granting a university's willingness to provide the teaching resources, the increase in both student and faculty numbers might diminish the sense of a cohesive community, because they would no longer meet with one another or share a common learning experience to the same degree. It would be a risky experiment.

A more promising way of making the benefits of a teaching and learning community available to more students would be the creation of small undergraduate programmes with distinctive aims elsewhere at the university. They might be distinguished by having a broader core curriculum within a cluster of disciplines, for example, within biological and physical sciences, or within the social sciences and humanities, than is the case in existing Departmental programmes. McMaster's Engineering and Society Programme, which combines the full engineering curriculum with courses that examine the place of engineering and technology in society, as well as elective courses taken in other Faculties, is a positive case in point.

A recurring issue in the design of programmes of liberal education in the arts and sciences is the role of specialization. Should students be required to specialize to some degree? How much time should be available for specialization? How can the core curriculum with its new courses be designed to articulate with the courses that comprise a disciplinary specialization within a Departmental programme? The Planning Council's proposal ventured some answers to these questions, but other more specific answers have evolved with experience.

We do not require specialization, but students who wish to specialize accomplish that almost entirely through the way they use their electives. With minor exceptions, the core courses remain intact for all of our students. We continue to believe that whether specialization is a good choice for a student depends on that student's image of his or her future. A student who, for example, aspires to be a civil rights lawyer might benefit from a degree in, say, history, but he or she might benefit as much from a mixture of courses including philosophy, literature, sociology, and government, to cite just one of many plausible sets. We do not believe that specialization offers a royal road to mental discipline, nor do we believe that the association of specialization with depth is a necessary one.

What degree of specialization should be accommodated in a liberal programme? We believe that the answer is, enough for students who choose that route to prepare themselves for graduate work in most of the major academic disciplines. That is a large order, but it would be a serious drawback for a programme that is able to attract outstanding students to then leave them so poorly prepared to meet the requirements of specialized graduate programmes that they could not do so without years of further undergraduate work.

Although the Planning Council did not propose this option at the outset, McMaster's Combined Honours Programmes offer an opportunity to combine the core courses of the Arts and Science Programme with sufficient work in a Departmental degree programme to meet the requirements for Combined Honours Degrees. Although heretofore such programmes had always been a combination of two disciplines, now it could be the combination of the entire core of the Arts and Science Programme with another subject. The completion of a combined honours degree in a subject almost always meets the course requirements for entry into graduate programmes in Canada, the United States, and elsewhere (p.46).

Students who take a combined honours degree have a schedule of courses that rarely has any space for electives outside of either the department of specialization or the required Arts and Science courses. In our view, however, the balance between the need to offer an avenue for specialization, on the one hand, and the need to offer sufficient work in the arts, sciences, and mathematics to warrant an arts and science degree on the other has been struck in quite a satisfactory way within the Arts and Science Programme. Combined Honours Programmes have been chosen by about one third of the graduating students (see p.199 for information on choices).

Final word

We have been fortunate at McMaster to have a set of circumstances that no doubt eased the way for the acceptance of a programme like ours. The University had already been innovative in education, notably in its radically different approach to undergraduate medical education. Moreover, when acceptance of this Programme was being debated, the University had received a large endowment from which start-up funds were made available.

In the absence of systematic data we can only speculate on what, in general, it takes to institute a programme like ours. Obviously, there must be a substantial group of faculty members and university leaders, including administrators, who really want to bring it about. If there is such a group, our experience suggests that some of the other conditions necessary for success will be available to them. There exists a group of exceptionally able students who are attracted by the prospect of a broader university programme. There are faculty eager and able to teach them, and who find the experience rewarding. An approach to pedagogy that encourages teaching and learning as an active collaborative enterprise is now quite widely championed by university educators. The value of creating a community for teaching and learning within a coherent programme is also widely recognized. We are strongly convinced by our experience that when these elements are brought together in a programme of undergraduate education, the rewards for both the students and the university as a whole are great. We hope that this account of one such programme will encourage others to work towards making their own vision of liberal education a reality.

Notes

1.   Christopher Lucas, *Crisis in the Academy: Rethinking American Higher Education.*(New York: St. Martin's Press, 1966) 171.

2. Boyer Commission on Educating Undergraduates in the Research University, *Re-inventing Undergraduate Education: A Blueprint for America's Research Universities* (Princeton, N.J.: Carnegie Foundation for the Advancement of Teaching, 1997).
3. Thomas Pocklington and Allan Tupper, *No Place to Learn: Why Universities Aren't Working* (Vancouver: UBC Press, 2002).

Contributors: Chapter Authors and Editors

With one exception, all of the authors of chapters and the editors of this book are, or were, faculty members of McMaster University.

Sylvia Bowerbank is Professor, Department of English and the Arts and Science Programme.

Barbara Ferrier is Professor Emeritus, Department of Biochemistry and was the second Director of the Arts and Science Programme.

Louis Greenspan is Professor Emeritus, Department of Religious Studies.

Bill Harris is Professor, Department of Physics and Astronomy.

Bob Hudspith is Retired Associate Professor, Department of Mechanical Engineering.

Herb Jenkins is Professor Emeritus, Department of Psychology and was Chair of the Arts and Science Programme's Planning Committee and its first Director.

Les King is Professor Emeritus, School of Geography and Geology and former Vice-President (Academic) of McMaster University.

Graham Knight is Associate Professor, Department of Sociology.

Miroslav Lovric is Associate Professor, Department of Mathematics and Statistics.

P.K. Rangachari is Professor, Department of Medicine.

Michael Ross is Professor Emeritus, Department of English.

Jennifer Smith Maguire is a post-doctoral fellow in the Department of Sociology and graduate of the Arts and Science Programme. She was a student in the course about which she writes.

Roman Viveros-Aguilera is Professor, Department of Mathematics and Statistics.

Gary Warner is Associate Professor, Department of French and the third Director of the Arts and Science Programme.

Jean Wilson is Associate Professor, Department of Modern Languages and Linguistics, and Programme in Comparative Literature.

The many students and graduates of the Programme who submitted contributions to the book are named in the text.